CHRIST OR THE RED FLAG

CHRIST OR THE RED FLAG

by

Michael Wurmbrand

HODDER AND STOUGHTON
LONDON   SYDNEY   AUCKLAND   TORONTO

I WAS BORN INTO AN ERA OF POLITICAL MURDER. One after another, the 'politicians' killed each other off. Fascists murdered Fascists of a slightly different political shade. Hitler had Brownshirts, Mussolini his Blackshirts. We had Greenshirts. They killed and were killed: one renegade from the Party was murdered by his former comrades, who filled him with bullets from ten different guns, then hacked him to pieces with axes. Another Fascist leader garrotted ten rivals who aspired to replace him. After many tribulations, the Greenshirts were able to seize power for a brief time — time enough to slaughter the Jews; then they turned to murdering their own friends, Fascists like themselves, super-nationalists and Rumanians of the 'purest' blood. Next, Greenshirts were rounded up and shot in droves by the dictator who emerged from the power struggle, Antonescu. And then Antonescu himself, at the end of the war, was shot by a firing squad.

Thus it happened that from the time I first began to understand and think for myself, I heard in our home in Bucharest of people being jailed, killed and simply vanishing without trace.

My mother and father were Jews who had become Christians. It made life harder for them, since Protestants were a persecuted minority in Orthodox Rumania, and they had to suffer twice over: because they loved their Jewish race, and because they loved their evangelical faith.

Since they had become Christians, their faith was enthusiastic and deep. Father soon revealed an innate gift for communicating with people and influencing crowds: he was a speaker of extraordinary power. He became particularly well-known as a missionary to the Jews.

During World War II, our home became a refuge for the homeless. Every day we sat down to eat with a host of relatives, strangers and brothers in faith, each with his story of grief and woe.

It should, clearly, have been a wretched childhood — one with which I might bore you to distraction. But as I recall, it was a time of crystalline happiness, because my parents had the power to turn complaints to laughter and tears into the giving of thanks with their love.

But I puzzled over all the talk of killing. One evening when my father came to kiss me goodnight, I asked him: 'Daddy, will we be killed too?'

This stopped him in his tracks. He thought for a while, then decided on the truth:

'We may very well be killed, because we also are Jews.'

'How do they kill us?'

'They come in a big car and drive us away, out of town.'

I was very pleased. A ride in a big car! And then to be killed at the end of it. That was when one got to see Jesus. I had never driven in a car; or encountered Jesus. My two greatest dreams!

'When we are far from town,' father went on sadly, 'we get out. Then the police shoot us with machine guns.'

I felt a hush of sadness too. But then I brightened: 'They kill us a little bit, and then we go to heaven. But why can't the police come after us there?'

My father said: 'Because they don't know about the ladder that we have, which is belief in Jesus.'

When I was a boy, my father spent at least two hours a day teaching me: telling stories, singing songs, explaining why one prayed and what one should pray for. By the time I was four, I could read anything that was given to me.

The relatives and refugees, beggars and gypsies who came to our door, came first and foremost because of my mother. They knew that no one was ever turned away. She might slice the bread thinner or stretch the soup with water, but everyone was

6

welcome at our table — a big beautiful walnut table at which, I am sure, I never in my life sat down alone with my parents, although I was an only child.

Jews who had escaped from the Nazi extermination camps slept often at our house. Then later, we gave room to Nazi officers whose lives were endangered by vengeful people who wished to kill all and every German, because some of them had slaughtered Jews. After them, father filled the house with Russian soldiers whom he hoped to convert.

My wife Judith, whom I knew as a girl, says: 'At first I wondered what everyone was doing in your house: if you didn't have thirty visitors a day, I began to feel something was wrong. It was a constant carnival. No one in Rumania got married or had a baby or encountered trouble but they came to your mother for advice!'

Bucharest is a city of wide boulevards lined with trees, of parks and shady squares filled with flowers and open-air cafés, where you may take refuge from the sticky heat of summer, sipping a cool drink — raspberry soda is very popular — or tasting the cool breeze from the lake in Cismigiu Park. Even during the war it could be gay and lively — for some.

Our home was on the outskirts of town, where rents were low. We were the one non-Greek Orthodox family in an old apartment block. Along the road outside went trucks and tanks and troops and sometimes members of the *élite* Iron Guard, Rumania's Fascists. In the cause of 'Aryanisation', green-shirted squads of Guardists roamed the streets looking for Jews to assault. They raided and looted Jewish homes on such pretexts as 'looking for hidden money'. The absurdity of talking about 'racial purity' in a Europe that is a hodge-podge of Anglo-Saxon, Latin, Slav, Gypsy, Turk and Tartar worried the Jew-haters not at all.

Early in 1944, when I was five years old, father came home from the Ministry of Cults, which had been persuaded — thanks to the intervention of his friend, the Swedish Ambassador — to permit the opening of a Protestant chapel. The one difficulty was that he had no chapel and no money to

7

rent a building. But we did have a three-room apartment. In a minute, the decision was taken.

'We'll live in one room. The two others we turn into the chapel. Sabina (turning to my mother), you'll go and buy about a hundred chairs. The others must stand. We'll have no altar, just a lectern. We can't afford the space.' There was no arguing with my father. It was done.

Baptists, Pentecostals, Plymouth Brethren were all forbidden sects. So they came to us, the only Protestant chapel with services in the Rumanian language. Father would preach to one congregation of two hundred, while another two hundred filled the yard, waiting their turn. One service after another, five times a day. It was stuffy and hot. The perspiration ran down his face. The chapel was lit by one big oil-lamp which helped to consume the air. It was like some service of the early Christians in the catacombs.

At that time Bucharest was being bombed by the Allies, and the Russians, too, only their bombs very rarely exploded. I was the black-out inspector for our chapel. One lady would always creep under a table when the bombardment began and cover her head with a newspaper. She would tell my father, 'Stop laughing! If a bomb falls on us, it will help a little.'

Often we took refuge in the shelters. Bombs shook the earth with a monstrous thump, sometimes extinguishing the single light that burned in the ceiling. People huddled around father and mother as though they could protect them. My father would talk or lead everyone in song or prayer.

I prayed too: my prayer was, 'Oh God, make all the bombs fall in the Dîmbovitza (the river that ran near our home). Don't let any bombs fall on houses or men.'

At the height of the raids, my parents were arrested. The charge was 'holding illegal religious meetings'. The givers of father's permit had not foreseen that he would create a church of love where every persecuted and forbidden group might worship. But that was what had happened.

While they were in jail, friends took me to the countryside. They thought that I would be safe in the home of an elderly couple who were brethren in faith. But strangely, there I was arrested too. It seemed to be my family's fate. Word went around the village that the son of a Jew had arrived. And it was forbidden, by a Nazi decree, to evacuate Jewish children from the capital. The militia came to arrest me, and carried off their five-year-old prize to the police station. But there I created such a hullabaloo that they were only too glad to release me after twenty-four hours to the old couple.

So I also experienced prison early in life.

A few weeks after the fighting ended for us, in 1944, I went down with mastoiditis, an infection of a bone behind the ear. The doctor said it might be fatal. There was at that time no penicillin. It was essential to operate on the following day. That evening, before I left for the hospital, my parents gathered a dozen brethren in faith in our home to pray for the operation's success.

I had a fever of 104F. I asked what was happening. And my father, who concealed nothing, told me that I must go to hospital and that I might die.

As the brethren stood round, father read from the Epistle of St. James: 'Is any sick among you? Let him call for the elders of the church; and let them pray over him, anointing him with oil in the name of the Lord: and the prayer of faith shall save the sick.'

He anointed me with oil while everyone knelt in prayer.

Then one of the brethren cried out, 'Alleluia! I thank thee Lord that thou hast healed this child! We believe it with all our hearts!'

Father put his hand again on my forehead. It was hot as ever with the fever. He turned dubious scrutiny on the kneeling man. He had asked them here only to pray.

But then a second visitor and a third cried out, as the spirit took them. And a fourth and a fifth. All thanked God for healing me.

Then I began to pray: to get better, to play here on earth a little longer, to stay with my mother. And after a while father once more put his hand on my forehead. He looked at me strangely and called mother. She took my temperature. It was not yet normal, but it had fallen.

9

Next morning the doctor came for a last examination before I went to hospital. On hearing my mother's account of what had happened, he smiled. But the smile faded as he examined me, to be replaced by a look of puzzlement.

At last he put his instruments away.

'The infection has gone,' he confessed. 'Very strange.'

In two or three days I was up and playing in the yard. The operation was forgotten.

The physician said, 'It's really quite miraculous!'

Dr. Laurian Segall, a Bucharest specialist, was Jewish and not very prone to believe in miracles wrought by Christ.

For a time Rumania was under attack by both the German and Russian forces. On August 23rd, 1944, King Michael overthrew the Antonescu regime and declared war on Germany. The Luftwaffe bombed Bucharest; but by then the Germans were retreating everywhere. Soviet tanks rolled unopposed into the capital on August 31st.

On the following day I was with father in a general store, when we saw our first Russian couple — a captain, who was shopping together with his girl-friend, an army sergeant. They spoke no Rumanian, the salesman had no Russian.

Without a moment's hesitation, father offered his services as a translator. The couple gladly accepted and we spent some time helping them.

The woman complimented father on his Russian. 'You've been so kind. But I really wanted to buy some clothes. Do you know a good shop?'

Father saw another fish falling into his net.

'I don't know about these things. But why don't you come home to lunch with us and meet my wife? She'll take you out in the afternoon and show you the best place. If you go alone, you'll only be cheated.'

They were delighted and wrote down our address. Why, I demanded, hadn't father immediately told them about God?

'Remember when you planted that apricot pip and kept digging it up to see if it had started to grow? Nothing happened, did it? Some things need patience. A kind invitation is a seed. It will grow.'

Now even the birds and the bees learnt on the first day that what Russians really liked was alcohol. The occupation began with a looting of all liquor stores and wine shops, and we had heard the stories of drunkenness and theft long before they reached the capital. They were healthy young peasants. They had never seen anything remotely resembling the wealth of Bucharest, even in its impoverished wartime state. They were the conquerors and they did what they pleased. They had to have anything that glittered. Startled citizens were relieved of their watches in the street. You saw soldiers with three or four on each wrist.

I suggested we bought a bottle of wine for the captain and his friend — if they drank a little, they might be in a mood to listen. So we took the wine home with us to lunch.

Father put the bottle on the table and said to an astonished mother: 'As it is written, "Be a Jew with the Jews, Greek with the Greeks and a drunkard with drunkards." We have Russians at table.'

When they had arrived and sampled a glass of wine, we sat down to eat.

'First we always say a grace to God in this house,' said father. He prayed in Russian.

The Russians put down their knives and forks and lost all interest in food. What was it, they asked — faces alight with interest. Could we say it again? What did it mean?

'I remember my granddad had some holy books,' said the sergeant. 'But the word "God" was taboo. In home and at school we heard that religion was invented by the bourgeoisie to oppress the people.'

In the end father talked to them for nearly three hours. They forgot why they came and never mentioned the shopping expedition with mother. Before they departed, both knelt down with father while he said a prayer, and gave themselves to Christ.

They came many times to see us before they left for the front. I boasted that my strategy with the wine had turned the trick. Without it, they might never have been won.

We moved to a new house, rented from a friend of father's, a wealthy Jewish doctor. It was a spacious, rather elegant place, long and narrow in design with room after room joined by a corridor, and one big ballroom that could hold 200 people easily. Father at once turned it into his church, and all the extra rooms into a mission. In a week the place was filled with our strange guests. Russian soldiers whom father found on the street now joined the rest, and left us their fleas in exchange for the tableware or whatever they took with them on departure.

Father had become pastor of the Swedish Israel mission, and represented, together with a Norwegian pastor, the World Council of Churches, then in the process of being formed. They handled relief funds sent from the West for famine-stricken Rumania. Father drew a regular salary — which meant that now we had as many as thirty stray guests sleeping in the hall, in the church, even the bathroom.

My mother worked so hard for everyone that she had never a moment to herself. Then she began speaking to meetings of the women of our church. And from there she began a second career as a preacher. She joined in street corner meetings, drawing great crowds. Such gatherings had been unknown in Rumania until then. It meant that my parents were often absent and much of the time I was looked after by a lady who came as one of our transient guests and stayed five years. 'Aunty Carlie' became our housekeeper. 'She is the boss here,' said my father — but only when Carlie could not hear. If he grumbled, she would immediately threaten to leave. I sided with her always, and father was powerless.

A friend brought a gift of oysters once. He loves oysters and was looking forward to eating them at supper. But when he sat down to eat, Carlie said, 'I threw them away. You are a pastor, and you should not be eating luxurious foods like that.' I agreed.

Another time she made some of her very tasty sausages. Father was given two. He ate them and said, 'Fine, I'd like another.'

'It says in the Bible that pastors should eat little,' replied Carlie. 'What you've had is quite enough.'

When father went into the kitchen he found her eating a whole plateful of sausages. 'The Bible also speaks of justice and equality,' he complained. 'Why should I have two when you eat eight?'

'Because I'm not a pastor,' she snorted. 'You should be a model of abstinence.'

Aunt Carlie was a Hebrew Christian. She taught me what she considered to be German, though a German would have fainted on hearing it. It was not even good Yiddish.

I drew immediate conclusions from father's stories. What he said, for me, was just exactly what he meant. This made for some interesting results.

A story that impressed me deeply was of a rich lady who gave a round of mouldy cheese to a beggar. The beggar was very pleased: stale cheese tastes good to the starving. She also was pleased with herself. So everyone was happy. But that night she had a dream. She was in heaven, and the saints were feasting at one table on good things. She tried to sit with them, but an angel touched her sleeve and pointed to a small table set apart, on which stood the mouldy cheese she had given to the beggar.

'Be so kind as to sit here,' said the angel. 'What you gave is what you get.'

My father said this meant that when we obeyed St. John's injunction to give one of our two coats to 'him that hath none', we should give the best we have to others.

I said, 'Father you have two suits, you'll have to give one away.'

Father had just been able to afford a new suit, the first in many years. He took out the old rusty suit I had always seen him wear, and the brand new one.

He asked, 'Which shall I give?'

'The one you want to wear in heaven,' I suggested. 'The new one.'

Books were my favourite food. When I tried to read at table, my mother became angry.

13

'Put that away and eat your dinner!'

I suggested a compromise: I would eat, if she would put the food in my mouth while I read. She didn't agree. It seemed a very reasonable arrangement to me.

It was not long before I clashed with our religious instructor at school — a Catholic school run by priests. Father Joseph warned us against swearing.

'When our school was being built,' he said, 'a workman hit his thumb with the hammer and took the name of the Holy Mother of God in vain. That same day he fell from the scaffolding and broke both legs! The Blessed Virgin punished him!'

It did not sound very just. 'Father,' I wondered, 'can this be right? My Daddy says that Jesus's mother was the kindest lady who ever lived. Our hearts are icicles compared with hers. She wouldn't push him off the building. She would forgive him and try to help him.'

Father Joseph told me crossly not to contradict him. The workman had fallen because he had blasphemed, and that was that.

'I think he just missed his footing,' I said.

Slap! The Father had a strong right arm. It hurt — but not nearly so much as my feeling that the punishment was unjust.

That evening I told my father I would not attend any more religious classes. He did not ask why, or tell me that I must go. In this matter, he said, I was free to do as I pleased. Eventually I poured out my story. He said nothing then, but later he told my piano teacher — a Catholic — why I was no longer attending classes in religion. The story reached the Bishop's ear and Father Joseph was reproved. He apologised and said that my father's teaching was right, which was a lesson in humility to me. We had no more quarrels.

Years afterwards, this priest shared a prison cell with my father. In their affliction, they laughed over this memory.

I was taught not to accept ideas passively. And when my father read once from Matthew 11, 'Come unto me, all ye that labour and are heavy laden, and I will give you rest ... and learn from me; for I am meek and humble,' I objected:

'A humble man never says he's humble — that's boasting!'

My father replied that sometimes self-assertion is also a virtue. 'When Koch discovered the bacillus of tuberculosis, he was contradicted by the whole German Academy of Science. Should he have humbly yielded to these great authorities? What a loss to humanity! But he simply disregarded them, and said what he knew to be correct with great force. Many great men have had to assert themselves in the face of opposition. Humility doesn't consist in not considering yourself. It lies in knowing that what you have is not from yourself, but from God.'

Seeing how my parents won souls for Christ, I decided one day to try my hand at it, too. My mother had taken me with some children to the park, and while she sat on the grass I approached a man who lay reading a book.

'Do you know how to get to heaven?' I inquired.

He looked very startled. 'I can't say that I do. I've never even been asked such a question. What makes *you* ask?'

I explained that if he didn't know how to get to heaven, then he would go to hell; and in hell there were no toys, or sweets — in fact, nothing but a fire which burned you up. It was quite a long speech.

'Where did you learn all this?'

As I explained that my father was a pastor, he arrived in the park to collect us. The stranger was a professor, it turned out; and soon he and father were deep in discussion. He visited our home later and eventually became converted. He and his wife joined our church and have remained family friends ever since. Thus began my missionary career.

Soon I moved on to greater ventures. The streets were full of Russian soldiers who had been for years away from their homes. They loved to talk to children and pick us up and give us candy — Russians are sentimental — and give us a little of that affection which they longed to lavish on their own children at home. In return I would give them Gospels — it was a work that we schoolchildren could do at times when it would have been extremely dangerous for older people.

But my favourite task was to put up posters on walls by

night. We made flour and water paste and together with the others I would go out after dark and stick them up around the neighbourhood. Already the Communists were taking control of the country and cracking down on religion. Every day communist cadres would tear the posters down — and every night we'd put them back again.

The Russians had imposed on Rumania a puppet premier named Groza. The Communists promised anything and everything while they took over one ministerial post after another in the coalition Government formed after the war. Their masters in Moscow ordered our country to be stripped of its resources, oil, ships, rolling stock, food — until by 1947 Rumania was bankrupt and starving.

A time of terror had begun. The peasants, who formed the strongest opposition to Communism, had to be crushed. Now that Stalin's armies controlled all Eastern Europe, any pretence of freedom was abandoned. Hundreds of thousands of innocent people filled the prisons. In Rumania alone, some 60,000 people were executed. They ranged from Lucretiu Patrascanu, first Communist Minister of Justice, shot by colleagues who thought he was too powerful, to small farmers who objected to the seizure of their land and goods.

The terror had a deep effect upon the young. An eight-year-old like myself felt it hardly less than older boys. A sullen, silent generation began to grow, suspicious of friends and enemies alike, aware that anyone, schoolmate or teacher or priest might be an informer. This system of informing is the heart of the Communist machine. The state seeks to know and control every detail of your life, so that it can blackmail and pressure you into submission and crush even the thought of dissent. My generation learnt to fight it as a way of life. One watched every step, knowing that the slightest indiscretion would go down in a file, and might be used against one years later. To tell untruths, to cheat the Communist machine in any way possible became the honest thing to do.

Thousands saw parents persecuted, their churches closed, their schools made into indoctrination centres. Our church, being active, was a prime target of the Communists. They organised gangs to shout down my father as he preached, for his sermons were not in accordance with the Party line. He had to speak sometimes with a phalanx of the congregation close around him, fighting off thugs who would try to strike him, or throw things. It was frightening, yet exciting for a boy. I enjoyed the services more than before — often now they looked more like a boxing-match.

Father was granted an audience with young King Michael, shortly before the Communists deposed him. On the way to the Royal Palace, he observed that an American pastor who was with him had a hole in the heel of his sock, and he remarked politely on this, thinking that the man was unaware of it. But the pastor took deep umbrage.

However, after this bad start my father and the pastor, who was a representative of the World Council of Churches, became friends. The American had been duped by the Reds' talk of liberty and freedom of religion, and he was going about making pro-Communist speeches. Father was able to convince him of what was really happening.

More little mishaps enlivened the royal audience. The King and the Queen Mother received the visitors standing, but pointed to where they should sit. My father immediately sat down: only when he was comfortably settled did he realise that the King was still standing. At last they entered the scarlet and gold salon for luncheon. It was the custom to put down one's fork if one had had enough of a dish. My father, while answering the questions of the King and Queen Mother, put his knife and fork down several times without tasting a mouthful, and each time a footman would sweep away his plate. So my father went hungry.

King Michael showed them the wall in his study, which had cracked when Vishinsky, the Soviet foreign minister, slammed the door after delivering Moscow's ultimatum to form a Communist-dominated Government. After having eaten at the palace, father and his colleague left and went to a restaurant.

King Michael's reign did not long survive. On December 30th, 1947, the Communist who would soon take over the country went with his stooge, Groza, to present the King with abdication which he was told to sign there and then. King Michael refused, upon which the palace was encircled by troops. The Communists said that he was an 'unsettling influence' — his would be the responsibility for the bloodshed and civil war that would follow his refusal to sign. So the King acquiesced, and the Kingdom of Rumania ceased to exist.

The People's Republic began its life on the same day. My mother explained what this so-called 'abdication' meant. King Michael would be driven out. He must leave his palace and the country. This made me most unhappy. Though not too sure what kings actually did, I knew King Michael was young, and his picture in school showed him to be handsome. Besides, he was 'Defender of the fatherland'. I liked him. I suggested he come and live with us.

'We have no room,' said my mother. 'The house is already full.'

I said he could share my bed. It was big and I was small.

'Ah, but the Queen Mother will have to come too,' my father said. 'And all the court. They will fill sixty cars, at least. You cannot ask a king without his courtiers.'

So I abandoned the idea. I cut King Michael's picture from my history book because we were ordered to by the teacher. But I kept it for years, until it was lost in the seizure of our belongings.

Our church faced fresh persecution. One evening, while I was being bathed by Carlie, the doorbell rang. I emerged to find father arguing with two members of the secret police. He was being taken from us by the Communists, as he had been by the Nazis.

'I will not leave this house quietly,' father warned, 'unless we are allowed to sing a hymn and pray. If you want no trouble, you'll sit and listen.'

Nonplussed, they sat. We sang and prayed together, and my father took his time reading a psalm from the Bible. Then they carried him off.

On this first occasion, he was held for six weeks. Then, through the intervention and protests of friends — we still knew a few people of influence who had not been arrested — he was released. But this, of course, was only a trial run, a momentary relief before the storm.

My father realised that his being arrested for good by the Communists was now only a matter of time. He sent me to stay for a while with friends in the countryside. When I returned, he was gone. He had simply vanished from the street, one Sunday morning in February 1948, as he walked to church.

My mother tried to comfort me by saying he would be gone perhaps for only a month or two. But the months passed while she tramped from office to government office in the snow. She waited in the halls of the People's Security H.Q. and the icy yards of prisons. The officials shrugged: they had no records of Richard Wurmbrand's arrest.

It was months before we learnt the truth: he had been kidnapped from the street, bundled into a car by agents, then placed in the cells deep below the great square in front of the Ministry of the Interior. I must have passed a hundred times over his head. Here, in a windowless cube measuring three paces by three with only a pipe in the ceiling for air, thirty feet below ground, my father lived for nearly three years, seeing no man but the guards and interrogators.

Men from the local Party branch came to look over our home. We had far too much living space, they said: a ten-year-old boy could not have a room to himself. I must move into my mother's room. The rest of the house would be requisitioned and the mission would follow later. We might expect new tenants very soon.

The first arrived a few days after this: he was a captain, with the blue tabs of an officer of the People's Security — a nice name for the secret police — on his Russian-type uniform. We never knew to which of its many branches he belonged — I suspected he was involved in the 'discovery of hostile elements', or perhaps their creation, artificially, by provocation. These were the biggest departments.

He moved into my bedroom, sleeping in my bed and using the furniture that had been mine. When he wanted a larger table, he simply took the one in our living-room which my mother had kept polished for so many years, plus a few other items that caught his eye.

But my mother had one thought uppermost in her mind. She warned me, 'As long as he stays, don't offend him. He's a powerful person, and he may help us to reach your father.'

But the captain had nothing to communicate beyond his immediate needs. In these, girls figured prominently. Two or three times a week he brought women back to entertain in my old bedroom. He kept a supply of liquor in the chest of drawers which I had used for my clothes.

We saw little of him. He was out all day. He ate in his officers' mess and worked long hours. My mother, still hopeful that she might obtain news of father, tried to run into him 'accidentally'; but he avoided us as much as he could.

Oddly, it was we, the counter-revolutionaries, who were asked about him. Two agents in plain-clothes called while the captain was out and questioned my mother about his habits.

'We know nothing,' she said. 'We hardly ever see him.'

Then, in 1948, the confiscation of all property by the state began. The doctor from whom we had rented this house lost everything. Now we paid rent to the state for our room. It was difficult. Mother had no income, and her small savings had gone on attempts to bribe officials who might supply information about father. We lived on the charity of friends.

It was the same for all. Did not Lenin say that private ownership creates capitalism and the bourgeoisie? Peasant and landlord alike lost all they possessed, and a vast Communist bureaucracy grew up to handle the affairs of the monstrous state machine.

Party membership rose from its natural level of a few thousand to more than half a million. A party card could mean the difference between eating and starving.

The Communists closed down my Roman Catholic school. Some of its priests were arrested, the rest dismissed. The Roman Catholic Church was one of the first Communist targets. The Reds knew their enemies: my father, himself a Protestant, saw in jail how Catholic priests resisted torture and coercion better than other clergy. This is one value of celibacy: it trains a man to resist temptation.

At school, we changed overnight from Latin masses and daily prayers to science-worship and classes in atheism. Our hymns of praise were now dedicated to Lenin and Stalin. Visits to church were replaced by tours of the 'House of Culture'. Each pupil had to contribute a regular essay to help 'the fight against religion and sorcery'. They copied them from newspaper articles ridiculing churchgoers as illiterate fanatics. All these were pasted up in the 'Red Corner' — a corner of the classroom filled with atheistic propaganda and pictures.

Our new principal was a stern Jewish lady, a good teacher who played the Communist from necessity. She wore her grey hair drawn back into a bun and lectured to us daily on natural science: how Old Testament views of cosmology and creation were fantastic in the light of today's knowledge; how new discoveries made the Bible's version of man's development look absurd. She harped repeatedly on the trial of Scopes the American teacher who wanted to bring Darwin's theory of evolution into the classroom. (He was fined $100—opponents of atheism are killed by the Communists.)

I used to ask questions. What made great scientists like Einstein and Newton believe in God? How could creation happen by accident? — it was as if the lunch we were about to eat appeared without being prepared by our mothers. They could not really answer these arguments I had learnt from my parents. But they could talk around them, and silence me.

Yet I got good grades. Some teachers were secretly pleased to see a pupil argue against the propaganda they were obliged to spoonfeed to us. Finally, I ran into bad trouble.

The Communists organised the 'Pioneers' — a youth movement with cells in every school. Its chief purpose was to take children more and more out of their parents' influence and into the Party's arms. Outstanding pupils were given a red 'Pioneer' scarf. They could not be bought or sold. Not to wear this prize was unthinkable.

We sat behind our scarred desks while the principal extolled the joys of being a 'Pioneer'. Because this was a People's

Democracy, she said, the class would be allowed to nominate some pupil as the first candidate. They proposed me.

She looked displeased. The boys grinned. Then she turned to the class and said doubtfully, 'Well, Wurmbrand is a very lucky boy. I hope he appreciates the honour.' I stood up.

'I don't want to wear the scarf,' I said. 'It's the badge of the Party that keeps my father unjustly in prison.'

My voice sounded unnaturally loud. Everyone stared.

'Won't wear it!' the teacher bridled. 'You'll regret this, my boy!' She scolded on a few minutes more. It was annoying for her: only recently she'd won the principal's job and her pupils' behaviour reflected on her. Ten-year-olds were not supposed to call Party insignia symbols of oppression.

It seemed likely that I would be expelled. I told my mother what had happened. She had so many troubles, carrying on the work of the church and helping people whose relatives had been arrested, and looking every day for some way to reach my father, that I hated to upset her more. But she sent a friend to the school to see what they intended to do about me. This friend explained my situation.

To begin with, the principal had thought I was a boy from the German minority, and that my father had been thrown into jail as a Fascist. When she heard that we were Jews who had been persecuted by the Nazis, her attitude changed. And when she understood that my father was suffering for his Christian beliefs, she altered completely: in her heart, like almost everyone else, she loathed the Communists.

Next day I went back to school. She took me into her private office and asked a series of questions about my parents, then bent down and hugged me. From that time on I was the most protected boy in the school. All the teachers knew the story of the red scarf and were secretly delighted about it.

After the birth of the state of Israel had created an exodus of Jews from every part of Europe to the Holy Land, the Communists began to sell Rumanian Jews to Israel for dollars. Jewish agencies in the West would pay this desperately needed foreign currency to the Communist Government. And the Jews in

Romania scratched together their savings to make further bribes to the officials who controlled the waiting lists.

Some of our Jewish friends simply agreed to turn over everything they possessed — homes, furniture, all their private belongings — to officials in return for a visa. Night after night long queues of people wrapped in blankets waited outside the visa office. They brought food and slept on the pavements. The lucky ones left for the coast on trains that departed secretly by night from obscure sidings. It could not be admitted that people wanted to escape from the delights of the People's Republic.

Every few weeks a teacher would suddenly vanish from school — having enthusiastically praised Communism the day before. The class would turn up as usual: but their professor never appeared. He had packed his bags quietly and left, with no goodbyes, for Israel. They did not boast that they were escaping — some official might have cancelled their visa. They simply vanished and were replaced by others of lower standard. Finally, our principal herself made off to the Promised Land. One day she was present, the next she was gone and a new teacher occupied her office.

It was a situation that led to many jokes. A favourite one was about the two ships that passed in the Black Sea. The Russian ship displayed a huge banner: 'For the cause of Marxism and Leninism, forward'. The ship carrying Jews to Israel also had a banner with the slogan, 'Because of Marxism and Leninism, forward'.

Next the Communists passed laws making it impossible for the children of political prisoners to obtain a state education — and there was no other kind. My father's story, the red scarf incident, what was officially described as my 'rotten social origin', all combined against me: I was expelled.

That was the end of my schooldays. I was too young to get a job. There were no private schools of any kind. There was nothing for it but to stay home. Perhaps I was fortunate, in a sense: I did avoid daily indoctrination with Marxism in state schools. However much you fight against this, it is insidious and it can take over your mind almost before you realise it. Children are highly susceptible. Already I was DAC agent. The

DAC was a co-operative enterprise for collecting scrap iron. Organisers in every school handed out DAC buttons and urged us to collect more. With ten million toothpaste tubes, the Government could build half a battleship, and so on. I did not want to help the people who had taken my father in any way, but I was caught up in this game of collecting. I found myself pledging to collect so much scrap by August 23rd, day of the Red Army occupation. In many ways, through red corners and red scarves, through DAC and Pioneer groups, through Marxist and atheist indoctrination, we learnt to think as they meant us to think.

I obtained an erratic but very broad education from my father's books. Shakespeare, Voltaire, St. Augustine and the Greek myths; St. Catherine of Genoa and the Hindu *Vedas*; politics and sex manuals; medical dictionaries, psychology textbooks; Kierkegaard, Kafka, books of Jewish mysticism — the legends of the Baalshem and the Hasidic stories. I spent entire days reading. Some were in French, which is almost a second language in Rumania. I knew some, and soon grew more proficient. There was a treatise on yoga in French, and I was fascinated. I learned to stand on my head for long spells. But when I demonstrated this accomplishment to my mother, she said only, 'I think feet are made for standing on.'

In the heat of the summer my mother sent me for a short holiday with family friends in the northern province of Moldavia. When I returned, happy and full of my adventures some weeks later, I found my 'Auntie' Alice, an old friend of mother's, waiting for me alone.

She wept as she explained that my mother had been arrested.

Now I was without father or mother.

The secret police had come on the night of August 22nd, 1950. (I remembered that a state factory near us in Moldavia had been burnt down that night. There had been similar incidents across the nation.) It was the day before the national celebrations arranged to mark the anniversary of our 'liberation' by the Red army. The Communists feared an uprising.

They feared sabotage in the towns and a peasant revolt in the countryside against collectivisation. There had been arson in state factories, pitched battles between unarmed villagers and soldiers on the land.* So the Communists had cause for alarm. More than 5,000 people were arrested in the night before August 23rd. In their panic they were afraid even of my peace-loving mother.

They had taken her at five in the morning. She was in bed, and they made her dress before the eyes of grinning militiamen. The secret police tore the room apart, looking for heaven knows what. No one knew where she was held.

Pastor Solheim, too, had to go. My father's associate in the mission for many years was forced to leave the country.

I recall nothing about the weeks that followed. Despair threatened to swallow me. But human beings can bear only so much pain and fright: then a barrier comes down to shield you, and you suffer dumbly like an animal. It was a horribly strange time. I felt utterly abandoned. I think I wept at night, alone in bed. It became very clear that, however much my father might take the lead in daily affairs, my mother was the rock of love, to which we clung.

Her Bible, big and beautifully bound, remained behind. My father gave it to her years ago, when they became Christians. Between the printed pages were pages for notes. Over the years these had been covered with the daily thoughts of my parents.

I read the psalms. They are the most effective medicine against grief like mine. In them are cries to God of anger, rebellion, remorse, confession, praise and deep expressions of strength in adversity. One's woes seem so like the sufferings told here.

* Ten years later, in 1962, the then Prime Minister Georghiou Dej, shocked the country by admitting that 80,000 working peasants had been tried in 'infamous frame-ups'. 30,000 of them in public 'courts-martial' quick sessions before army officers in public to terrorise the people. An undisclosed number of thousands were shot at this time.

I read for many nights. Then I turned back to the Book of Genesis and began to read the Bible, a chapter each day. As I read, the writing and notes on the pages in between brought back my mother and father.

I heard that my father had been 'tried'. A military court-martial — the military dealt with 'political' cases — held a hearing that lasted ten minutes and sentenced him to twenty years in prison. He had been held at that time for more than three years without trial.

What was my father sentenced for, I am sometimes asked by people with the bourgeois prejudice that nobody should be arrested without reason. In a Communist country, the question put about a faithful pastor, or any honest man, is: How has he escaped prison?

Never was any sentence read to my father. Ten years later, I attended his second trial. Never was a motivated sentence read to us, his family and sole audience to the hearing. So you must decide for yourself what he was sentenced for; almost any accusation will do.

Watchman Nee, the renowned Chinese evangelical writer, was imprisoned in Red China partly on the charge that he committed adultery with numerous women. Catholic nuns there were condemned on accusations of murdering the children they had nursed. In the Soviet Union, Pastor Krivolapov is in prison. The reason? He has slit the throat of a child of three, while the congregation around him sang hymns, this being part of the ritual taught by Baptists and Pentecostals. Cardinal Mindszenty was a spy; the Hungarian Bishop Ordass, a black marketeer. In Czechoslovakia, Rumania, Bulgaria, men who worked to establish Communism such as Rajk, Slansky, Artur London, Patrascanu were tortured or executed as 'agents of foreign powers' or police informers for the old regimes. Some of those who were killed have now been rehabilitated. Except that Marxism teaches the eternal soul does not exist. The dead are dead and that is it. So whom did they rehabilitate? In our country the Catholic bishops were sentenced for spying or preparing armed insurrection, the priests for sexual immorality. They all confessed to these crimes. So

26

anyone may choose, according to his taste, the reason for a twenty year sentence.

After the sentence on my father, they seized our last belongings. One October morning three inspectors came to make an inventory. Chairs, desks, books, our stove, cups, saucers, knives and forks, pictures, the radio, my mother's sewing machine: they took everything. Except the most useful thing of all to me — father's typewriter, a heavy old Smith-Corona, the kind that lasts forever. It had been hidden under some old clothes that they had thrown about the room. God blinded them for the moment: the typewriter was put to good use for the Underground Church in the years ahead. It was our first underground 'printing press'.

I watched the inspectors turning over my father's books — luckily I'd put most of them in the attic — then ran downstairs to telephone Aunt Alice. She arrived just as they were finishing the job.

'You responsible for this kid?' asked one. 'Then sign here.'

He pushed the inventory towards her.

'But you've taken even his bed,' protested Alice.

'We are here just to make an inventory.'

She signed.

'The premises must be vacated within twenty-four hours. A worker's family is moving in tomorrow.' They left, with a final warning not to move any of our things.

I packed a bag with a few clothes. She helped me to carry the cumbersome machine to the tram halt. We boarded a number nineteen for the other side of Bucharest.

Alice shared her apartment with only three other people — her father Mr. Grigore, a twenty-year-old girl who was studying medicine at the University, and an orphan of my own age, Radu, whom she had taken in off the streets.

Mr. Grigore was very much head of the house. Once he had been well-to-do, a top inspector on the railroads; now his expert knowledge kept him in his job. He didn't like the new regime; but he knew it couldn't do without him, nor he without

27

the pay-packet that kept his household going. At seventy, he still worked an eight-hour day, six days a week .

There were only three bedrooms in the house, so we, the children, had to share Alice's room. From the window, across the tree-lined street, was a big cemetery; on the corner, a children's hospital.

There was a terrible epidemic of polio that summer. Thousands of children were left paralysed, although the Salk vaccine was available by that time. The Communists refused to import it: they had to practise medicine 'in the spirit of the class struggle', which meant doing without such imperialist drugs as penicillin and streptomycin. Many lives were lost, not only for lack of these drugs but through the vast black market which sold them adulterated with other substances that often killed the patient.

Old Mr. Grigore gave Radu and me money to visit the cinema once every two months. He was a mine of stories, and loved to make jokes about the new regime.

One concerned a teacher who asked his class at the end of every week what good deeds they had done. His pupil Paul said, 'I helped an old lady get on the bus.' 'Good,' said the teacher. Michael said, 'I also helped the old lady get on the bus.' 'Well, good.' Then Stephen said, 'I helped Paul and Michael put the old lady on the bus.' 'But why,' asked the teacher, 'were so many of you helping this lady on to the bus?' Paul replied, 'She didn't want to get on.'

Mr. Grigore cackled. 'That's how the Communists make our country happy! Get on the bus, or we'll kill you!'

But he warned us to be very careful about repeating the scores of anti-Communist jokes that went the rounds. Distrust everyone. Many were now in prison for telling jokes to the wrong person. Anyone could be an informer.

Mr. Grigore was at work all day. Radu could still go to school, while Alice was out for long hours searching for food in the empty stores or doing church work.

So I was much alone. It wasn't a happy time. Thoughts of my mother and father tormented me. Would I ever see them again? What would become of me? No parents, no education, no job; nothing to do, nowhere to go. I sat staring out of the window at the graveyard across the road for hours at a time. I tried to learn English, so that I could read some books by Conan Doyle which were in the house. (I even imagined I could speak it, until years later I met an English person who couldn't understand a word I said.)

I must have read my mother's Bible from cover to cover half-a-dozen times.

I played a lot of chess with Radu, and quarrelled with him a lot, too; frustrated and envious, with all my tensions locked up inside me, I took it out on poor Radu. He was very different in personality from me: stolid where I was temperamental, gliding with the stream, while I was always fighting against it. He was a good boy, and I loved him. But sometimes I just had to explode.

When Radu finished elementary classes he found a place in a technical high school and encouraged me to apply as well. But I was too green to lie about my father. The application was at once rejected.

I spent entire days waiting in line for food for our 'family'. Rumania had been called 'the granary of Europe': though small in size, it had been the world's sixth largest producer of corn, but now we were starving. One queued for hours to buy a loaf of bread and the joke went round, 'Have some more bread with your bread.' There was nothing else, though we had lots of coloured coupons for unobtainable foods. One day I visited seven stores, one after the other, and discovered nothing but bottles of vinegar and ersatz coffee.

When a store received a few kilos of oil or rice, word flew round the city in a flash. A giant queue would form, of which perhaps a tenth could be served. It was not only food: everything was in short supply. In another joke, a listener asks the state radio:

'My wife will have her first child in a couple of weeks. But because of our great economic plan, the state stores will have no diapers until nine months from now. What should I do?'

Answer: 'Have another baby as soon as possible.'

Aunt Alice was a member of the keenly evangelistic

Plymouth Brethren, which had many followers in Rumania. Because of the persecution of minority churches she had started coming to my father's services — the only Protestant services in Rumania during the war. She became one of his most devoted disciples.

She was a little set in her quiet ways, and not used to coping with two noisy boys who missed their parents and were reaching an awkward age. Now I see how kind she was: then we seemed just a burden.

After my mother's arrest, the congregations at our church dwindled. Sixty would attend, where there had been 500. My mother had taken on all father's work. She had discussed with the leaders of various churches, how to resist the pressure we faced. Pastors needed state permission now to preach. We knew that some were acting as informers. So more and more we held our services in private homes or in the open. The Underground Church had been born.

Our former church remained open, but the man who had replaced my father had none of his gift. He was more Lutheran than Luther, and his wife invited the church members to call her 'Madam Pastor'. St. Peter's wife had not been called 'Madam Pastor'.

Then the secret police went to work on this pastor. Afterwards he became known as an informer.

Inevitably, I also began to question my faith a little. It was not a rejection but rather a feeling of abandonment, of losing God along with my mother and father. Would I ever see them again? Would I ever be allowed to go to school, or to work? Would I ever make friends of my own age, or would most of them always be scared to talk to me? I seemed to be becoming a non-person, living life in a vacuum.

I could not even go into the public library because I had no student or worker's card. And I quickly exhausted Mr. Grigore's collection of books.

I could not go to the movies. My mother had asked me not to go to the Russian films that were shown everywhere. Despite that, I went with the money Mr. Grigore gave us. But not for long. The first we saw was about the Korean war: scene one – defeatist doctor tells gallant Red soldier that his leg must be amputated immediately, but it's impossible because the nearest hospital is miles away: scene two – gallant Red soldier amputates own leg with lid from rusty tin, singing patriotic songs to deaden the pain: scene three — soldier is back in the front line ready to crush the imperialists. And so on.

I tried again later. This time the film concerned a thirteen-year-old Russian boy who runs away to the front in World War II. Before his age is discovered he becomes a hero by spying behind the German lines. As a reward, he is permitted to serve on at the front.

All these films were the same, long glorifications of military might with sometimes a peace message thrown in during the last minute. (After the other side had been wiped out.)

So movies, too, were not for me. I could have no fun and no future.

And then a postcard arrived from my mother.

It was only a few lines — they allowed no more. She was in a labour camp at the canal. She was well. I could come to visit her on the last Sunday in February. She loved me.

I read the message again and again. I placed it inside her Bible, only to open it and read the words in her beloved hand-writing a dozen times more, all my troubles gone for the moment.

The canal was a huge slave-labour project. It was to run for scores of miles across a plain from the Danube to the Black Sea. It would cost billions. Tons of rock had to be blasted out, factories built, whole towns set up to house workers on the spot. It was to become the industrial Ruhr of Eastern Europe. Probably Stalin saw it as being of military use, too: alone among Rumanian development schemes he approved this one; and when he died, so did the canal.

The tens of thousands in the labour camps were mostly political prisoners: politicians, priests, intellectuals; dispossessed farmers, 'idle' workers, Chritians, absentees, anti-semites and Zionist leaders. Anyone, in short, whom the state thought might prove troublesome, including a large category of Communists who had fallen into disgrace.

My mother's camp was near Cernavoda, a small town on the Danube where a long bridge crosses the great river, a three-hour journey by train.

On the Sunday I rose at five a.m. Snow lay in the streets. Alice had scoured the shops and found some dried fruit and nuts to put into a jar of preserves to go with the bread that would be the staple of my mother's diet. There were some hard-boiled eggs and other rare things. In all, it had cost an average worker's monthly salary. We had used some money sent by our family abroad.

I arrived in Cernavoda at nine a.m., then walked for an hour towards the camp against a bitter wind mixed with sleet. The basket of food grew heavier with every mile.

On Sundays even the 'politicals' who had lost all rights were supposed to be allowed some rest; yet all the women were out at work. The guards herded the visitors into a wired-off compound and took down their names. There we waited for two more hours. Towards midday it began to rain. There was no shelter and an east wind pierced us to the bone.

Then, through the grey rain that came at us slanting across the low level country, we saw approaching a long column of suffering beings. The road was muddy and the fields on either side were wet and soggy. They came towards us very slowly, stumbling sometimes because of the wind and the mud. Some of the women had wrapped their feet in rags bound up with strips of cloth. Others wore boots that were too big for them. On either side of the column were guards, big uniformed men with guns who seemed not to belong to the same species as the thin creatures they drove along like the column of lost souls from Dante's *Inferno: si lunga tratta di gente* . . .

I could not believe that my mother was one of these people. They came on down the road trampling indifferently through the pools of standing water and went past us. I could not see her. The column halted and the guards outside shouted at the guards inside and then the column moved on into camp.

We waited another two hours in the compound. The rain

began to slacken. There was nowhere to sit down. I wished it was all over.

I could not feel angry. I could not feel anything much, except a little fear. The rain and cold had washed everything away.

Sometime in the afternoon a guard came and unlocked the gate.

'Everybody out on the road!' He was a big, hook-nosed man who looked like a gypsy. 'No visits today.'

A woman asked a question.

'They've been slacking. This is a punishment.'

There were murmurs of protest.

'Shut up. Those are my orders.'

By the time we got back to Cernavoda station it was dark but the rain had stopped. The train lurched through the countryside where nothing showed but patches of melting snow.

Some weeks passed, blank weeks broken by Sundays of much bustle and incident. With Alice we attended two, sometimes three church services in a day. Each service lasted hours and included a dozen hymns. Everyone knew me and wished to show kindness to 'the martyrs' child'. My mother and father had grown to heroic stature. And the pastor who had replaced them was simultaneously shrinking in authority as he and his wife became more unpopular.

Every Sunday I found myself at a gathering in a strange house. I was the only true representative of Pastor Wurmbrand and Mrs. Wurmbrand. I was the centre of all attention. Old ladies, young mothers, schoolgirls crowded round, all eager to feed and fuss over this little doll. At twelve years old I was expected to pronounce judgement on all kinds of personal and religious problems. How traumatic this could be for a child thrown into maturity like a non-swimmer into deep water.

A month later came a new card from my mother. I should come again next Sunday and hope for better luck. Once again we scratched together the money for the fare and a basket of food.

It was a cold dry day. After a few hours of waiting in the compound we saw women lining up before their huts inside the camp. Some waved to us but they were too far away to recognise a face.

There were several hundred visitors and the guards watched us as closely as the prisoners. They marched us into an open field where rows of trestle tables had been set up in the mud. The visitors were lined up behind one row of wooden tables. The prisoners stood behind another. In the corridor between patrolled a short fat grey-haired woman.

The tables were ten yards apart and across the space were bawled tearful greetings and tragedies and news of births and deaths. The east wind carried away their voices but above the crying and the shouting rose the gross leathern voice of the woman officer.

'That question is not permitted!' She bellowed, with all the cold command that comes from having a gun bouncing on your hip. 'That question is not permitted.'

Not many questions were permitted. Some people simply stood and gazed at each other and wept.

They called my name. I struggled through the crush to a place behind the barricade of tables. Across the corridor I saw my mother. Her face was grey and pinched and she looked very ill. I had never seen her so thin. She wore a ragged dress and a scarf round her head. She held out her hands and smiled her beautiful smile.

I was shaking badly and couldn't find anything to say.

'Is there any news of Daddy?' she called.

'That question is not permitted!'

My mother was weeping. I could not bear to see her standing in the cold wind and crying. They had taken everything from us and now they would not let us talk. She looked very beautiful and I started to weep as well. So not much could be said between us anyway. All around us people were yelling and I was confused. Then I saw they were leading her away.

'Mihai, believe in Jesus,' she called. Then she was gone.

Someone was shaking my shoulder. It was their turn now.

I walked numbly away from the labour camp along the muddy road over the plain to Cernavoda. Poor, poor mother. This was the price they made you pay for being yourself, for having faith. She was so incredibly thin. This was what you got for the crime of loving others with all your heart.

I didn't get home until very late. I couldn't tell Alice and the others anything of what happened. I kept shaking my head. I felt numb and empty and I just wanted to be alone and sleep.

In the morning I took out the Bible my father had given me years before and sat for a long time reading. All the other books had lost their importance. I wanted to read a psalm of David. It was the only prayer that could calm my soul. All that week I read the Bible with a kind of passion. I thought that if my mother could go on believing in God under such conditions, then I could not do without him either. I understood it better now. Her poor body, her proud intellect could not have withstood. But faith upheld. Not understanding, simply believing, she clung to Jesus.

Not for years did I understand the crisis I passed through at this time. But I mark that day as the day of my conversion, the start of my real life as a Christian.

I am a slow starter. Ideas lie a long time in my mind: then one day I wake up knowing exactly what I must do. In the Bible God says, 'My strength is made perfect in weakness.' Thus He will conquer whatever we impose upon our souls. You cover the earth with concrete but sometimes the grass bursts through. The soil is in conspiracy with the grass. It is not meant for asphalt. So the love of God is in conspiracy with the human heart.

We heard that mother had become too ill to work. (Later we discovered that guards had thrown her into the river, breaking two ribs.) But her next postcard said only that she was working on a collective farm and visits were allowed. There were fewer restrictions. Alice could come too. It was only a few miles outside Bucharest.

On Sunday we went by tram to the outskirts, then took two buses out to the *kollektiv*. She was thin still with hollows under her eyes. But she looked stronger. The summer sun had tanned her face and arms and she was more cheerful. Her eyes shone and she cried only a little.

'How is the work?' we asked.

Very hard, she said, but because this was a collective that supplied only top party members, food was plentiful and varied. She worked all day in the fields. Sometimes the heat made people faint. But it was better than the canal.

I told her some of my troubles and a great tenderness and warmth passed between us. We did not have long together. Alice promised to take good care of me: I promised to take care of Alice. We said goodbye.

The months turned to years. I continued to live with Alice and Mr. Grigore and Radu, resigned to living a life insulated from the things boys go through, school and games; joining clubs and going on expeditions. The summer and the winter went their way. The days were uneventful and if one believed the soothing propaganda in the newspapers so was the world, except for America where things went from bad to worse and everyone was starving.

I remember that I was able to bring two people to Christ. The first was the mother of a boy named Constantine who helped me study maths. She was herself a teacher. One day at Constantine's home, she asked about my parents. She listened quietly and said that her own husband, a professor of philosophy, had died recently. She seemed lonely and unhappy and I invited her to come next Sunday to our church. I gave her one of my father's books to read.

She was really impressed.

'Tell me more about your father,' she asked.

So I told her about my childhood and our life together and my visits to the labour camp and my mother. I explained how reading the psalms had kept me from despair.

We saw a lot of her that winter. She came to prayer meetings and we read together in the Bible. We grew to love her and she us. Eventually she came to Christ.

The second convert was a boy only a few years older than myself. I was leaving church one Sunday morning with my mind far away and I walked straight into him. He dropped some books and I helped him pick them up, apologising.

We fell into step and talked as we went along. I sensed soon enough that he was a Jew.

'What was that place you were leaving?' he asked.

'The Lutheran church. You should look in.'

'I am a Jew.'

'So am I.'

I explained a little my circumstances.

'Well, my family are very strict and Orthodox.'

'So was Jesus. So were the disciples.'

We talked for hours that Sunday. He was curious and had a lively mind that time had not closed. We met again and at last I persuaded him to look around the church. We argued about the hatred many Rumanian Orthodox people had towards the Jews, and the anti-semitism of the Lutherans.

'The sins and crimes are theirs,' I argued. 'But Christ's teachings are really the religion of the Jews expanded to include the whole world. The Jewish religion is false because it is Jewish: you never hear of Polish science or French medicine — these things are international. So is Christianity.'

He came to supper at Aunt Alice's house. He had never seen a New Testament. I showed him one and as we talked I read passages to explain what I meant about the relationship of Judaism and Christianity.

He was surprised by many things. 'But that is beautiful,' he said. 'I never knew!'

He began to read more deeply in the Gospels and from week to week his conviction grew. At last he told us he wished to be baptised.

Today he studies theology in Scandinavia.

But these friendships could not fill the void inside me. I felt lonely and hollow.

A few weeks later I took a walk down Victory Boulevard. The main thoroughfare was empty of traffic. A gang of women were clearing the pavement of melting snow. Another winter had passed and I still lived in my private limbo. I was resigned to having only a past. The future was blank as ever. I tried not to think all the time of my parents. It hurt too much. I turned back towards Alice's, past the huge portraits of Marx, Engels, Lenin, Stalin. The bearded ones flapped in the stiff breeze.

There was a faint scent of spring in the air. The trees along the road had small green shoots on the branches.

In my room, I tried to read. I heard a knock on the door and then Alice's voice, crying out.

I ran into the hall and saw my mother there smiling her fantastic smile.

'Mihai!'

'Mother!'

I kissed her and hugged her, weeping and laughing.

'I think I'm going to faint,' said Alice. 'Oh, I can't believe it!' She began to cry and went into the kitchen.

We looked at each other. She wore old patched rags like a gypsy woman and her feet were lost inside man's boots that were too big for her. She carried a straw basket that held all she possessed. I saw how thin her shoulders were and how the bones stood out in her lovely face. I was taller than her now.

At last she began to weep.

'Don't cry too much, mother.'

'Of course not.'

But we went on weeping anyhow.

Alice came out of the kitchen. 'I'm so happy!' she sobbed. Her eyes and nose were red with the tears. 'Don't mind me. I'm not crying.'

My mother laughed. 'None of us are.'

She had been released only that morning from Ghencea, the transit camp outside Bucharest. She had set out from the same camp nearly three years before for the canal. Now the canal project was dead those slave camps were closing down. It had been all a waste of money and human life. She had passed through many prisons and worked on many collective farms since leaving the canal and they had freed her as they had taken her, without explanation. She had not even a few pennies to pay her tram fare. But as soon as people knew from where she came, everyone offered to pay.

Alice began to prepare some food. By the time it was ready we were calmer and after we had eaten we sat up talking for a long time.

My mother at once took me in hand. After years of hunger and privation, she began at once to work for others again. She had never stopped, really. In the camps, she was the one they all turned to for comfort. She saw my situation and she thought about finding me a job. I was fourteen now and I might work. But who would give a post to the son of a political prisoner?

We walked by the lake, through the trees in Cismigiu Park. There was much to talk about. The talking eased the pain that had been there for so long. I felt in my heart a great wish to live again.

My mother spoke to many old friends but none of them could help. Most were as poor as we were.

'Why don't you ask Mr. Constantine?' said Alice. 'He works at the Opera now. He used to know many people.'

Mr. Constantine was an elderly aristocrat. He had a little pointed silver beard and pince-nez and no money. The family were descended from the nobility and his father had been a famous general in the First World War. Those parts of their property not destroyed by the Nazis were taken by the Communists. A few things he treasured had been saved and he kept them with him in his single room.

The room was one in what had been his own house. I went there one morning in March after my mother had talked to him. He thought he might find work for an assistant at the Opera, where he was now the tuner.

The house was a big old mansion in a quiet street not far from Alice's place. It had heavy old doors that you had to push with both hands to open. The hallway smelt of bad cooking and damp. Workers' families had moved in on every floor. The stairs were clean enough but everywhere plaster was cracking and paint was scuffed and boards showed where carpets had lain. The vanished pictures had left cleaner patches on walls. I heard voices arguing, children crying, radios playing.

I climbed three flights of stairs and knocked. Mr. Constantine opened the door, smiling. He had beautiful manners. They seemed very natural and made all the people who were shouting 'comrade' at other people, whom they hated, look even more stupid. He was wearing an old silk dressing-gown.

Almost everyone called him 'the Maestro'. He had studied music in France and Switzerland and found the tuner's job at the Opera before the Communists took over completely, so that he had a worker's card. He could buy food and drew a salary from the state. Not many of his class had so much foresight.

'Tell me about your father,' he said.

I told him. He asked about my own life and tastes and beliefs. I loved music and we talked about that; then we discussed books. There was a piano over on the far side of his bed and many books. Bibles, dictionaries, concordances; Lenin and Kierkegaard and Martin Buber; titles in French, German, Russian and English as well as Rumanian. He spoke six languages.

'I have some prestige still at the Opera, Mihai,' he said. 'I daresay they would take you on as my assistant, if you would like that?'

'I'd like it very much.'

'We must see what sort of ear you have. For this work one needs perfect pitch.'

He talked about my duties. He looked very fragile in the light that came through the tall window with the faded drapery.

'One thing; you must never say to anyone what has happened to your father.'

I promised.

He made us coffee on a small stove jammed behind the door.

'To your success,' he said.

I obtained from the employment bureau the sixteen-page form that every candidate for a job must fill up. It took me an entire evening. Form-filling in Communist countries requires the making of many ink-blots. You take your first form back to the personnel officer, explaining that you have spoilt it. He gives you another. This for your own records so that you will know what untruths you have told to get the job. Over the years you may fill in a score of these forms. They detail every part of your life: from cradle to grave — and your parents' lives, too. One question asked on all such forms is whether they have been arrested or imprisoned for political reasons. I simply left it unanswered, putting a line through the space. After all my father had been kidnapped, not arrested; and my mother never received a trial.

I gave such details as seemed safe about my education, record and beliefs. They wanted the names and addresses of two neighbours in every place we had lived during my lifetime. You had to be careful to give always the same names, names of people you trusted not to talk too much when the secret police came checking on you. The information in your dossier follows you through your life. An untruth told because you wish to eat some bread can cause you serious trouble perhaps ten years later, if discovered.

Permission came through, and I started work at the State Opera House. It was a large baroque building near the river. The drapes were red velvet and the chandeliers glittered like frozen fountains. Music is not amenable to Communisation: so, with the introduction of a few Russian works into the repertoire, the Opera continued its bourgeois ways.

My job had its advantages. I did not have to clock in — in itself an astonishing piece of laxity. The state usually controlled every minute of the working day. But with so many singers and extras coming and going and most of the rehearsing done in an annexe with sound-proofed rooms nearby it was difficult to keep check on everybody.

The Maestro and I tuned the pianos in rehearsal rooms or repaired instruments for only a few hours each morning. Then we set out together on private house calls, among his wide New Rich clientele. The top Party men all sought a bourgeois musical education for their offspring and the Maestro had more customers than he could handle. I had a good ear and I'd received some music lessons before my father's arrest. So I took on many of Mr. Constantine's house calls. I made about $10 a month as my official salary from the Opera (the Maestro's was only $40), but twice that sum came in from private clients.

Some members of the *ancien régime* had also kept their pianos. So I moved from the cramped single rooms where the families of the old ruling class lived among relics of the past and would not chop up the Bechstein for firewood, to the bare apartments of the new masters, determined to give little Georghe the proper education. From one came long denunciations of the regime; from the other paeans of praise.

The Maestro steered a careful course, never allowing himself to be provoked. He was much loved in the homes of the old bourgeoisie. I was quickly accepted.

'Whatever Mihai hears within these walls,' said the Maestro, 'he knows better than to repeat.' And he would tell my story.

The talk was often about U.S. intervention. People could not believe that the Americans would let the Russian armies occupy half Europe and install by force Communist Governments everywhere. They clung to the hope of rescue long after the possibility had faded.

The young were more cynical. If there was a loud noise in the streets, someone would joke, 'Hey, quiet! I think I hear the Americans coming!'

The Maestro asked me to talk as little as possible to the Opera staff. We feared every day that my 'counter-revolutionary' parents would be discovered — which would mean the end of my job. When the artists threw little parties, I stayed away. The girls would giggle and tease me for my supposed shyness.

My mother could not work: her husband was a 'political prisoner'. A restriction order prevented her from leaving Bucharest.

'I'm lucky,' she said. 'Lots of former prisoners have been exiled to remote villages.'

We lived on my small income and the charity of friends. As the family breadwinner, I felt my importance. My name was on the vital worker's card that allowed you to buy rations. One day I wanted to buy something for myself.

'Mihai, we can't afford it,' said my mother.

'I'm supporting you now! I should have *some* spending money!'

I rushed out, banging the door behind me. The fit of pique soon passed and I came home to apologise, feeling ashamed of myself. How sharp the memory of childhood tragedies is.

My mother was never idle. She worked at home, making

clothes on an ancient sewing machine that broke down every other day. These were sold at the local flea market by a woman friend. She did all the queueing and cooking. She contacted all the old members of our church and organised prayer meetings and Bible studies all over town, learning day by day how to keep the church alive underground.

Shortly before her release, Stalin died. It was not a significant event for me. Conditions did not change in our country. The prisoners remained in prison, the people remained enslaved by the Russians. Perhaps there was some feeling of satisfaction: he had died on March 6th, the day on which he had imposed upon our king the first Communist Government.

Everywhere you saw pictures of his corpse lying in a coffin surrounded by a guard of Communist leaders who soon would also lie in coffins, but not before disowning the one whom now they honoured, and being disowned themselves a little later.

The schools were closed on the day of his funeral so that everyone, man, woman and child without exception could take part in the mourning procession. Loss of your job was among the lesser penalties for failing to attend. There were news-papermen and film cameramen from around the world. They took pictures of scores of children weeping bitterly. Many years later, the Rumanian magazine *Contemporanul* mocked at 'capitalist stupidity' and explained that if the children were crying it was because they had been given a good slap around the corner by their parade section-leader. Everyone in the parade had his numbered place and knew when and what slogans to shout. But how could a foreign newsman know that the cause of grief could be something other than the death of Roosevelt's 'good old uncle Joe' or Churchill's 'wise general-issimo'?

My adventures with the Maestro were more important to me than all this. Mr. Constantine had been giving piano lessons to the seven-year-old son of a party boss. After each session the boy would grandly order 'comrade chauffeur' to drive the Maestro home. Mr. Constantine had difficulty in persuading them to let him travel by tram. He had no wish to be seen driving through the streets in a secret police car.

At the Opera, an elderly odd job man had been appointed administrative director by the 'dictatorship of the proletariat'. This was a nice name used by Party leaders when elevating their friends to the highest posts. If a janitor becomes school principal, you may be sure that the proletariat has dictated it; and that the results will be unhappy.

One day the Opera's first harp required repairs.

'Comrade Maestro,' the new director ordered. 'See to it at once!'

'I'm sorry, comrade director, but this is an extremely delicate task, harps are specialised instruments that require an expert hand. In fact there's only one man in Bucharest at the moment who can do the job.'

'What does he charge?'

The Maestro suggested a figure.

'Outrageous, comrade! We are in the middle of a national economy drive. Comrade Georghiu Dej has personally asked all businesses to carry out their own repairs.'

Indeed, Dej — who had wrested political power from his rivals and now sat unchallenged on top of the heap — was awarding medals for feats of economy. Our director hoped for one.

The Opera's plumber was sent for and told to set to work.

'But comrade director, I know about boilers and drains, not harps.'

'Comrade, the party needs men who are ready to venture into new fields.'

The plumber took the harp down into his workshop. Soon he confessed to failure.

'I shall come in person to help!' said the director. 'Two heads are better than one.'

At the end of a morning, their combined labours had put the instrument into a worse state than before. Dismayed, they broke for a cup of coffee, leaving the harp lying on the floor, where the plumber's mate accidentally put his foot on it.

Eventually they took the instrument to the expert, who declared it now beyond repair, but was ordered to repair it anyway. He charged ten times the cost of the original job and sent it back.

The first harpist said it now sounded very much like a boiler.

But do not laugh. Millions have gone hungry thanks to this exaltation of ignorance over experience. The economies and agricultures of half Europe, of Russia, China and Cuba have been placed one after the other in the hands of incompetents with disastrous results. For many, the mistakes have meant a death sentence through famine.

Incompetence at the top is matched by indifference on lower levels. When the working man has no interest in what he does, no pride in craft or product or ownership of land, then a vast apathy reigns in every field of labour.

We tell the joke that our President went one day with his secretary to find out for himself how business was going. He entered a big grocery store and found it almost empty of food. 'How was it before?' he asked the secretary. 'Oh, a very good store. It belonged to Mr. B. who is now is prison,' said the secretary. Ceausescu ordered him released and given back his store. Next they entered a restaurant and found the same situation. The owner was under house arrest. Ceausescu ordered him put back at once. After solving a series of similar problems in businesses around the city in this way, Ceausescu was heading up Bucharest's main thoroughfare when the secretary tugged at his sleeve. 'Mr. Premier,' she begged, 'please don't go up this boulevard.' Ceausescu asked why not. 'We would pass by the former king's palace,' said the secretary.

The state was a gigantic corporation that controlled everything. When everyone served one boss as a small cog in a vast inhuman machine, what reason was there to trouble oneself with a client's wishes, why bother even to be polite? Workers cared most about underproducing: if they exceeded an official norm, it went up. Woe betide the scab who did! The norm system was taken to fantastic lengths. Bus conductors had norms for the number of people they should carry on their buses. I knew a pastor who, on release from prison in 1956, was put to work as a lavatory attendant. He found there was a norm saying that so many people a day should use the coin-operated toilets.

My own work, however, was exciting enough. I was seeing new people and places and learning new things. Sometimes I watched rehearsals of operas. It was not the best company in the world. They kept to the old war-horses they knew best.

One morning I was standing on stage watching some singers from the chorus practising their movements when suddenly I had an urgent sensation of imminent danger. I moved away from the piano where I had stood and immediately at my back there was a shattering crash. A long heavy iron bar used to support backdrops had worn through its ropes and fallen. The piano was splintered and crushed. People rushed over.

'It's a miracle you weren't killed!' said one of the singers.

The Maestro looked at my white face and suggested I take the rest of the day off. But I preferred to stay. I said a prayer of thankfulness at that moment.

Later, on our rounds, Mr. Constantine and I talked of miracles.

'If you believe in a God, it is not difficult to believe that a miracle can occur. But to believe there is no God is to believe in the most fantastic of miracles: that the universe came into being of its own accord. There is as much probability of that as of spilt milk returning by itself to the bottle.'

I had attended prayer meetings with Mr. Constantine and I knew he worked for the Church in secret. At the Opera, many people came to him with their problems, including famous artists and singers. He was able to bring some of them to Christ.

The Maestro was a fine speaker and I wished to learn his art. At fifteen years I began to speak at meetings, repeating what I had heard from my father and mother at small secret gatherings in private homes. To this I added my new 'knowledge' of archaeology, gained from the Maestro's books about recent research in the Middle East. They opened a door into the historical world of the Old Testament. I was fascinated.

I found I could talk for an hour or more and make myself understood. Twenty-minute sermons are unknown with us. On Sunday expeditions to the villages with Mr. Constantine, I addressed fifty or sixty people crowded into stuffy overheated rooms. The congregations were all nearly illiterate farmers who did not know the word archaeology; but they knew my father, and they knew thousands of Christians to be behind prison walls. My explanations of how British archaeologists had found the walls of Jericho with clear evidence of great cracks and fissures that showed the walls to have crumbled before 'some kind of earthquake' had a special significance for them. A clever boy, they would tell each other, he knew how to put it! The walls will crumble again and our imprisoned friends and relatives will be set free! Even the fact that the head of the expedition was British had its own meaning for them. The British were admired as lovers of freedom. As one speaker said, 'On the tomb of the unknown soldier in Westminster Abbey are the words "He died for the freedom of the world", and this is the spirit that still prevails in Britain today.' At that time we believed it.

I gave other examples that showed the historical foundations of the Old and New Testaments and how science was authenticating religion. This they liked, for they were forced to listen to atheistic lectures claiming that science had destroyed religious beliefs. The farmers were happy that such a 'learned boy' — one driven out of school, and still only fifteen — should prove the Bible to be true.

The meetings lasted sometimes for five hours. There was never merely one speaker. I listened to fiery peasant preachers who had wonderful story-telling gifts and not a few knew the Bible by heart. They would ask the congregation for a topic — then repeat, verse by verse, what the Bible said about it. There is not much to do in an isolated village and these speakers were immensely popular.

Between sermons, they sang. Not hymns in the Western sense. More like folk-songs, though they always had a Christian message. They were songs of love. Rumania had good song-writers.

47

Sometimes they would sing twenty songs in a row, each of a dozen or more verses. They had no song-books because the Communists had forbidden their publication. But they wrote them out by hand or cyclostyled copies for clandestine distribution. And they loved to sing the psalms, especially those that dealt with the wrath of God against the enemies of Israel. Or those that remembered Israel's captivity in Babylon, and held a promise of freedom:

'If I forget thee, O Jerusalem . . .'

When they sang, they sang with all their heart. It was lovely to hear them.

That summer the Communists organised a youth festival. Visitors from Communist Parties all over the world were invited to a three-week celebration of music, drama, art, science and sport. The Government decreed that Rumania's poor food supplies must be hoarded so that Western visitors would see a display of Communist prosperity. For months the stores were empty. Long lines waited to buy a little flour or fat. Bucharest lived on dry bread.

But on the day the festival began the shops filled with things we had not seen for years. Real coffee, white bread, butter, sweets, even steak. There was wine in the windows occupied for so long by bottles filled with coloured water.

Western Communists were not awfully impressed. The city was dead, the stores bare by their standards. But they knew that one did without in the cause of international Communism, a cause for which the visitors had more enthusiasm than their hosts.

Valeria, an old friend of my mother's, acted as guide for some of the tourists. After nearly five years in jails and labour camps, she had been freed and had found a job with O.N.T. — the National Tourist Bureau, who needed anyone who spoke languages. One day she was sent to the frontier to meet two youths from London.

'They sang Communist youth songs all the way to Bucharest,' she sighed. 'The "Internationale" every twenty minutes!'

48

One student's father owned the largest bakery chain in London, the other's was a wealthy executive in the car industry.

'Tomorrow we have to take them on a tour of the Royal Palace.' (It had become the House of Culture.)

'Poor Valeria,' said my mother.

To tell a visitor what Communism was really like when you had to live under it was dangerous and not very rewarding. They would not or could not believe it.

A friend of mine, Maxim, tried to mix with the foreign students. He met a boy from Paris, an enthusiastic Marxist who spoke about the need for an 'objective study' of problems arising from putting Marxism into practice.

'Right!' said Maxim. 'But you'll land in jail if you do.' He would not have dared to speak frankly to a Rumanian. But he assumed a young French student would be safe. He said that tens of thousands were in jail, many of them Communists, the best voices in the Party. Men who had fought all their lives for Communism were now being tortured to extract fake confessions.

'Dissent isn't being stifled here,' he said. 'It has been murdered.' Scores of political leaders had been executed for no better reason than that they were in the way of the men who had clawed to the top.

The French student was silent.

Maxim tried to explain some of the fear and suspicion that ruled in a country where neighbour was forced to spy on neighbour, and friend on friend.

He explained how the people's contempt for the regime had created a great store of underground jokes, and he told one that he liked especially:

A professor asked his class, 'Who took Troy? Geamănul, can you tell us?'

Geamănul, knowing the heavy penalties for theft of public property, said, 'It wasn't me, sir!'

The professor threw up his hand, flung his book at the boy's head and walked out of the classroom, crying, 'Our culture is dead! I cannot go on.'

In the master's common-room he found the head of the school, who was formerly the janitor.

'Why so upset, comrade?' asked the head.

'Comrade headmaster, what else can I be when I ask "Who took Troy?" and Geamănul stands up and says it wasn't him!'

'Comrade professor, I have known Geamănul since he was a little boy, and if he says he didn't take Troy, then he didn't take it, believe me.'

The professor, ready to tear the director into pieces, rushed from the room and went for a drink at the local bar. There he encountered the head of the secret police.

'What's wrong, why so upset, comrade professor?' asked the police chief.

'What else can I be, when my pupil Geamănul says *he* didn't take Troy when I ask him, and the headmaster sides with him and tells me this silly boy really didn't take it.'

'Very interesting!' said the police officer. 'But never mind, things will get better.'

They drank a glass of wine together and the professor went home to bed. At 4 a.m. his telephone rang. On the line was the head of the secret police.

'Comrade professor, you can stop worrying! After we parted, I arrested Geamănul and the headmaster and they have both confessed that they really did take Troy.'

The French student smiled politely.

A day later there was a knock on Maxim's door. He was ordered to go immediately to his local party headquarters, where he was severely reprimanded for criticising to foreign visitors. The French student had informed on him to the police. Because of the presence of foreigners in the country, he was not expelled but the black mark in his record troubled him for the rest of his life in Rumania, causing him to lose jobs and be kept under constant surveillance by the police until at last he obtained a visa and went to Israel.

Other students who had criticised Communism were arrested as soon as the Youth Festival ended. I was cautious, I talked to lots of foreigners, but chiefly to find out what they thought about us, and what life was like in the West. I was horrified and astonished to find that they knew almost nothing about real conditions in Russia and Eastern Europe, and when they did know something they simply concluded that 'you can't make an omelette without breaking eggs'. It was perfectly okay to have a slave population of millions, to allow the new masters to massacre whom they wished in the cause of creating 'a new society'. Their own criticisms of Western life seemed to me quite mad and plunged in confusion.

The festival meant that the Opera was working at high pressure. Night after night I worked backstage while free performances of Gounod's *Faust* were put on for the benefit of the visitors. It was preferable to other entertainments offered — Scottish Communists with bagpipes or Bulgarian folk-dancers.

When the festival ended, food vanished once more from the stores. But we had found a secret source of provisions. One day my mother heard that a girl student on the floor below Alice's apartment was leaving her room. We arranged for one of the brethren of our Underground Church to move in. He was a cook — a cook in the secret police mess where only the best was served. Ion the cook brought us real white bread, butter, sugar. He had access to the store-room which contained delicacies unheard of since before the war: real coffee, beef steak, ham. He could not bring out much, but every scrap was welcome.

You may say: It was not his property. Then whose was it? The Communist secret police had not worked to produce it. The Communists had stolen from everyone. Should he have had scruples about the overfed officers, or scruples about the hungry families of Christian prisoners? He acted in a comradely way with what belonged to comrades.

To have such a neighbour was real luck. Even workers like Mr. Grigore who had been a supervisor on the railroads could not find decent food. All the best was kept by Party officials and secret police officers for themselves. The black market was meagre and dangerous. You could be sentenced to long terms as an economic saboteur for selling a few eggs if caught by the special 'economic police'.

My mother faced a peculiar problem: a secret police order

denied her the right to leave Bucharest; but a Government regulation forbade her, as a person without legal occupation or worker's permit, to live in the city. The Communists had solved the problem of beggars and street peddlars by sending them to the labour camps or collective farms. Now the same was happening to middle-class people who were prevented from working legally, but managed to live by selling things they made at home, or on the charity of friends and relatives.

A secret police agent came to the door one day when I was out and tried to bully my mother into divorcing father. She had only to sign a form and it was done. Then she could get the precious work permit. They wanted, of course, to break my father's spirit.

Throughout his diatribe, she kept quiet.

'Even God cannot contradict someone who remains silent,' she said.

The agent left with the warning that as long as she remained married she would not work. So we lived in constant fear that she might be deported.

For weeks we had lived in cramped quarters with Alice and her father. Now a friend found a place for us. It was the little attic of our old mission, a big four-storey building with a score of rooms all of them occupied, after my parents' arrest, by brethren of our church.

When the living-space bureau sent investigators round, they found the entire place filled with busy mothers and their children. They had no excuse to move them out; or others in.

The two tiny rooms — one no more than a scullery — were made smaller by sloping ceilings. We were close under the eaves of the house and when it rained the roof leaked. Radu came with us to the new home. We shared the smaller room, sleeping side by side on two ancient, stained mattresses. There was just space for a small desk under the window. When the rain came through we caught it in enamel buckets and it came through often that winter. There was nowhere you could be alone and sometimes I wanted to be alone very badly. We moved into the attic in the autumn of 1954 and stayed for eleven years.

My mother had the bigger room — bigger by about two

square feet. She brought her friend Valeria there to live. They had been together for a while in the camps.

There was no water and the toilet was down three flights of stairs. But it was a home.

To write to the West was less dangerous now. My mother wrote to her brother who had lived in Paris since his student days and he sent us some parcels.

The Western clothes he and his wife mailed to us were beautiful. We had not seen things like them for ten years. As in all Communist countries, clothes were in short supply because of bad economic planning and poorly made because there was no pride in workmanship.

We had a joke about it. Brezhnev wished to honour Russia's oldest man on his birthday. What, he asked the old fellow, could he do for him? 'When I was a hundred,' said the peasant, 'my wife had my youngest son. He grew up and left us, and I haven't seen him in twenty years. I long to meet him again.' Brezhnev ordered a national search and some possible sons were found. The old man was asked if he could recognise his own. Without a moment's hesitation he rushed to the end of the row and tearfully embraced the man there. Brezhnev was puzzled. 'But how could you be sure about a man you haven't seen in twenty years?' he asked. 'How not?' said the old man. 'Isn't he wearing the coat he left in?'

My mother was still using an old, broken-down sewing-machine on which she made clothes for sale at the 'flea market'. This was the country's last refuge of free enterprise, an open-air market held in a big field on the edge of the city. The Government let it be, and even charged vendors five lei for a permit to sell. The economic police mixed with the crowds, checking papers from time to time. On a fine Sunday you would get 50,000 people there. The vendors spread blankets on the earth to display their offerings and people sat in the sun with handkerchiefs and hats made from newspaper on their heads.

It was like a big museum of the bourgeois past, an end-of-an-era show. Travelling clocks. Pigskin cases. Wedding rings. Hat-boxes. Fine table silver. Stamp collections, Oil paintings. Sets of medals. Drawing instruments in leather cases. And tens of thousands of books, including many Bibles. It was the only place in Rumania where you could buy a Bible. It was also a gathering place for underground believers.

We took the number nineteen tram out to Talcioc with the clothes mother had made. I carried some Bibles and copies of father's books, which we had unearthed from an underground store room in the mission known only to us. The mission house was connected by a subterranean tunnel to another building and there we had stacked piles of an edition of the Bible, the last printing before the Communist take-over. The Bibles were bound in rough board on coarse paper because we had nothing else, and because we were working against time. My father knew already that they would arrest him.

There were stacks of his own books, too. *The Passion of Christ* and *The Crucifixion of Jesus*, and dozens of pamphlets, and copies of his church magazine *The Friend*. He had published about twenty Christian books, and some had been best-sellers. At the flea market I gave bundles of ten or twenty to villagers who would come in from the countryside. There was a great demand for them.

'If you're going to Bucharest, visit Mrs. Wurmbrand,' villagers asked friends. 'Bring some books back with you.'

Our best 'distribution agency' was a family with a photography business in a small northern town. The father was a former political prisoner and he, his wife and eight children were believers. There was a boom in the photographic business — everyone needed photos for the innumerable forms and documents of the Communist super-bureaucracy — and members of the family travelled widely, setting up their cameras in a village for a day then moving on. As they went from place to place they took help to the families of arrested Christians and held secret prayer meetings.

I sometimes travelled with them. While one brother was taking photographs at the village school, I and the others would be organising an underground prayer service. My father was a symbol of resistance to them. Legends were created around his name, and his books went from hand to hand. As his son, I had always to speak.

How many hot and crowded peasant rooms I preached in, so airless (with all the windows closed tight and curtains drawn for safety) that the oil lamps guttered. And I had never been taught to preach. How many straw mattresses I slept on, bitten all night by a special brand of giant flea that apparently liked only my flesh!

The villagers needed an excuse to gather a crowd in one house. They would celebrate their patrons saint's day three times a year, keeping open house. Any and every anniversary was put to use. Weddings, birthdays, baptismal days, burial days . . . all these events provided a 'cover story' for a religious service attended by several hundred people. Afterwards I came back on the train through the mountains which were thickly forested and green. There were hardly any cars on the roads but you could see some fine horses in the fields. We passed a gypsy camp, circles of straw-covered caravans around a bright fire. It looked like a good way to live.

One evening when I returned from a trip in the north I heard my mother and Valeria talking excitedly even before I opened the door.

My mother's face was bright with joy.

'Mihai! There's a postcard from Daddy!'

It was a few lines long. He was safe, he was well, he loved us and — God willing — he would see us soon. We could send a parcel, to the prison hospital of Tirgul-ocna, a town in the mountains to the north. But something about the way the card was written puzzled me: I read and re-read it. Why should he ask us to send a parcel of 'Dr. Filon's old clothes'? Filon, a physician we had known for many years, was a little over five feet tall; and my father is six feet two inches. If he wanted something from Dr. Filon, it was not clothes. What did you want from a doctor when you were in hospital?

'He's asking us to send medicine! Things they can't get there!'

It was known that Tirgul-ocna had a jail for prisoners sick with tuberculosis. Streptomycin was the new drug that was defeating T.B. Obviously, he needed some. 'Socialist medicine'

55

was then just coming round to conceding that the drug — available in the West for years — actually worked. It could only be bought on the black market at a high price.

When we told the news to Alice she said little. But a couple of days later she came to the attic carrying a small package.

'This is for Richard's parcel,' she said. 'From father and me.'

It was a hundred grams of streptomycin.

'Alice, it has cost the earth. We can't take it!'

At least 6,000 lei, I thought — my salary for a year.

We tried to persuade her to resell the drug. She would not hear of it.

'It is not all my money. Others have contributed, too. It could be put to no better use.'

So the streptomycin was sent.

(Years later, we discovered that my father gave the drug to prisoners whom he thought closer to death than himself. His own recovery, said doctors who examined him on his release, was 'a miracle'.)

About two months later, a new postcard came. It said that we could visit father at Tirgul-ocna. After seven years, our first prison visit! At last the terrible oppression of the Stalin years was easing a little. Since Stalin's death two years before, Kruschev had climbed to the top, eliminating Beria on the way, and now, in 1955, he was preparing for his famous Twentieth Congress denunciation of the dictator. Besides, the Geneva Conference with President Eisenhower had been agreed on and Kruschev wished to throw a favourable light on Communism everywhere.

But my mother still could not leave the city. She had to report daily to the police. An infringement of her restriction order would mean deportation. We agreed that I should go alone.

I travelled on a slow overnight train to the north, passing through the Carpathians at dawn. Tirgul-ocna is a town of 30,000 people, situated in a mountain valley overlooking the River Street. Its biggest building is the jail, a neo-Gothic heap of turrets and towers and crenellated walls.

The train got in at six in the morning. I carried my bag of food and clothes down the empty road. It was cold up there in the mountains and the sky was very bright and blue. The big ugly main portal of the prison was closed and remained so until 10 a.m. A handful of other visitors arrived and they let them in alphabetically so that I was the last. Sometime in the afternoon, a small wooden door in the big gate opened and they called my name. I went through into a cobbled courtyard.

The questions and the search began. Prison officers checked my credentials and took out one by one the things my mother had carefully packed. I watched them hack up the bread with a penknife and then spoon out the jar of preserve she had made on to a grubby sheet of paper.

'Put that back in the jar,' one of them said.

They even cut the hard boiled eggs in half. I tried to wrap up the mess that remained and pack it into the bag. I did not want them to see I was nearly crying.

I waited another two hours in the courtyard. It was damp and smelt of carbolic and I could hear boots clashing on stone and the echoing shout of prison voices. Then they let me into a big gloomy hall shaped like a railway tunnel with the end blocked off by a huge door that went up to the ceiling. In it, at eye-level, was a small barred window. Under the window was a table, and on either side of the table, two guards. They did not mean you to get too close.

After a few minutes, a face appeared behind the bars. It was a gaunt, grey face. The head was shaven and the stubble on it was white. The bones stood out and the eyes seemed enormous. I suppose I recognised him by the eyes.

I began to shake. It had been seven years, and I remembered my father as a handsome man, wise, loving and strong. I'd been nine-years-old then, and now I was sixteen.

He smiled and asked about mother.

'She's well at home. She couldn't come. She says to tell you that even if you die in prison, you must not be sad because we'll all meet in heaven.'

'Have you food at home?'

'Yes,' I said. 'Our Father is very rich, he provides.'

The guards grinned. They thought I was saying that my mother was living with another man.

'Have you appealed for me?'

'Yes, we . . .'

'That's not allowed! No questions about trial or sentence!'

'Why couldn't Mummy come?'

I was so badly shaken — at seeing him, by the yelling guards — that I lost my tongue. I couldn't get the words 're-striction order' out. I stuttered something.

'You have two minutes left,' said the guard.

He asked about my schooling, about the church, about our friends.

I don't know what I said, probably some Bible verses.

'Time's up!'

I called, 'Mother sent you a parcel!'

Then he vanished from behind the grille. They led me out into the courtyard again.

I walked back to the railway station down the hill in the dusk.

My mind was blank, I was not thinking at all. I stood in the inevitable line for a ticket and when I'd bought it I saw the train begin to move. I ran and caught the rail with one hand. My body swung out as the train gathered speed. I was flattened against the side of a carriage. Whistles were blowing and people shouting on the platform. I was on the point of losing my grip and falling on the track when hands seized me and hauled me in through a window.

My life had been spared for a third time. God had a task for me.

The shock of seeing my father in these conditions, the shock of the accident, knocked the stuffing out of me. When I got home I could not talk much. In an agony of frustration, poor mother tried to draw something more out of me. But it wasn't there. I felt hollow and lost. I could only say that he was well, he sends his love, he's well.

For a long time after that I had nightmares about a long tunnel with a grating at the end of it, where uniformed men were beating my father silently in the dark.

Not long after this I lost my job at the Opera. The authorities had discovered the blot in the family history. Almost everyone at the Opera House knew my story by now. The management let me 'resign' instead of firing me. That meant a lot: I had references, and nothing went on my record.

I went about Bucharest still, tuning pianos in people's homes. Collette, a friend of mother's who taught piano, recommended me to her pupils. I did repairs, too, at 100 *lei* a visit (about 75p).

While I still had the worker's card I enrolled in a technical school for an electrical engineering course. You could take a couple of lectures a week, study at home and sit an examination at the end of the year. The men in my class were middle-aged workers. People of my own age went to college. More than a hundred of us sat the exam. I was one of the fourteen who passed. It didn't do me any good: next term the polytechnic was shut down. The state had changed its educational policy for the umpteenth time. They were constantly tinkering with the system to 'raise the cultural level of the people'. Now they were slowing down the big plan for quick technological education to divert money elsewhere.

Throughout my life under Communism I never once finished at school or university. The state machine always intruded, either accidentally because of some new educational plan, or because of my 'social origin'.

But the examination I had passed was a valid contribution towards obtaining a school leaving certificate. If I could study at night and pass the other subjects, then I might get into university and 'steal' another year or so of education before being caught again.

It would not be easy. There were 500 candidates for every thirty or forty places at the university and Russian — of which I couldn't speak a word — was a compulsory subject. Nobody wanted to learn Russian. We took a kind of pride in not knowing it, just because it was forced on us.

Christian, a friend of mine, boasted that he would pass *without* Russian.

'That's ridiculous!'

'Oh yes? You'll see!'

On examination day, he went before the board of three professors. You had to pick a numbered card which carried the questions. Luck of the draw — you couldn't possible know what questions you were getting.

Christian drew a card — then hastily and very obviously stuck it back in the pile. The examiner's eyes popped.

'What do you imagine you're doing!'

'Sir, that was number thirteen! I'm bound to fail if I take that!'

'Rubbish, boy. Take card thirteen immediately!'

'Oh, sir. I'm finished now. But I'll show you I've learnt something just the same.'

Then he proceeded to answer the questions perfectly.

We were all astonished when he passed. His Russian was abominable.

'You see,' he explained. 'I found a boy who'd drawn card thirteen earlier and learnt the answers by rote. All I had to do was persuade them to make me choose that card!'

June 1956. A hot summer, a long drought. Dust on the leaves of the plane trees that lined the street. Swallows skimming by the attic window as they nested in the eaves of our house. I worked hard for the exams in the stuffy little room under the sloping ceiling. I wished for a desk that I could get my knees under and prayed sometimes for an hour to be alone. Mother had turned our attic into a centre of the Underground Church. Brethren came up the stairs day and night often from far-off parts of the country. And since my mother was often out on church work, I had to look after them.

Suddenly, I knew I had to get out into the hall. I dropped my book and ran outside. There in the hallway was my father.

He was thin and gaunt-faced, his head was shaved, he wore patched and ragged clothes and carried a greasy bundle. But it was my father.

'Is it really you?' I asked. It was too much for me to believe ... and he was so changed. But I soon found that the change was merely physical. Close on nine years of suffering had not broken him.

My mother was out. We went into her room and father laid down to rest. He had been released that day from Jilava, and he had walked to the city along country roads. We talked for a while. He said:

'Mihai, you know that in prison I had no Bible. I have forgotten it. I have forgotten all my theology. But these things I know for sure. First, there is a living God and he is our loving father. Second, Jesus Christ is the saviour and bridegroom of our souls. Third, the Holy Spirit works in us to make us more and more Christ-like. Fourth, there exists beyond question an eternal life. And lastly, love is the best of ways. This is what I have learned in prison.'

Suddenly, my mother was in the room with us, laughing and weeping and hugging us. When at last the greetings and the explanations were over, we tried to make father rest. But word had spread that he was home again. All that evening old friends and brethren came to the attic. People left only to allow new visitors into the tiny room. With them were many strangers, hoping for news of loved ones in jail. To a few, father could give more than words of comfort.

We walked next day in the park. The pale sunlight of early morning slanted down through the trees and the air smelt good. I think he found me a tougher character than he expected.

'You know how much I admire you,' I said. 'You were always right about things, you've always had the best arguments. Maybe your influence on me was too great. If God hadn't taken you from me, and then mother, perhaps I'd never have developed a personality of my own at all. Perhaps taking you away was one of the means God used to let me develop!'

He was a bit taken aback. But I had to make it plain to him from the start.

'I love you very much, but you are you and I am I. I have read your books. I don't think like you in many ways.'

'Truly,' he said, 'I'm glad. Because to find yourself as a personality in your own right is to receive one of God's greatest gifts to mankind.'

Pigeons rose from the path, shattering the quiet with their wings.

'In prison,' he said, 'I used to dream about the child I'd left behind and make up stories to tell you when I came back. In prison time stands still. You do not realise the world is changing. But I find I have no child now. No one to tell my stories to. So be it.'

Father could not sleep for an altogether hour. His nerves were in shreds and he would wake and walk about and read until dawn. He found it almost intolerable to be alone.

I was due to sit for my *baccalaureate* in three days, and he would constantly come and talk to me while I was trying desperately to catch up on last minute studies. Then he would feel guilty about interrupting me, and shut himself in the other room. And I would feel guilty about leaving him alone. The beatings and the years in solitary confinement had left indelible mental scars.

Sometimes he came into my room at 2 a.m., while I slept after working late.

'I was lonely,' he said. 'I wanted to see you, please go on sleeping.'

But I was already awake. We sat and talked.

I studied almost nothing in the last days before the exams, when I'd counted on doing all my revision. But in the event I passed, notwithstanding.

I discussed with father my future.

At that time a theological seminary had just been permitted to open. It was part of the so-called 'new course' that followed Stalin's death. Stalin had been denounced by Kruschev and the old Stalinists were falling in several eastern European countries. A short-lived retreat began from the most disastrous Communist economic policies: forcible collectivisation, total economic submission to Russia.

A few concessions were made to the Church. It was the summer of the summit conference between Eisenhower and Kruschev and dubious gestures of goodwill were made. Communists gained a foothold in the World Council of Churches to which they sent the stooges they had chosen to run show churches in the occupied countries. They attended W.C.C. conferences, they sat in Geneva as permanent representatives. So the West formally recognised the infiltrated, spied-upon, state-approved Church and praised non-existent religious liberty.

By way of return, in Rumania, a theological seminary was permitted to open. It would be a place to show foreign visitors who doubted Communists claims. The state felt sure its pressures and persecutions would control the situation.

Still, I was eager to study — to study anything, though above all I wanted to be a pastor. I tried first to enter a medical school, but my background was discovered. The seminary also seemed out of the question for me.

We learnt that Bishop Müller, leader of the Lutheran Church, would have a say in the seminary's conduct. The bishop was one of the courageous few who chose to stay and work inside the 'show church'. He dealt as best he could with the oppression, and at the same time he carried on a parallel secret ministry. He played the cowed, obedient priest, but aided in hidden ways the martyred Church.

The bishop and father were old friends. They discussed the seminary and agreed that indoctrination lectures and other pressures would make studies difficult. But all life under Communism was a compromise. At least students would have Bibles, a library, the chance to learn Hebrew and Greek. Informers there would always be, but also many honest pastors doing their best. The classes would be on a high scholastic level, since this was to be a show place. The professors all had degrees or doctorates from foreign universities. Some girls would also study there.

Then came the blow. Free education was the great Communist boast, but here students would have to pay 3,000 lei a term; an average worker's pay for four months, and quite beyond our means.

Because he loved my father, the bishop offered to support me from his own pocket. Like other Church heads, he drew a state salary and could afford it. I disliked taking his money, but saw no other way out of my *impasse*. I wanted to escape from my confined, oppressive life, the spying and the lying and the scraping to survive. A couple of months later, I left Bucharest for Sibiu.

The little town is beautiful. The blue-grey medieval roofs, the stout, thick-walled castle, the narrow streets, the gilded weathervanes danced and sparkled in the clear mountain air.

I strolled about, carrying my fibre suitcase, my head filled with doubts and hopes. It was very relaxed and gentle after the capital's harsh atmosphere. In the square, plump German burghers nodded and chatted and people everywhere were friendly. The German minority of Rumania was then about 300,000 strong, and most of the students at the seminary would be from among them.

The seminary was housed in the bishop's palace, a heavy Germanic residence with big black iron gates. I rang the bell and was admitted into a stone-flagged quadrangle. A student took me to the second floor.

'We sleep twenty to a dorm,' he said as we entered a large sunny room. 'Better get some straw for your mattress. I'll show you where to buy a sackful in town.'

So much for free education: we had even to buy our own straw!

My companion was named Otto — a large fair German boy of about eighteen who grinned all the time. He was bursting with health and heartiness. I felt suddenly conscious of my Jewishness.

'There's a bit of anti-semitism around here,' said Otto. 'A lot of lads are not so much German as Saxon.' Which meant, usually, chauvinistic.

'If they give you trouble, tell me. I'll soon shut them up.'

'Thanks.'

'We have only ninety pupils here,' said Otto. 'But 700 applied to get in. So many wanted to come, the Government was really annoyed! All the years of propaganda against religion, and then all those boys wanting to train as pastors!'

'Have they given you any trouble?'

'Oh, they tried to make me drop the idea. They called everyone who applied, you know, and told them, "you're young, the Party needs you: don't ruin your life by entering this superstitious, unprogressive place."'

'Did it work?'

'A few people dropped out. Then they called the parents to Party headquarters and warned them they would lose their jobs if they let their sons enter the seminary. That worked with some of the intellectuals and professors. Didn't they try all this with you?'

'I think we are considered hopeless cases.'

I talked later to Bishop Müller. Because of his friendship with my father and our special relationship, he could speak freely with me.

'Little by little, we will be worn down,' he said. 'They are already beginning to put pressure on the ninety boys who remain. One father — a professor at Cluj University — was told outright that he would lose his job if his son stayed with us. The lad has gone.'

At the start, however, I was happy. The Germans were good boys, more open, less suspicious than the Rumanian city-dweller. They had spent their lives in small towns and hamlets where only Hungarian and a German dialect was spoken, and they had a poor knowledge of Rumanian. They never used it among themselves.

The students were a healthy lot: no trouble sleeping here. I lay listening to the snores in the darkened dormitory and felt the spiky heads of straw in the palliasse pricking my back. We were to be actors in a show school — but actors don't have such a bad life.

I rose at six and attended my first morning service. Classes began at eight, but they were few.

We dissected the Bible slowly and painfully, as if in a laboratory. With a few honourable exceptions, the professors followed the modern fad of examining not what the Bible said, but how it came to be written. Only that just as it is not possible to debate the things of the spirit without subtracting from their purity, so you cannot take apart the word of God without losing sight of its global meaning.

How many authors had contributed to the Books of Moses? Three or five or six? Who wrote the heroic 'Song of Moses'? Or the discourses attributed to the Prophet?

I used to believe of every page in the Bible that 'thus says

65

the Lord'. One might as well have dissected a living person one loved to find out how his inside worked. Shakespeare wrote Shakespeare and Moses wrote Moses, as far as I was concerned. But we continued dating Deuteronomy, doubting Joshua. It was not without interest: but how totally irrelevant to the struggles we would face if we became pastors!

When the four lectures of the day were over at noon, I went to the library. What a disappointment! They had only a couple of hundred theological books, and most of these were works of analysis and criticism by Dr. Nobody, M.A., D.D. and his contemporary colleagues.

The young seminarists were not to be tainted by the writings of the holy fathers or the great mystics. The books of the great reformers, the lives of saints and martyrs were not for us. Good books of apologetics proving that Christianity was true? Debate against Marxist poison? What good would such books be in a theological seminary? I saw I had been foolish to expect anything else. I found later that even in the West you can finish a seminary education without having read St. John Chrysostom, without ever having seen a book of Meister Eckhardt, without having learnt to preach from the writings of Spurgeon, the greatest preacher of the last century.

The library at the Orthodox Institute in Sibiu was close by. The students said it was kept under lock and key, but I walked over anyhow, to investigate.

The doors were open, but no one was about. I glanced through the catalogue. The whole collection seemed to consist of books on rearing pigs, crop diseases and the like.

'You are looking for something?'

I jumped. A priest had entered behind me, a severe looking man in a rusty old soutane. Who gave me permission to come in, what was my name?

When I told him, the cross look vanished.

'The son of Pastor Wurmbrand?' He had met my father years ago. 'A remarkable man! Unstoppable! He came to the Ministry of Cults where I worked during the war, demanding a permit to preach. That took courage in those anti-Jewish, anti-Protestant days. I thought they'd clap him in jail. But he got hold of Minister Sandu, an unpleasant fellow, and told him he'd have to answer before the judgment of God, and he'd better make sure he was saved, no matter if he gave him a permit or not. And really — it was unbelievable — he had that minister running out from behind his desk in five minutes shouting, "What can I do to be saved?" Hee-hee-hee! I daresay he needed it.'

I told him of father's years in prison.

He shook his head, sadly. 'Your father had a gift for touching people and no doubt he could help them even there. Some Orthodox priests have little love for Protestants, but your father was deeply appreciated.'

I explained that I had come in the hopes of finding some good theological books.

He scratched his nose. 'We have some. But it is strictly against the rules to let students at them. We keep them in a locked room.' He thought for a moment. 'I can see you are a boy who has learnt how to keep silent. I'll let you in, if you promise never to breathe a word.'

I found in the locked room the best library of religious books I had ever seen. It was superb. With the old priest's permission, I came every afternoon, and read as I'd never read before. St. Augustine, Meister Eckhardt, Erasmus, all the great saints and mystics and thinkers were there, and many curious authors and visionaries I did not know.

Here I did my real studying. The rest was worthless, apart from some of the instructions I received from our handful of good professors.

We were taught to write sermons in didactic, pedantic style, with no hint of evangelism, or personal witnessing. Our constitution guarantees only liberty of worship for Christians. Freedom of propaganda is reserved for atheists. Professor Rapp, the deputy bishop at Cluj, taught that God had given three revelations: one through Moses, one through Jesus and one through Karl Marx. He was fair to Jesus, and granted that he was a little bit bigger than Marx.

Our pastors had mostly studied for their doctorates in Germany before the war. Their lives had been passed in provincial towns. Bishop Müller had hand-picked them to teach here and, within the limits imposed, some were often very good. The bishop knew personally Petru Groza, the grubby little politician who had been elevated to the presidency by the Communists. Groza had no power but some influence, and Müller drew on this old friendship in setting up the seminary. A compromise here won concessions there. But along with his own choices, the bishop had to accept the state's appointees. Men like Pastor Novicov, who was able to combine his office with atheistic propaganda as our lecturer in dialectical materialism.

Novicov liked to fish in the cold streams in which Transylvania abounds, and he liked still more to tell about his angling adventures. In the classroom we could always divert him from Marx to mullet, though which was the more boring is doubtful. Our course included a year of lectures in Marxist dialectics, another year in Marxist economics, a third year in scientific socialism.

Some of Novicov's lectures were read from typed manuscripts supplied by the Ministry of Cults, and based on *The Atheist's Handbook* (known to us as *The Moscow Bible*) an enormously long attack on all the world's religions, prepared in Russia. It was required reading throughout the Communist bloc. He dared not depart from his text. He knew there were informers among the students too, watching to report any step out of line. A bad report to the ministry could lose him his job and those fishing trips. We liked to ask him awkward questions.

When he told us that in every school but this, it was taught that Christ never existed as a historical personage, someone wondered: 'Sir, could you tell us if Pontius Pilate ever existed?'

'Hum, well. Why don't you look this up yourself? You'll find the answer somewhere in Roman history. Not my speciality.'

Pastor Novicov would not be drawn into any dangerous discussion. Better show ignorance than that!

Other professors warned us on the quiet against Novicov. Most of the others kept to a strict academic line.

The students were very gullible. They were Lutherans with

deep, simple convictions. They knew nothing of the great body of Christian defence against atheistic attack created over the centuries. I knew some from my father and I was learning more. When I put these ideas to the other students, they were thought novel and inspiring.

'Nobody ever talked to me with such words,' said Otto. 'Why don't the pastors teach us this?'

Why indeed? I provoked the professors into discussion whenever I could. I knew that some of them secretly approved. I tried to steer the class away into channels that opened up matter for meditation.

But how cautious they were! Once, when we made an end of term gift of flowers to a certain pastor, he pulled out a piece of paper to read his thank-you reply! They kept written records of everything they said publicly. Communist officials usually do this also: they never know when they may be accused, in some Party upset, of saying things contrary to the new line years before it came into existence. Fear rules their lives.

It deeply affected us, too. At home, we always considered our cover story: what did we say if it came out that more than three people had met under our roof and talked? We would agree: three games of chess were played, I won the first, you the other two. And so on.

We saw our friends arrested and telling contradictory stories under questioning. You had to exercise in saying the wrong thing which was politically 'all right'.

We studied a little Hebrew, Greek and Latin — which made a welcome change from Russian. Being the only Rumanian not from one of the minority groups, I often drafted official letters for the seminary. It made a good excuse to talk with Bishop Müller. Out of his affection for my father (and perhaps because he had lost his own two sons on the same day in the war) he made me his protégé. He told me some strange stories.

Once we had a visitor from the West. Pastor Hansson, a representative of the World Lutheran Federation came to look over the seminary, but, feeling the room could be bugged, the bishop could not get him alone to tell the facts about the conditions we worked under. The Ministry of Cults took him about like a bear on a chain.

Hansson exchanged a few nice words with various pastors, admired the old buildings and left. But later the Bishop attended a dinner for Pastor Hansson, with other Church leaders. The bishop was upset that he should be going back to the West full of false propaganda. He dropped some hints of the truth.

Next day the Bishop was visited instead by the secret police. They played back to him a tape of the dinner-table conversation with Hansson.

'I don't know where they had the microphone,' the bishop told me. 'I imagine the equipment was American, because it worked really well.'

Bishop Müller escaped with some hours of questioning and another black mark against his name. At seventy-one he was considered pretty harmless.

All foreign visitors, delegations and news teams are given this official run-around. They stay at the best hotel in a Black Sea resort, they visit a show school, or a show farm, always the same ones; the same guides take them about. It is amazing to Rumanians that Westerners should fall for it. The big television networks in the U.S.A. spend millions on documentaries attacking American institutions. Towards them, Westerners are critical. But when they come to the East, they accept any drivel that is told to them by the Communists. There is, it seems, something intrinsically wicked when the U.S. army spends money advertising for recruits. Television exposes the 'scandal' and paints the blackest possible picture. But when, in April 1971 — to take only one example — a leading American T.V. team went to Rumania, what did we see? A fat girl reading an anti-war poem aimed at America, a Party official telling frightened lies about the economy, some film about the famous hotels (foreign visitors only) and a band in fancy dress playing Enescu's Rumanian Rhapsody! The reporters did not say one word to suggest the oppression, the persecution, the corruption, the misery and the murders.

Every two months, an official Party spy was sent to the seminary from Bucharest. Comrade Dimitrescu, a short, cold-eyed man of about forty-five, came to gather information from his informers and inspect the place personally. He would appear in dormitory and classroom nosing out scraps of non-conformism. His spies reported to him any student who had begun to lose his faith under the propaganda barrage. He would be called to secret police H.Q. or approached by an agent and invited to become an informer. Often, it was done subtly with little bribes, then threats. But with those who would not bow the head, they were brutal. One boy, from an old aristocratic family, was proud of his name. But he had to be made ashamed. He was taken to police H.Q. where they knocked the resistance out of him. Every week he had to go, till at last he broke and became their informer.

Those students who did work for the secret police stayed on at the seminary, of course; and they went on to become informer priests. And the informers had to be spied upon by others! There was no end to it. And with good reason: this fear is the thing that holds the system together.

The janitor at the seminary was a known informer. But who was it that watched the janitor?

One morning I found at the seminary gate an old man with a barrow selling sweets and nuts and sunflower seeds. Now all the thousands of street-vendors, once so common in every town, had been swept away into factories or camps by the Communists. I had not seen a vendor for years.

I remarked on this to Otto. I was sure he was an informer.

'That old chap? This isn't Bucharest. People still carry on a few little businesses up here.'

'Well, we'll see.'

Over the years I had developed a sixth sense for small oddities. When you live in a police state you learn to be a detective. You look always for the tell-tale weakness.

The vendor did a brisk trade. I was one of his best customers. We talked. He was interested in the students.

'Are you from these parts?' I was very friendly always. 'You have a better accent than the Germans.' Perhaps to curry favour with me, he explained, after we had met several times,

71

that he had been a member of the police under King Carol. With a display of allegiance to the old order, he hoped to win my confidence.

I asked, 'Were you ever arrested by the Communists?'

'Oh, I wasn't important.'

I had never heard of a police officer of the old regime who had not been jailed by the Reds. Either he was lying, or he had avoided jail by turning secret police spy. The whole tenor of his talk was to lead me into some indiscretion.

I told Bishop Müller that we had a new member on the staff. We stood at the window looking down. The vendor was talking and smiling with a student.

The bishop believed me. An inner circle of some twenty-five trusted students was warned. It was the revolution in Hungary and its Rumanian aftermath that finally gave the vendor his big chance.

For days after the uprisings in Budapest, and in Poland, the Rumanian Government tried to suppress the news. The trouble was nothing; it was the work of a handful of imperialist agitators. But all over Rumania spread the wave of student unrest. Demonstrations broke out in Bucharest, Cluj and other towns. The Politburo raged against the students who 'despised socialist achievements and showed total servitude towards the capitalist nations'. To no purpose. Large areas of the country were placed under military rule, and big round-ups began. But before open rebellion could burst out, the Red army had crushed Hungary. In Rumania, trouble was quelled before it could spread.

Later, when the Kremlin made some economic concessions to Hungary and Poland, Rumania received next to nothing.

'It's always the same,' said Otto. 'The Rumanians have no fight in them. They think they can get somewhere against the Russians by cunning. But they can't.'

It was discovered that anti-Communist youth groups had formed in Cluj, Sibiu and Brasov. All the members were arrested, including relatives of many boys at the seminary. They had been hopelessly naïve. Mostly Germans, they had organised all too thoroughly, keeping journals and records and lists of names, even lists of friends they thought they could count on when the uprising came.

One would say: 'I know so-and-so, he hates the Communists too.' And poor so-and-so would be added to the list. All of them were arrested.

'They quarrelled over a girl,' said Otto. 'Some of the German lads were stupidly nationalistic and said they'd never marry Rumanians. That led to the quarrel and someone turned police informer.'

A seventy-year-old pastor was arrested, simply because he had been on the list. He didn't know the group existed. A boy from Brasov, whom I knew, was badly tortured to make him reveal more names.

It emerged that the police had known for months about the group. But they had waited for more and more to fall into the net. Several boys were taken from the seminary.

The day after the arrests, the vendor of sweets disappeared. He had done his duty.

One day my father came unexpectedly to the seminary and was taken aside by the lady secretary. I was in trouble again. This time, expulsion threatened. I had written to the dean protesting against a plan to hold a dance in the seminary; girls would be invited and beer drunk, and I thought we had come here rather to learn about God than to enjoy ourselves and dance. There were plenty of places for this. Why do it here, I had written, where we were supposed to be made pastors who would bring God to souls and souls to God?

'Mihai asked me to give the dean his letter,' explained the secretary. 'But I kept it. I knew they'd expel him.'

My father talked it over with the bishop. They asked me not to make trouble that might interfere with the Underground Church work they did together. Bishop Müller could not, in his official position, risk being exposed as my father's collaborator. Neither could father show any outward sign of friendship towards him, until the day he died.

But there were no more dances at the seminary.

Every year the army draft board would summon students

from our seminary and the Orthodox one to the induction centre for a medical and documentation check. We would have to do military service of two years as soon as we finished our training. We were weighed, injected, examined, all by women doctors. We filled up the inevitable questionnaire.

Once, we found ourselves in company with the Orthodox students. We all sat about naked, waiting our turn. They were discussing the draft, and some were swearing as if they were already old soldiers. 'Why do you swear so much,' I asked. 'Aren't you Christians?'

'No, we're atheists,' one replied.

'Then why are you here?'

'Theology is a subject like any other,' he shrugged. 'It has its historical interest. Besides, we had not much choice. Not being of proletarian origin, most of us couldn't study what we wished.'

Many of them knew nothing about the Bible, or Christian writing, or Judaism. God was the old man in the nightshirt of the Communist jokes.

I tried to reason with them, but they were stuffed with atheistic indoctrination, and pseudo-scientific reasoning.

'Think a little about the mathematical probability that this universe, so amazingly ordered and governed by physical laws came into being by accident,' I said. 'A British scientist said once that there was as much chance of this as there was of a chimpanzee making marks on paper and accidentally writing the complete works of Shakespeare.'

I flipped a coin. 'What's the mathematical chance of this falling heads ten times in a row? It's once in every 1,024 times. And a coin has just two alternatives, heads or tails. Now, when we walk the foot employs some twenty bones with a million alternative movements, directed by the fantastic computer that is the human brain. What's the probability, with its billions of alternative calculations, that it's the product of chance?'

They had no answer. Many of the Orthodox students sided with me, and five of the 'atheist' boys were interested enough in our discussion to meet with us again another evening. We discussed many things, from the archaeological discoveries that showed Biblical history to be accurate, to the prophecies that we now saw coming true in the world today, such as the rebirth of Israel.

The Kruschev 'thaw' was quickly over. In 1958, signs of a new era of oppression and hardship appeared. In 1959, a fresh seven-year plan to eradicate religion, ordered by Moscow, went into operation.

We had our first hint of it one morning, when a call went up to the dormitory for one of the German students, Klaus Knall. A visitor downstairs was asking for him. That night Knall's bed was empty. He had gone. The secret police had called again. We wondered who would be next.

Soon, several others were taken for questioning. This was the aftermath of Hungary. Eighteen months after the uprising they were still arresting students who'd said a word in its favour. They watched and waited, hoping that the victims would lead them to others.

Pastors and teachers began to disappear in other parts of the country. I worried about my father. He had preached at Cluj, to the fury of the Ministry of Cults, which clamped a ban down to prevent him speaking anywhere. Now he was preaching secretly, as he had done among Soviet soldiers during the war. His re-arrest was only a matter of time.

In Cluj, two pastors from the Hungarian minority had been taken, allegedly for listening to the Radio Free Europe. It was jammed, but sometimes you could pick up fragments of broadcasts from the West. The Dej regime was frightened of the Hungarians in Rumania. Petru Dumitriu, Rumania's leading novelist, who escaped to the West in the sixties, described how Central Committee members were dispatched by plane to Transylvania to pacify the Hungarian minority after Budapest's rebellion. They circled around a couple of times, then turned tail: even the secret police there were not trusted. When the uprising had been crushed, they made some concessions to the Hungarians, then cracked down on any suspected trouble-makers, pastors and priests included.

We gained one new student: another boy from the German

minority, who had been thrown out of the secret police training school. Call him Fritz Neumann. His story was comic — and suspicious.

Neumann was coerced into joining the secret police. The force already had some 40,000 men, but could never have enough. You couldn't walk a block without seeing the hated blue uniform. They recruited boys directly from high school and put them through a training college from which they emerged with a 'degree' and the highest-paid job in the country with a car and many other perks.

Career officers never escape — even if they are dismissed. They are always given other jobs in which they can spy, such as personnel officer in a factory. The state does not waste its time and money. But nor will it maintain any officer who shows the faintest hint of disloyalty. I knew one who was dismissed for failing to report that his brother had asked him to put in a good word for a friend in prison who was sick.

Neumann, I was sure, was still spying for the secret police. They had their hooks in him. He told how he had been sacked:

'You see, if you're joining the People's Security, they check all your relatives to make sure about your social origins. I had some very distant cousin in the U.S.A. whom I didn't even know about – he'd emigrated there before the war. So I wrote down that I had no relatives abroad. Then this fellow wrote out of the blue to my family from Washington, and they found out.'

'But how?'

'Well, they were watching my Dad's mail.'

'You mean, you were in your third year of training and they were still reading your father's mail?'

'Certainly . . . and that was the only letter we've received from abroad since the end of the war.'

'Didn't you tell them you didn't know this relative?'

'I had an interview with one of the top officers. I asked how I could be blamed if some tenth cousin in America wrote to my Dad. They said, "If we ask you one day to shoot that cousin, how can we be sure you'll do it? You have relatives who have sold out to the imperialists." '

76

Vast quantities of private mail are rifled by the secret police. They have a whole department for it. I know from first-hand experience how they are steamed open in batches in special compartments, micro-filmed and sent on. My father under interrogation was shown copies of letters he had sent years previously.

Neumann claimed to have had a religious conversion during the difficult months of his life that followed expulsion. Other boys to whom he confided his secret refused to believe that he had connections still with the secret police. But I had no illusions on that score.

That January of 1959, the snow was very deep. It covered the streets and the rooftops and made the mountains beyond them look chalky white against the grey sky. It was very cold and we did not go out much, but I had made some friends in the town and sometimes I would speak at underground meetings in their homes.

One morning the small son of one of these friends came to tell me that a lady from Bucharest wanted to see me urgently.

'She is waiting in the little park across the road,' he whispered. 'She says she'll stay until nightfall.'

I hurried out. A grey figure wrapped in shawls was seated on a bench under the bare trees. She saw me and came quickly forward over the icy paths.

'Aunt Alice! What is it? What's happened?'

'Mihai, it's your father. The police took him again last night.'

'Is mother all right?'

'Yes, they didn't touch her. His last words to her were: "Give my love to M. (the informer who betrayed him) and to Mihai." '

This M. had denounced him to the secret police. They would have arrested him anyway, sooner or later: my father was always an open man. He trusted people; and he had trusted M., a pastor he had helped since the time of the Nazis, and whom he looked on almost as a second son. How deeply the betrayal must have wounded him!

'Alice, it's risky for you to be here. If father's in jail, then I'm under surveillance, or soon will be.'

'I had to come. Your mother couldn't.'

Her breath clouded on the cold air.

'Your mother offered each of the secret police an apple when they came. You know how she always offers any guest food! But the strange thing was — they took the apples!'

'Was the search very thorough?'

'They took many of your father's notes for sermons and for his books. They even took the book he gave her as a birthday present — the one he wrote all those verses in!'

They let them pray together before my father was taken off in handcuffs.

Alice had to leave at once. It was getting dark. I bent to kiss her and she hurried away down the hill in the winter dusk.

Why had M. done this? Pressure, I supposed. Blackmail, perhaps. They were experts in breaking minds and hearts. But we knew trouble was coming. The new drive against religion had been carefully planned. On one hand, atheistic propaganda re-doubled. On the other, the persecution of the clergy increased. False charges of womanising or homosexuality, theft or embezzlement were the pretexts for hustling priests and pastors back into jail. Drunkenness, 'parasitism', spywork betrayal of the Party or of the state, black marketeering — anything went in the campaign to defame the Church. I found later in the West clergymen stupid enough to believe these allegations.

I requested permission to return to my mother's side. I told Bishop Müller that I would try to find work in Bucharest.

'Don't be too hasty,' he said. 'When your mother is over the shock and if you think you can leave her, come back and finish your third year. Perhaps I can help her with a little money. I'm an old man, my needs are few. I owe your father a great debt of gratitude.'

I could take a leave of absence which would not go on record.

While my father remained in prison, Bishop Müller sent

mother 200 *lei* (about £1.50) a month. For her, it was the difference between eating and starving, sometimes. We knew the bishop was giving away all he had to the families of many other imprisoned pastors.

After some weeks I returned to Sibiu. My mother had taken up father's work along with her own and was more deeply involved in the Underground Church than ever before. She would not allow herself to weep. Work would be her salvation.

With the end of my three years at the seminary, the spectre of army service arose. I believe in serving one's country, but not in serving those who have stolen it. Patriotism does not consist in joining the army of anti-Christ. But I saw no way out.

Then a curious thing happened. Draft board time came round again, and I went up for interview. They had a row of small cubicles at the induction centre. After the medical, you entered one and gave details to an interviewer who made out a long form.

'Nationality?'

'Jewish.'

He looked up: a Jew studying Lutheran theology? To my surprise he gave a brief smile and said in Hebrew: 'I've been in Israel.'

When he came to questions about my father, I said he was in jail.

Then he began to talk. We had privacy in the little box. Although not Jewish himself, he said, he had been to the Holy Land. When the Jewish Welfare Agency JOINT was helping people reach Palestine in the late forties, he had gone there.

'It was tough in Israel then. Fighting everywhere. I told myself, you've landed yourself in another war — and now there's peace in Rumania. I knew nothing about Communism — from a distance, the propaganda made it sound good. So I came back. God, I've regretted that!'

He was strongly attracted to things Jewish. He'd even had himself circumcised, so that he could pass for a Jew.

I told him something of my story.

He shook his head. A sympathy had grown up between us. A

bond. We knew the enemy. I couldn't ask his name or shake his hand, but it was not necessary.

He tapped the form before him. 'Perhaps I can do something for you,' he said. 'But it's better that I say no more.'

I didn't know what he meant. The incident slipped from my mind over the next year, nor did I think of it when draft board time came the following year, and passed without a call. But as the years went by and I heard nothing from the army I grew convinced that my military file had been lost. Or destroyed.

For accidents will happen in a totalitarian regime. People hate it so much that they are willing to risk their lives to sabotage it.

I returned to Bucharest for the summer holiday to learn that my father was to be 'tried' by a military court. Mother had received notice that this time we could attend.

We took the tram together to the address they had given. The sitting took place in a small bleak room with a bench on a raised platform at one end and a red banner above it. JUSTICE FOR THE PEOPLE IN THE SERVICE OF THE PEOPLE. There were portraits of the Communist leaders on the walls, heavy meat-faced men with sour stares. How many tragedies had started here!

The chief judge was a colonel. He had red epaulettes on his uniform and a red angry network of veins in his cheeks. The two 'assessors' with him on the bench, and the state prosecutor were all heavy suety men. They had the bored detachment of small officials going about their everyday work — of men who dealt in death and life, but were touched by neither.

The fat, grey-haired little colonel sat impassively through the prosecutor's five-minute speech concerning my father's 'crimes'. He did not specify their nature, though he referred once or twice to testimony from people whose names we did not know, and who did not appear in court. Perhaps they were informers who had come to our church under false names. Perhaps it was sheer fiction. It did not matter. This was just a legal charade. The defence lawyer had never heard of these witnesses either, nor were their statements on record. He had not even talked before to my father. There was a two-minute recession after the prosecution speech and they exchanged a few words. The defence could not contradict the prosecutor, or even demand clarification.

The colonel-judge was named Hirsch. He was probably Jewish.

'Wurmbrand, do you wish to say anything?' he asked.

My father was given one minute. He ignored the rigmarole about being an 'enemy of the people' and said a few words about his faith. If the court took into account that he had been three times imprisoned by the fascists during the war and had helped many Jewish children escape Nazi pogroms, he said, they could not consider him a 'reactionary element'.

'That's enough,' interrupted the judge, and together with the assessors he walked from the courtroom. Trial by jury is unknown with us and the sentence had been dictated beforehand by the Party, so no time was wasted. My father had looked steadfastly at us while he spoke and now he smiled tenderly at my mother as the guards took his arms and led him out.

Very soon, the clerk handed us a piece of paper. It said that my father had been fined so many *lei* and sentenced to twenty-five years. That was five years more than his last sentence. There was also a bill for legal expenses! Nowhere on the paper did it give a reason for the sentence.

We came out into the hot summer afternoon. The wind was careering along Victory Avenue.

A few mornings later, two officials in grey suits came to the attic. They wanted to inventory our belongings before re-quisitioning everything again. But now we knew what to expect. I had taken my books and the few other things we wished to keep to friends. The inventory did not take long. We were allowed to keep some sticks of furniture.

We had no idea how we might find money to pay the fine. They took the few *lei* we had as a first payment, and we went on paying for the rest of our lives in Rumania. (On the eve of our departure for the West, six years later, two collectors came to the attic demanding another instalment.)

That summer I obtained permission to study at the library of the Rumanian Academy. A friend of my father's, Professor Titulescu, who had himself spent seven years in prison, helped me get it. A permit like this was almost a supernatural privilege, something like permission to enter the Vatican's library of ancient manuscripts.

It was unlike any Western library. There were no open shelves. The librarians gave out what books they were asked for, and each night sent the record of who was reading what to the secret police. Books were perilous things. The people could not be allowed to study Plato, Kant, Einstein and their like.

Professor Titulescu had met father during his prison years. He is a great mathematician who has written treatises on his speciality. Now he was a 'ghost' who wrote works which were published under the names of 'academicians' who could barely put two sentences together, but had been elevated to the heights for Party purposes. We had some 200 academicians, many of whom were idiots: the best of them might have taught ten-year-olds. They employed the real, but politically unacceptable professors to write books for them. Titulescu turned out two books a year in this way.

The professor told me about his arrest. In 1950, when groups of *maquis* were fighting the Communists in the mountains, his great-nephew Ion had given them food. A captured man mentioned Ion's name under torture. And every man and woman related to Ion was then arrested. Titulescu had not seen Ion since he was a baby, he had not been in the mountains since before the war. But the relationship was enough to keep him seven years in jail.

'In prison,' said the professor, 'my great-nephew gave a cup of soup one day to a new arrival. The man thanked him and asked why he was in jail. "Because," said Ion, "I did what I have just done for you. I fed a starving man." The new arrival said angrily that only swine would condemn a man for that. Ion told him, "Obviously you don't remember me, Mr. Prosecutor. You were the man who got me my sentence." '

The professor shook his head. 'We are a small country. Your father and I saw not a few encounters like that in prison.'

From early morning until closing time, for an entire month, I could use the library. It was like a dream. But how I hated the librarian, a foxy middle-aged man who sat at his desk all day reading only thrillers. With the most wonderful books all round him, books which so many people longed for, he preferred rubbish. He hated serving me and would always finish his page before looking up, while I stood waiting.

I told my mother that I would not return to Sibiu. I must find work and help pay our way. She argued with me, of course. But I joined the queue at the labour office, and there spent many dim hours. When the state controls everything and every worker must be processed for every job, the official machine must be enormous. The Communist mania for centralisation and control of the workers meant that millions had to pass through the very few centres in each district. The queues form when they opened at 5 a.m., and stood until midnight. Once I found myself sixth from the counter as the midnight closing hour approached. But you could reserve your position. I put my name on a list and resumed the wait at five next morning.

In a People's Republic everyone must work: there can be no unemployment. It is an article of faith. But what to do with the political outcasts, the 'social lepers' who may not receive the precious worker's card? Them you offer the lowest menial tasks in towns far from their homes. You don't want to be a dishwasher in Bacau, a lavatory cleaner in Craiova? Too bad, comrade. If one did accept, that meant surrendering one's Bucharest identity card and the right to live or work in the capital. Movement from the countryside to the cities was rigidly controlled. Once you were in a job, it was difficult to change.

There were vacancies for translators. I applied, sat the examinations and passed. Then they discovered that my father was in jail. We decided that I was wasting my time trying to find work.

Late one night I was reading in my room when I heard a noise on the stairs. I thought immediately: they have come for mother. They were banging on the door and shouting. But my mother was out, and in her room Aunt Alice and friends were making plans for a prayer meeting.

And it was Alice they wanted. The secret police had been first to her home. They had bullied someone into revealing that she was here. Now they hustled her roughly out. She was not allowed to say anything. She wept as they led her off.

A little girl on the stairs gazed at her with wide dark eyes. Then a door opened, an arm reached out, seized the child and pulled her inside. The door slammed. Those Wurmbrands! Making trouble again!

Two secret policemen had remained to question us. One was poking about in our belongings. Everyone has something to hide in a Communist state.

'What the devil do you need all these books for?'

I had written some notes in the margins, and he screwed up his eyes trying to read them. I could see how his mind worked, if it worked. He was a young man, very proud of his authority. We were enemies of the people, and we wrote bad things about Communism in the margins of books.

'What is this?'

It was a dedication in English to my father. I told him so.

'We'll see!'

He found another book inscribed to my father, this time in German.

'So many dedications! We will take these books. They contain material critical of the Party!'

He wrote something on a pad of paper. I began to gather up clothes they had pulled from drawers. There were two big exercise books on the floor and I put my hands on them. The officer put his boot on my hands.

'Give those to me!'

I surrendered them. He flicked the pages. Both notebooks were filled in a careful spidery longhand script.

'This is in German?'

I said it was. I tried to explain that these were notes about a medical cure which an old lady had copied out from a book and given to my mother.

'Shut up!'

I saw that the more I tried to explain, the surer they became that I was concealing a terrible secret. Pages and pages of German! It was obviously a great cache of counter-revolutionary material. They left at last, the secret policeman carrying the books under his arm.

In our unhappiness at Alice's arrest, we forgot the books. But comedy often mixed with our tragedies, and some days later the owner of the notes arrived. Old Mrs. Tomaziu was a keen devotee of the system of saline baths at different temperatures prescribed by a German quack as a cure for everything from dropsy to diabetes. The patient was kept in water for about a week, it seemed. She urged my mother to try it. People believe that they want to believe and Mrs. Tomaziu had copied out by hand the German doctor's entire cure from a book. It had taken her a year: she was not a very fast writer.

'After I had my fifth, dear, I said "Never again!"' she told mother. 'But those baths put me on my feet. I don't know where I'd be without them.'

My mother likes to make people happy. She promised to read the notes.

'Take care you don't lose them,' warned Mrs. Tomaziu.

Now they were gone. Nothing we could say could convince the old lady that we had not stolen them. My mother wanted to keep the cure to herself. While I was out of the house that day, she returned with some oaf who threatened my mother. With some difficulty, she managed to persuade them that we really did not have the books. From the secret police, we heard no more about our counter-revolutionary writings. The famous cure was lost to the world.

Now began the business of trying to find where Alice had been taken. The long waits in halls crowded with relatives of prisoners, the silent endurance of insult and the contemptuous indifference of officials. We could not trace her.

The summer ended, and we agreed that I should return to Sibiu. I knew in my heart that it would not be for long. Many friends and neighbours in Bucharest had been arrested in the new drive.

At the seminary, the number of students had been reduced to

twenty-three. We had started out with ninety. One after another, boys had been expelled, arrested, or made to leave by parents under pressure.

The girls had gone first. The Ministry of Cults simply ruled that the Church needed no woman pastors or Sunday school teachers. All religious instruction for children was banned. Atheistic lesssons increased. Party hacks turned out scores of books and pamphlets attacking religion. *An Anthology of Atheism* was one of the biggest. The pamphlets had titles like *How Religion Appeared* or *Are Adam and Eve our Ancestors?* It was a big campaign and thoroughly organised.

On my first day back at the seminary, Bishop Müller called me in. He looked very tired and old.

'I have to tell you that they mean to expel you,' he said. The Vice-Rector at Cluj wants to see you personally.'

The seminary was administered through the university at Cluj, where the Vice-Rector ruled. A Communist Party member who had the title of a pastor, he kept the Rector and staff in line.

I went by train to Cluj. It was two hundred miles north, through the mountains. The Vice-Rector's office was the best in the pile of grey Gothic buildings.

I could no longer study at Sibiu, he said. Why?

'Because the law states that the son of a political prisoner cannot be educated at a public institute. The order comes from Bucharest.'

There was nothing to say. I caught the next train back to Sibiu and sat staring out at the bare wet fields and the mountains, green and dark until they reached the forest-line. Beyond that only the hardiest shrubs survived. I felt hollow and empty. After years of work and waiting and sacrifices by others on my behalf, I was back at the start. Except that now I was twenty. That is how it goes, I thought, for millions like me on this side of Europe. Some of them would think me pretty lucky. I was no longer frightened or curious about the future: it was not going to change soon. They broke everyone in the end, however brave. Even the very bravest were twisted and marred in ways they could not see. I felt sad with a universal sadness; not for myself but for all those who had been cheated of their freedom by Communism.

At the seminary I told Bishop Müller what had happened. I asked if I could sleep a night or two in my dormitory. I had work I wanted to finish and friends to wish goodbye.

The Bishop looked unhappy.

'Mihai, if only I was concerned, you could stay. But already someone has been in here, asking if Wurmbrand has got out yet . . .'

'I see.'

Many were watching Müller. How they would enjoy reporting he had harboured a counter-revolutionary against Party orders.

I put my things in the fibre suitcase and placed my Bible on top. The corridors were empty and only one of the dormitories was occupied now. I drank a glass of tea with two of the boys.

A professor who had never before spoken to me outside the classroom shook my hand and said, 'I do hope everything goes well for you in the future.'

He walked away quickly, worried in case anyone should witness his crime.

I stayed on a few days with a Christian family in Sibiu. I wanted to see all my friends there before I left for good. It was autumn now and the trees were bare and the leaves rotted darkly on the roads. I went from house to house in the October mists and saw the rain falling over the mountains. When I was walking, I did not think so much.

Sometimes I stopped and sat for a while in the yard of a small Catholic church that had been closed. The grass was very tall and rank and glass from the broken windows littered the paths. Around the back of the church a line of abandoned beehives lay toppled on the earth. I wondered where the priest was now. Was he in prison? Or did he sit in a bureaucrat's chair collating the reports of informers on his brethren? I prayed for him and for my father and mother and for all Christians in the Communist-dominated world forgotten by their brothers.

On walls everywhere posters announced the formation of a new medical school. The Party had suddenly realised that the nation's health services were in a bad way, thanks chiefly to the process of selecting only students of 'healthy social origin' in every field. Doctors, dentists, inspectors and many other kinds of personnel were needed. The Health Ministry was to create a huge new cadre of medical students. That autumn some 30,000 were enrolled all over the country. Officials toured schools and clubs seeking students who had been kept out of the universities that year.

I decided to apply for entrance. The alternative was unskilled manual labour, either in the army or out of it. (I'd not yet realised that my draft-office ally had done away with my file.) People of my unhealthy social origin went into a pioneer corps and worked on the roads or the railways. It was another kind of slave labour for boys who'd made the mistake of choosing non-proletarian parents.

I sat for the special entrance examination. It was simply a formality that any schoolboy could have passed: the Ministry had to report that its new schools were open and full by the end of the year, and it did.

The medical school of Bucharest had moved into the pleasant old buildings of a former Catholic monastery, shut down by the Communists! Life here was much more relaxed. All the rebels, the rejects, the intellectuals and counter-revolutionaries were gathered in one basket, nearly 2,000 of us, and the lecturers let us know what a gang of undesirables we were. We must mend our thoughts, or else . . .

I didn't care. I would soon be thrown out. I enrolled in a class training health inspectors. We would examine food stores and state restaurants, grim, bare places like army canteens. (A few good restaurants still existed, but only foreign visitors or the Party *élite* could afford to use them.)

The course of study was hard. We had more than forty hours a week of obligatory classes, then long hours of preparation. The harder we worked, the less time we would have to think about other things. Besides the study there were hours of 'voluntary' labour. Every Sunday we dug ditches, planted parks, worked on collective farms. My course had one advantage: we did so much 'field work' that it was sometimes unnecessary to punch the time clock.

In the evenings there were exquisitely boring political meetings, also called 'voluntary', at which speeches by Dej or some other Communist boss would be read in their entirety. They went on for many hours. After that the lecturer would ask us what we had learnt from them.

You could not dream, or surreptitiously read. You were expected to take notes and expound the relevance of Comrade X's drab rehash of Marx in one's own life.

Worst were the days when the lecturer announced that we should criticise Comrade So-and-So. Some luckless student would have to stand there while the Union of Working Youth members said how ashamed they were not to have noticed earlier his anti-Party tendencies.

And last but not least, there were lectures in atheism. Travelling speakers went from town to town spreading the gospel of materialism. We would be warned by local Party headquarters that all students must gather in the main hall for 'Professor' X's talk on the 'Origins of Christianity'. This ended in a question and answer session at which pre-arranged questions were asked, designed to expose the failings of the Church and the corruption of the clergy.

Some of the atheistic lectures angered me so much that I could not keep my mouth shut. They would tell such stupid lies. It was Party doctrine that no evidence existed of the historical figure of Jesus. I thought that Jesus had always had many enemies, but until now none so desperate that they must deceive people into believing that there was no Jesus.

'Sir,' I asked. 'Isn't it true that Jesus is mentioned as a historical figure by Josephus, Tacitus, Suetonius and other ancient historians; and not only by them, but in the Talmud? That work, which contains sayings by Christ's contemporaries, not only recognises Him, but also His miracles. Can you tell us why this should be? The Talmud is the holy book of the Pharisees, the fiercest foes of Jesus.'

No one had ever before answered back to that lecturer. He

was speechless. Before he could find a reply, I walked out of the room.

This was dangerous; but I was angry, and we had so many people of 'unhealthy social origin' at the school that open discussion was more common than in other places. I was not punished, but another black mark went on my record.

Everyone at medical school had a story to tell: they had been mishandled ruthlessly by Communist society, expelled, dismissed, victimised for political reasons. They had been deprived of any kind of private life, spied upon, gone hungry. Not a few had been in jail: one because he had tried to get across the border into Yugoslavia, another because a relative had fought in the resistance movement ... it is never difficult to enter a Communist prison, almost any reason is good enough. One was sentenced for having shown agreement by his silence to counter-revolutionary talks. The medical school offered a kind of freedom.

I became friendly with a student named Werner Brink. We had both discovered Buddhism and Indian religion and he was delighted to find I had a few books on these subjects and how they relate to Christianity. We lived in the same neighbourhood and were often in one another's homes. His parents were of German origin. They had been hunted by the Nazis during the war for trying to help Jews. On one occasion Mr. Brink had only escaped by hiding for hours under piles of dirty linen during a house search. They received me with great love.

Werner was dark and wiry, with a short spruce body and a large head that was usually bent over a book; he was clever, and earned a reputation for leadership at the school. We were alike in many ways, including the fact that we both had to exist every month on the 'scholarship' that passing school's entrance examination brought with it: 300 *lei*, about £4·00.

We shared a loathing for the class 'leader', Josif Gigurtu, a U.T.M. (Union of Working Youth) secretary. Every class in every school had its secretary, who combined the duties of informer and cheer-leader. Josif made life hell for everyone. If the lecturer was a minute late, he would start to lead us in Party songs. He had a propaganda kit of Marxist leaflets, anti-religious booklets and mimeographed sheets containing the latest hymn of praise for Communism from the composer's union. Sometimes the lecturer was called away to the Party office, and we suffered an hour of unadulterated Josif.

At last the truth came out. All this enthusiasm was generated by fear: Josif's guilty secret was that his papa had been a leader of the right-wing Iron Guard. There was no more unhealthy social origin than this, and he was expelled.

The scientific materialism seminars seemed interminable. Apart from one or two U.T.M. informers, all the students were tired to the point of nausea with indoctrination and would pass the latest political jokes around in an effort to relieve the boredom. Why are Rumanian cows the world's largest? Because they're fed here and milked in Russia.

Many teachers were incompetent hacks who had been raised to professorial status in exchange for collaboration with the Party. After ten or twenty years, they were as bad as ever. One of these instant professors, Nicholas Marinescu, used to intersperse his readings from Marx with asides about the incredible improvements in the life of Siberian peasants since the revolution. The place had been transformed into a garden. Whereas in the U.S.A. starving people grubbed for food in the dustbins of the rich.

Marinescu's voice would rise to a scream as he ended! 'Yet there are people here who still admire the imperialists and denigrate the achievements of the socialist countries. They are enemies of the people, and they will be punished! People have been sent to Siberia for less!'

'Sir,' asked Werner innocently, 'why send them to happy Siberia? They could be deported to hungry America — that would really teach them a lesson.'

That year spring came late. The roof of our attic was like a sieve and rain dripped through into buckets and bowls on the floor. The house was state property: it was therefore illegal to repair it. The state took care of that — on paper. All work was performed according to a schedule, and the co-operative said that our roof could not be mended until three years after the

91

first application. It was, and the job so badly done that rain still came through.

My mother went every month to the court to file a petition for clemency to my father. That meant long spells of lining up and waiting, and while there she attended some trials, hoping to glean news of Alice or other friends who had vanished. Once she heard the appeal of Klaus and some friends of mine from the seminary. They had simply disappeared one day. This was the first we had heard of them since.

My mother never told me details of her Underground Church work. 'We must put our lives in separate compartments to this extent if we are to keep things secret,' she said. I did not go to her room when she had visitors, not even to join a prayer meeting, unless I had been invited. She had her contacts, I had mine. Our rule was to keep matters as loose and disorganised as possible, to muddle whatever could be muddled to confuse informers. Her bedroom was strewn with papers and clothes and books: yet she knew always where everything was, in which old school textbooks a certain paper was kept, what battered box contained a certain letter.

'You are too soft with informers,' I complained. 'You know some of these people who come to you work for the secret police.'

'Better an informer that you know than one you don't,' she said. 'We are never going to be free from spies, and if you know your opponent then you can stop him doing real harm.'

Once an informer came to the door with a tale of woe, trying to borrow or beg fifty *lei*. My mother gave him five.

When she told me, I was furious.

'A kick in the pants is what he needs!'

'No. He was trying to find out what money we had. Five *lei* was right. If need be he will sit at table with us. We can manage him without giving anything away.'

The barber that father and I always went to was an informer, too. One day he became over-friendly and asked me some stupid questions. Then he came round to the attic to tell my mother his troubles. He had enough of them. He didn't get on with his wife, his mother-in-law (who lived with them) had cancer, he himself was a tuberculosis sufferer. Still, he had his subsidy from the secret police: he had been seen entering the office of the head of the department of Cults. (Bishop Müller had been waiting for an audience at the Ministry for months.) We knew, too, that he was trying to collect information from Christians who attended our meetings.

My mother showed him only love.

Years later, on a Paris street, we met him again. My mother asked how he had escaped, knowing very well that he was spending his police bribes.

'It's my tuberculosis,' he said, not meeting our eyes. 'I came for treatment.'

We let him go, without more teasing.

Most people become informers unwillingly: they are forced into it. But then they begin to justify themselves to themselves. They savour the importance of bearing little secrets to the omnipotent security police. They enjoy their ounce of power. They wish to prove their usefulness. It becomes a kind of passion. They report every trivial non-conformity in the lives of friends and even relatives.

Psychological tests have shown that a person who does a boring and worthless task for low reward puts a greater emotional charge into it than one who is well-paid. He has to justify to himself what his conscience tells him has little justification. The informer is a man of low status in the community, whether among the ordinary people or his masters, who may not wholly hide their contempt. He does a humiliating job that brings no social respect. When the external reward is small, then an internal reward has to be invented. So the reluctant informer becomes an eager one.

It is an unpleasant process, and it is the backbone of Communism in action. Among your friends, inside your family, there may be those who have taken this role rather than lose their jobs or go to jail. You distrust everyone, for you know it could happen to you. Your dear friend may have the best intentions: but can he resist daily interrogations, threats, harassment of every kind, beatings?

An old fable tells how the trees argued about how best to

defeat the woodcutter. The oldest tree said, 'He cannot harm us until he is able to make one of us into an axe-handle.' And that is the Rumanian nickname for informers: *cozi de topor* — axe-handles.

So my mother did not tell me whom she visited, where her prayer meetings would be held, what wives were most deeply involved in the Underground Church. It was better that I did not know. Nor did I tell her my little secrets.

One evening as we sat over a supper of fried potatoes and bad coffee, she explained that in her search for someone with news about my father she had found a high police officer with a proposition to make. Hundreds of people were escaping at that time, the early sixties, to Israel, travelling as Jews with forged papers bought with bribes. Our policeman also wanted to get out of the Communist paradise.

'If we can find a bribe for him, and help him to obtain a permit through one of the Jewish agencies,' she said, 'he promises he will try to get Daddy released.'

She had talked to a Jewish official in the Interior Ministry known to us, and it appeared that the police officer really had sufficient power to do what he said. When you see a ray of hope in circumstances of total gloom, you tend to think it shines brighter than it actually does. We spent the rest of the evening plotting and planning.

'If the top Communists with big villas and fat salaries would rather be poor immigrants,' said my mother, 'then we are due for harsher repression. Those who remain will be seeking, and finding, traitors everywhere.'

But we could not miss any chance to help father. My mother had a secret meeting with the officer. He gave convincing evidence that he had helped Jews in the past out of goodwill. He hated the regime and thought only of escape. A friend who had arranged the meeting swore we could trust him.

My mother came home elated. She planned to set to work on helping the man get the permit from the Jewish agency next morning. If my father was set free we might all get to Israel ourselves! Our friend had the necessary contacts.

That night I dreamt that this friend stood in a garden imploring two birds to nest in the hat he held in his hand. The birds fluttered about, but they would not go into the hat. Tears flowed down his cheeks and he left the garden.

In the morning I recalled the dream very vividly. Its meaning seemed quite clear: that our hopes in the fixer and the secret police officer were futile.

I told my mother and asked her not to waste more time or money on the scheme. It was dangerous.

'It's only a dream,' she said.

But I was so persistent that she waited twenty-four hours, perhaps thinking that I would come round. The following morning we heard that there had been a purge of 'opportunist elements' in the Party. Our policeman had been arrested.

I trusted my dream because it was neither the first nor the last of its kind. Several times I have had dreams foretelling symbolically events through which I would later pass.

The New Testament begins with the story of a dream which St. Joseph trusted. And then Jung speaks about premonitory dreams in his psychological writings. When one considers that of the six billion or so cells in our nervous system only some one per cent are utilised in the overt operations of mind and body, it is surely possible that the rest are given over to functions we do not comprehend. The subconscious is still man's dark continent. Inside us are stored the instincts and memories of generations. If a computer can predict the outcome of certain events, then cannot the human brain do more? Scientists say that if they designed a computer capable of doing something like the work of a man's brain, it would be the size of the Albert Hall. Could it not be that crucial events give cues to one's personal unconscious which tell you the outcome in dream?

This might be the mechanism. Behind it is the One who operates it: 'God speaks once, yea twice, yet man perceives it not. In a dream, in a vision of the night, when deep sleep falls upon men, in slumberings upon the bed; then he opens the ears of men and seals their instruction.'*

The director of the school, a dour, stocky man in his forties,

* Job 33: 14–16.

announced that everybody must attend a special evening political meeting on Good Friday. The idea was to spoil the holiday and keep people out of church. On Easter Sunday there would be forced labour. The night before — which is the high point of the Orthodox Easter — they had arranged a dance and a rally. Attendance was obligatory for all students.

The Easter celebrations of the Orthodox Church appealed to my emotions, though I am a Protestant. In former days, great crowds would pack the lovely old church of the Patriarchy to pray and join in the chants for long hours amid the incense and the candles and glittering images. Priests in rich robes celebrated the liturgy and led the procession. And as the first minute of Easter Sunday was born the whole city would explode in a joyous uproar. Bells pealed, firecrackers exploded as the great cry arose: 'Christ is risen!'

Now services were harassed by gangs of youths organised by the Party. They would wait outside churches, whistle against the chanting, light cigarettes from the candles. This hooliganism was most common in the countryside. In Bucharest, the Party preferred to keep the mass of students away, while at the same time sending along a token handful of elementary schoolchildren, with their teacher, for the benefit of foreign visitors.

My class discussed the situation, and we agreed to stay away from the political meeting. On the afternoon of Good Friday not one of the twenty-five in class turned up. A list of names was posted on the notice-board under the announcement of Saturday's rally and dance. You had to sign against your name to acknowledge that you would attend. Only two out of the twenty-five went.

On Monday morning, the director walked into our class, pale with anger. His voice shook as he summoned us all to a meeting in the main hall. There we found the school's Party secretary *and* the secretary for that district of the city. It meant real trouble.

The first target was our class secretary of the Communist youth organisation, a likeable boy who had replaced the expelled Josif. The school secretary, a short fat man with nicotine-stained teeth, launched the attack.

How could Marcel fail so criminally in vigilance, after all that he, the school secretary, had taught him? 'Knowing it was Good Friday, you were unable to convince your class to stay away from the superstitious church rituals, utterly discredited by scientific materialism. Why did you not use the dialectical skills I've been teaching you for months?'

Don't blame me, cried the secretary, in effect: he's the guilty one. If you want to keep your job in a Communist state, you point an accusing finger at someone else. The poor man was very frightened.

The twenty-five of us all had excuses ready, most of them backed by medical certificates — you could buy them on the black market, complete with health stamps. But that day they were not interested in excuses. It was time for another orgy of public confession.

The district secretary followed up with a second tirade, threatening everyone with expulsion and demanding some 'serious self-criticism'. The school secretary could start by confessing his faults.

The little man stood up.

'No one knows better than I how grave my failings have been,' he began. 'I have wronged the Party in failing to educate these students in political alertness and awareness. I have failed to see that their instructors went earnestly about eradicating the last vestiges of religious superstition. I — a man whose very existence without the Party is unthinkable . . .'

That, at least, was true. He carried on for some time. Then it was our turn.

'Now who is going to be the first to echo my words and really start the criticism . . .'

Silence. No one stood.

'Very well. We'll proceed alphabetically.'

One by one they rose to say how ashamed they were to belong to a class with such a secretary. Finally Marcel explained how ashamed he was to be secretary of such a class.

'Why didn't you stand up first,' shouted the district secretary, 'to tell us what sort of leadership you have given?'

Marcel was a decent boy with a lean country face. It would

be a bad loss to us, his expulsion as Union of Communist Youth secretary. He hardly ever called political meetings: we simply arranged our cover story every week. 'The political meeting was held on Thursday from 6 p.m. until 9 p.m., and we discussed so-and-so . . .'

While he was busy with his self-denunciation, I prayed for courage. Being a 'W' — and therefore a German or a Jew, since that letter doesn't exist in Rumanian — I came last.

'Wurmbrand!'

I said: 'I am a Christian and the Constitution guarantees us freedom of worship. If we continue like this we may upset the Party leadership by showing that we do not respect socialist legality. The Party is adamant on this point.'

Now it was the turn of the district secretary to be frightened. Jews are cunning. You never know what to expect from them. Would this Wurmbrand have dared to speak out like this without some backing? He began to wonder if he might not indeed get into trouble.

The meeting was brought to a hasty conclusion.

Afterwards, he found out that he had been a fool. And a heavy black mark went down against my name, to count towards my expulsion a few months later.

Marcel lost his position as class leader. I was called to the director's office for a reprimand.

I had learned to dissimulate, an art without which no one survives in the Communist world. But I was overwrought. When he reproached me for a 'hostile attitude', I burst out:

'Comrade director, isn't it Party doctrine that I am only matter, the random product of evolution? If I behave in a certain way isn't it because I am merely a creature of circumstance? If a fly bothers you, do you tell it to behave or do you kill it?' There were tears in my eyes. 'Many counter-revolutionaries are in prison. But weren't they simply reacting to these ineluctable laws of matter we hear so much about? Where is their responsibility? Sir, the fact is that the very words of your reprimand prove you don't believe all this "scientific materialism".'

The director stared at me for a moment, simply aghast. Then

he burst out — for once, sincerely: 'Do you suppose you're the only one who feels like crying sometimes? We have to live. My wife weeps every night. Because every day she teaches lies about our history and geography and everything else.'

Suddenly, he leaned forward and shook my hand.

'Now leave me alone,' he said, 'or perhaps with your God.'

That summer I befriended a student with access to the banned 'secret section' of the public library, where you found the truly dangerous books — works like Einstein's *The World As I See It*, in which he expresses his love of Judaism, his admiration for Christ. My new friend Ghiță who belonged to the history faculty of the university, lent me this one evening. I read it at a sitting and returned it to him next day.

Ghiță was studying for the job of re-writing history to conform with the Party line. That changed every few years, so he would never be out of work. Students in this faculty were carefully selected and groomed. Since they also turned out much of the anti-religious propaganda about the sins of the Church, they had access to rarely seen books of philosophy and theology. Rarely seen by us, that is.

Ghiță, too, had learned to dissimulate. He was a member of the U.T.M. and other Communist front organisations. He seemed like a dutiful student of Marxism, and his standing with the professors was good. But he was in fact a secret Christian.

His library pass bore no photograph. When he lent it to me I could let them suppose I was studying for an atheistic thesis and use the so-called 'documentary file' of bourgeois books which a good Communist needed only to document his attacks on religion and capitalism. (Every library had this division, and the open shelves of approved books were about as interesting as the Party newspaper.)

Here I found also books on brainwashing and psycho-political warfare which were allowed only limited circulation even in Party ranks. The most succinct and frightening of these was a summary of Lavrenti Beria's theories concerning techniques of bringing about revolution in a foreign country. Beria, Stalin's secret police chief until 1952, when he lost the battle for the succession to Kruschev and was executed as a spy, had all the evil genius of Hitler; but he was more intelligent and less emotional. There is a truly fiendish quality about this cold-hearted description of how to use what he calls 'psychopolitics' to undermine a people's loyalties and ideals and poison the mind of youth in capitalist countries with drugs and excessive, orgiastic emphasis on sex. The early destruction of religion is vital to his system.

Once again, books opened up new worlds to me. I read books written at the peaks of knowledge of God, and others by men who knew the lowest circle of hell.

In the spring of 1961 came the expected blow. A few weeks after the Good Friday incident I was expelled from medical school. The classleader told me to report to the office of the Party secretary one morning. With considerable relish he told me that the facts about my father's imprisonment had been discovered. I was to get out at once.

Once more I began looking for a job. Once more I tried for the post of translator. I sat for an examination with seven others in a state institute, translating pages of French and German science textbooks into Rumanian. I'd been reading and translating foreign books for years now, and I completed the test in an hour out of the two and a half hours allotted. The examiner congratulated me and the prospects seemed good. But I rashly let slip that I'd been attending the medical school. They checked on me there: and that was that.

I couldn't even get a job as a milkman. The state-run co-operative was hiring people to drive the motor-bikes.

We were interviewed by the personnel officer, who accepted others and rejected me, without explanation.

It wouldn't have been illegal for them to employ a political prisoner's son on milk delivery. But they had so many applicants for jobs, and they didn't want any complications. After many long fruitless hours of queueing at the employment office I began to feel again that sensation of utter hopelessness I knew so well: the malaise of the social outcast. The days passed without content or meaning. I couldn't read what I wanted, see what I wanted, go where I wanted.

I didn't like to meet friends like Marcel too often, because I knew people in our circle were spying on me, reporting anything 'anti-' that was said. But one day I ran into him on the street with a girl named Edith, who worked in the Rumanian film industry. Her complaint was too much work: she worked a fifty-hour week, had to attend political lectures and now she wanted a holiday on the Black Sea. But of course she couldn't have one, although she had money. The regime controlled everything, and the waiting lists for hotel rooms at coastal resorts were enormous. To take a train to Costanza and simply book into a hotel, as one would do in the West, was out of the question. Between you and the simplest goal lay so many obstacles that you hesitated to start out.

Edith told us about the mad, exciting life of the movie-maker in Rumania. Every script had to be approved by the Party and then, when perhaps a third of the film had been made, it would be shown to a commission which would judge it on a basis of political content. They, of course, felt obliged to find fault with it and the whole thing would go back into the melting pot to improve its propaganda value.

Rumania was in the happy position of being unable to make war films, since she had been on the wrong side most of the time. The Rumanian army had fought against the Russians and lost. However, there were lots of Rumanian and Hungarian films about our gallant secret police and their efficiency in catching American spies. Unfortunately, the leading Rumanian actor who always played the role of a Communist 007 defected to the West. All his movies had to be withdrawn from circulation.

When I told Edith about my own troubles, she offered to put in a word for me with a friend in the department that hired extras.

'It's ghastly work, really,' she said. 'You sit around most of the day twiddling your thumbs. Three hours waiting for the sun to come out, then ten minutes filming and then three hours waiting while they prepare the next scene.'

I said I was used to waiting.

A few days later Edith told me she'd arranged with her friend to slip me in quietly as an extra.

'Ever played a violin?' she asked. 'Well, now you're going to play in the orchestra of La Scala. They'll supply the clothes!'

The film company had tried to hire the Philharmonic to play, but the musicians' union wanted film extra rates instead of their usual concert performance fees. So the director had decided to use extras anyway, and dub the sound on later. It was the wrong decision.

The movie was about the life of Madame Darcleé, a famous soprano in the early part of the century, Rumania's answer to Dame Nellie Melba, who had actually sung at La Scala in Milan. All they wanted was a few shots of the orchestra fiddling away while Madame Darcleé gave forth. But the extras were mostly young students who'd never held a musical instrument before, whereas the conductor was a real conductor who wanted every detail of the miming to be perfect. Time after time, some bows would be up, others down as the camera finished a take. Individualism will out. The trouble was that the man who was supposed to be giving us the cues had to be outside the picture. Not every one could see him. Some followed the conductor and some the little man in the pin-stripe suit giving the cues.

'Hopeless!' The conductor shook his bushy head and waved his long slim hairless hands before it. 'Nothing to be done!'

At the end of Madame Darcleé's song, she had to bow to the audience — yet another crowd of hungry students in elaborate turn-of-the-century costumes ranged in three tiers of gilded boxes — who had to applaud and cheer enthusiastically. Six retakes and the cheers became maniacal, the conductor's bows more stiffly hinged and puppet-like. Until my neighbour, dressed like me in evening clothes and roseate make-up, burst into hysterical giggles. His head bent towards his knees and his shoulders heaved with suppressed laughter. I began to laugh myself.

Recovering at last, he looked at me, my ill-fitting coat, my Valentino make-up and started again.

'You are so b-b-beautiful!!'

I had to laugh. He was no picture, either. We recognised one another easily enough as Jewish. Walking away at the end of the session, through the high, barnlike sound stage, under the girders and catwalks and coldly glaring lights, we discussed the subject that always came up first between Jews in Rumania. How to get out.

We exchanged the latest news of friends who were leaving, or hoped to leave; stories of visits to the consulate and being followed by police agents; rumours of a speed-up in departure processes. After a long hiatus the regime was again permitting emigration to Israel, but the first flood of exit visas had brought angry protests from Arab countries and in 1960 the flow had fallen to a trickle. But that year, 1961, Jewish families were again being allowed to leave, but now the authorities demanded large sums in foreign currency for all who departed, ranging from £1,000 for ordinary people to £15,000 for undesirables like ourselves. Scientists were not for sale at any price.

From this, the conversation strayed into all kinds of philosophical and religious byways and we only parted hours later. Bruno gave me his address and we arranged to meet soon. But next day we ran into one another in the street outside my home.

With him was a remarkably pretty girl of about sixteen.

'Mihai, I want you to meet Judy — I've just been telling her all about our talk yesterday.'

Judith smiled and gave her long black hair a nervous toss. Her dark eyes sparkled mischievously.

'I'm certainly glad to meet someone that Bruno actually admits is cleverer than himself!' she said.

We chatted for a while as we walked. Feeling more than a little flattered and suddenly conscious of my uncut, uncombed hair and my scruffy heavily darned clothes, I asked where she lived.

'Just here, in this street.'

'So we're neighbours!'

And I showed them our attic windows, poking up from the rooftop of the old mission. Judith's home was only half a block away, round the first corner.

Bruno said, 'There's a party next Wednesday evening at the Goldbergs'. Why don't you come along?'

The habit of small evening gatherings to discuss the exit visa situation was common at that time. Bruno had received a tip that his family was high on the list. The parties tended to be rather exclusive, but Bruno was an outgoing, happy character and he had access to them all.

I went to one of his parties. Judith was with him. She smiled as I came into the room and soon she was asking me all kinds of questions about my friends, my interests, my love-life. Judith's curiosity was as tireless as it was flattering. What were these 'philosophical discussions' Bruno talked about? What did we discuss? She was so bored with school. All that doctrinal rubbish, over and over again, and always the same, and never anything to do with life! It was so dull. She longed, how she longed, to hear something different.

'It's like having to wear that horrible school uniform, day in, day out,' she said. 'It's so ugly, really ugly, I can't wait to get home and change! And if you wear anything else you're made to feel you're a sneak or some kind of freak. Ugh!'

She chattered, a babbling brook of innocent information and inquiries. In minutes she'd discovered that we had been born in the same hospital, but at a distance of six years, that I was a Christian, that my father was in prison because he was a pastor.

Judith's parents had met and married in a concentration camp during the war. A rabbi had performed the ceremony as best he could. They'd had one child in the three years spent in that camp, and it had died. After being liberated in 1945, her mother had travelled to Bucharest, seven months pregnant with Judy, perched on the top of a giant gasoline truck. They were determined to get home, and that was the only transport available. The journey of several hundred miles took many days. But Judith's mother survived and the child was born in a time of great hope: now, they thought, we are free at last. But their problems were just starting. They'd moved from their little Nazi concentration camp, to the vast national one that Rumania was soon to become. Her father had done well for a while and had even opened a small shop selling silk for ties and scarves. The next year it was taken from him as the Communists nationalised everything. Judith's first memories were of hunger, and standing in line to buy food.

'Mother would put me in one queue while she went and stood in another; how I hated that.' She grinned suddenly. 'So I found a way to beat them. You know how they always tell you in school that you children are the future of the country and so on. Well, one day I saw a line at a shop that had some cakes in. I was about ten and very small. But I just went up to the counter put my money down and said I wanted six. People started shouting for me to get to the end of the line. I turned to the first woman there and said, "Madame, I am the future of the country. I don't have to wait in line!" She was speechless!'

'And it worked?' I asked, laughing.

'Sure, I tried it on several times after that. It never failed.'

The family had lived in the Jewish ghetto area, Dudesti. 'We arranged a swop with an old couple who were looking for a smaller apartment, on condition that we paid them all our savings.' (Judith named a sum that was the equivalent of £6,200.) 'It was at the Iconnei Gardens, very central and much nicer. It had two bedrooms and a bathroom and a small kitchen, wasn't that sensational!'

I agreed that it was, for Rumania.

'What we didn't know was that a secret police officer was living in the same block and he knew this old couple were leaving. On the day they moved, he moved too: into our flat! He took the best bedroom and the kitchen and said to my mother, "One room is quite enough for you and your family. Jews, are you? Well, you'll probably be getting out soon anyway, ha-ha!'

Judith's family had simply lost all their savings on a deal that left them worse off than before, with a secret policeman in the house. They cooked in the bathroom and shared the toilet with ten other families.

'Apart from that, it was all right!' said Judith.

That lasted four years. Then they'd moved back to the Jewish quarter, close to our attic.

'I heard about your father of course. He's really a legend in the quarter. A lot of people say hard things about him who know nothing about what he did!'

The latter included, I later discovered, Judith's own parents. Among Jews there was, inevitably, resentment against one of them who preached Christ. Judith's father had seen his mother, father, sister and brother taken off to Auschwitz. His surviving sister saw them thrown into the furnaces. Her mother's family had perished, no one knew how, in Transmistrian concentration camps. Many Jews considered this almost as much of a Christian persecution as a Nazi one. Her father would say, 'Didn't they have *Gott mit uns* on their badges?!'

All her life, they'd tried to keep her away from Christian children. So that when she came with Bruno to our attic one evening to listen to a Bach and Mozart concert on the crackly old radio I'd found, she was shocked to see verses from the New Testament on the wall over my narrow bed. She'd heard the verdict of neighbourhood Jews on my father: 'Prison's the best place for him. Converting good Jewish people!' It was a tribute, of a kind.

Judith was also shocked by the place we lived in. You could see sky through the holes in the roof. I explained that we liked it this way for air-conditioning in the summer, but she didn't smile. The walls were stained and dirty with an invincible dirt, the sloping roof created an effect of claustrophobia, and, with the one narrow window, it was always half-dark.

Soon the talk came round to emigration.

'As far back as I can remember, I've been waiting to go to Israel,' she said. 'Mummy and Daddy had the chance when I was four. My grandmother went then. I was very attached to her. I used to walk around the house saying, "Israel, Israel, Israel!" I swear it was the first word I ever said.'

'Why were your parents so dumb, anyhow?' asked Bruno.

'They were not dumb! How could they see how bad it would be here, way back in '48?'

Once Israel was established and flourishing, and all Rumania had turned into a prison, other people began to envy the Jews. Many tried to marry Jewish girls or men, until finally the

Government refused visas to the non-Jewish partners of mixed marriages.

A few weeks later, Bruno's passage to Israel was approved. We saw him off on the train for the port, then came home together on the tram. For the first time, we talked seriously about my faith.

I did not work to convince her. The obstacles were many: religion was a joke among her friends, who were simple boys and girls indoctrinated with years of Communist propaganda. Christianity was an offence to her parents, who shared the anti-Christian feelings of many Jews. She had heard nothing from the other side.

One of the first objections she raised was to the idea of life after death.

'But if we have only to live here for a few years on this planet,' I said, 'where water, air, warmth and food are all provided in the correct degree, where everything works together so amazingly to create the ideal conditions for us—if we're here only to die, what sense is there in it all? Why do we struggle for knowledge that is quite unnecessary to our material existence? Why do we long to know about distant galaxies and pre-history? The highest minds seek spiritual understanding, not material things: doesn't that make sense only if there is a life after death?'

It was enough to raise a hundred questions in her mind.

That spring we met often. Discussing life, death and the hereafter, we walked several times a week in King Carol Park (re-named for some Communist leader—but still called everywhere after our first King). It was far from the centre of town, and the road leading to it was pleasant and lined with trees.

Watching her growing interest, I tried to persuade her to look inside a church.

'Mihai, we are good friends,' said Judith. 'Don't ask this of me, my parents will stop me seeing you.'

'Your parents have not thought about it, they are simply

reacting. Have they ever talked to a real Christian? Have they ever seen a Christian service?'

'I must be honest with them.'

'Also with yourself. You cannot condemn something you do not know about. You have a duty to satisfy your intellectual curiosity.'

I did not have enough confidence in her to take her to an underground meeting. I could not take her to the Lutheran Church; the official Baptist Church was led by Communist stooges.

So she came with me into an Orthodox church.

'You see the pictures?' I asked. 'On the left is Moses, a Jew, then Isaiah, a Jew. Next the Apostles, all Jews. And that one framed in gold is a Jewess, the Virgin. And this is Jesus, King of the Jews. But now listen: the priest is chanting a Jewish song from a Jewish book—the Bible.'

Judith smiled at me.

'Don't you feel at home here? It is really our house,' I said.

'It's also a bit of a Byzantine mixture.'

'True, but you don't mind sharing a little, do you?'

Judith was pleased with this adventure. The Christians had not eaten her, had they? I teased.

Easter-time came round again. I asked her to come with me to the great procession at St. Eleftherius' church. But again she shied away. It was the most beautiful of the Orthodox festivals, I said.

'Please don't insist,' said Judith.

So I did not insist. I simply walked her in the right direction. Suddenly we were among a crowd of happy onlookers.

It was the one day of the year when the Communists allowed religion out from behind the church doors. Bells were tolling as the procession wound slowly through the ranks of people. A verger with a lantern led the way and behind him came banners borne by priests, the deacons in rich chasubles, the Cross itself, then rows of women in black with crimson candles in their hands in a host of points of swaying, flickering light. The faces showed strength and dedication. A spiritual beauty shone out and their voices made a dark golden scaffolding of sound: 'Christ resurrected from the dead,' they sang, 'death treading upon death, and giving life to those in graves.'

I said something to Judith about leaving if she was upset. She did not hear me. So many of her relatives had died under the Nazis and lay now in unknown graves. And these voices sang that Christ gave new life to the dead.

The procession was only a shadow of its old size and splendour. But still at least 3,000 people had come to watch. Police and informers were everywhere, but they did not interfere and there was no hooliganism.

Judith turned to me, looking excited and a little dazed.

'I'm glad you brought me,' she said.

Years later, she told me that she thought of that evening as a turning point, the moment in which she said to herself: 'Perhaps Christians are not so stupid after all. Perhaps they know something other people don't.'

Sometimes Judith met my mother and Christian friends at the attic. My mother's strength and health had not fully recovered from the years in the concentration camps and she was often forced to take to her bed by sickness. On one such day, she and Judith had a long talk. Mostly they discussed family affairs, but the words my mother said about Christ also helped Judith towards an understanding.

She met also two Hebrew Christians, the Levys—a husband and wife who had been brought to Christ by my father years before. They were about to leave for Israel, and we talked of emigration, and the universal desire to leave in the Communist camp.

Mr. Levy told a joke: two guards were standing on the Berlin wall looking out towards the West. One sighed, thinking of the lies told about the Communist paradise and how much he longed to get to the West. Just at that moment he caught his companion looking out with the same expression on his face.

'Comrade,' he asked. 'Are you thinking what I'm thinking?'

'Of course, comrade.'

'In that case, you're under arrest!'

We talked for a long time about the problems of getting out, and how lucky the Levys were. Judith's eyes were a little bit wet when she wished them goodbye. She did not know how soon they would meet again, or what a vital role they were to play in her life.

I had no hope of getting into another polytechnic or finding a decent job. So I did what thousands of others had done before me: I became an illicit worker in the 'black market' of labour.

The illegal workers were the backbone of the building trade, a pool of cheap labour with no rights whatsoever which the state could exploit without damaging the false front of 'full employment'. Peasants left their villages without permission and joined relatives in the city. Without official papers, they could not work. In the same position were many middle-class people of 'unhealthy social origin', with relatives in jail who had lost businesses connected with the trade. All these formed the ranks of underpaid, unprotected, sweated labour.

I found a job on a building site where a new factory was to go up. My immediate overseer was a former political prisoner who had worked on the canal. He took me into his confidence, quickly realising that I had a head for figures and paperwork. I found myself more or less supervising some fifty workers. The chief purpose of this tightly closed leadership was to augment their own pay. The cheated workers were happy when I stopped this practice in my department.

One trick was to leave all paper work until long after an old building had been knocked down and no one could prove exactly what had been destroyed. So many cubic feet of wall brought down, so many cubic feet of earth moved meant so much pay for us, to be divided equally among workers whose existence the Party did not officially admit. The Party's accountants were idle and easily bribed. And only if a co-operative went bankrupt was a full-scale inspection of the books held. If the books showed a profit—not common in state-run businesses—no one asked questions.

All the officials concerned in the deal to build the new factory were illegally padding their salaries.

Desperately short of the basic necessities of life, the working man thinks constantly about making that little extra money. To the Western visitor, it seems that people in every Communist-dominated country live in an atmosphere of constant wheeling and dealing. To possess something from the West—a small record-player, say, or a pair of blue jeans—is to acquire an important status symbol. It is a way of expressing your disgust and contempt for Communist society, almost the only way possible with a degree of safety. It is the one form of dissent we can get away with. It is a means of resisting foreign domination.

The 'black' workers never dreamed of complaining about their wretched wages. They were glad to receive anything. None of the fifty on our site appeared on the payroll. All the names on that were false, so that of the 700 *lei* paid out by the state for these names the supervisors took half to divide among themselves.

But on the hated collective farms, the black workers would have received even less. The farms were manned by soldiers, guarding political prisoners, women and children. For all its repressive measures, the state couldn't stop the move to the towns. Some country people literally gave their blood to the state machine: their only income was the few *lei* they had received for donating their blood as often as they could to hospitals. I often saw men faint on the job because they had been giving blood too often.

The building trade was their chief hope of work, thanks largely to the spectacular confusion it was in after years of bureaucratic control. Nothing was co-ordinated. Each state co-operative had its own function, which it performed indifferently in its own time. When bricklayers had bricks, plumbers were out of piping; when carpenters had wood, electricians lacked light fittings. It seemed at times that the whole city was in process of reconstruction, so many half-finished shells of buildings stood about, spilling debris over roadways, untouched by workmen for weeks or months.

The chief superviser was a heavily-built, jovial man with a

bald head. We sat together in his drab little office looking out over the site. While I worked on the accounts, he smoked endless cigarettes and told stories.

One I remember was about the American and the Russian who arrived simultaneously at the gates of hell, only to find there is a capitalist and a Communist inferno. The American told his companion they'd be better off in the capitalist hell.

'No,' said the Russian. 'Come with me. When the Devil has wood, he'll be out of matches; when he has matches, he'll be out of fuel; when he has all these, he'll be called to a political meeting with the other devils. That's how it is under Communism: they'll never get round to lighting the fire.'

For the enterprising worker, there was the black market. It had millions of customers, but for dealers the risks were high and penalties heavy. It is illegal to own gold in Rumania, and all jewellery of value must be registered. When you have registered it, it is confiscated. Our friend Willie had offended against these laws and gone to jail. In prison he met my father.

He came to us on the first day of his release. 'Mrs. Wurmbrand, your husband asked me to say he is well and in good spirits at Gherla.' The ancient prison, built to hold some 2,000 inmates, now contained 10,000 men, said Willie. He had not been able to speak more than a word with father, but his name was a myth there.

'Many times, when we were sitting in the cell, someone at the window would cry: "Look boys, there's the pastor!" And we'd all rush over to catch a glimpse. He had such a reputation for helping others, and for courage.'

Willie, a Jew, had met members of the Army of the Lord at Gherla. They circulated the message asking anyone leaving jail to contact us in Bucharest. It was the first news we had had of father in a long time.

Willie had nowhere to stay, old business acquaintances, wanting no connection with an 'economic saboteur', had turned him away. We put down a mattress for him in my room. For a few days he shared our meals. Then he found another home.

We lent him perhaps 100 *lei*. In three months he turned that sum into 6,000 *lei*. Willie had a nose for business.

Everyone tried to buy things from Western visitors. But Willie always knew the most profitable items, the ones that brought in the best returns. He traded with visitors from Communist-ruled countries, too: Rumania has no cosmetics industry, Bulgaria has a large one. By meeting the trains and buses from Bulgaria, he accumulated big supplies of lipsticks and skin creams which he re-sold at a profit. He made drivers and railwaymen into his business partners, getting them to bring in boxes of the stuff for a cut in the profits. The commerce worked both ways: for Rumania is a gold-producing country, and the price of gold is much higher in Bulgaria.

Within a year, he had trebled his first 6,000 *lei*. He always listened gladly to the Bible, provided it was read by my mother. If he thought we needed help, he helped unasked. This Jewish black-marketeer showed more interest in helping a suffering Christian family than many Western Church leaders. Ravens not the priests, fed the prophet Elijah.

We asked Willie to receive; but he wouldn't accept it. The shell of anti-Christian prejudice had grown too hard. But who can say what was below the shell?

As a building worker, I saw how the Party spied on its own members. A friendly architect explained to me how his designs for new apartment blocks which would house important Party members always included plans for the installation of bugging devices in the walls. Every apartment was, so to speak, wired for sound.

The cost, the mis-spent time and effort of the huge secret police bureaucracy mattered nothing to the frightened men at the top: they had good reason for fear. Time after time, in one Communist dictatorship after another, they had seen their predecessors toppled, denounced and degraded by men who had been their loyal or servile aides. We cannot know how many of the two million Party members in Rumania are watched and live in electronically bugged homes; but it is a high proportion. The Communists spare nothing in this effort. Think only of the

U.S. Embassy in Moscow where no less than sixty bugging devices were discovered.

In many Bucharest apartment blocks you would find a 'secret' apartment, a flat unoccupied by any family, to which from time to time, strangers would come. These were places used by the police for meetings with informers who didn't wish to be seen entering some public office.

As a Jew who hoped to escape from Communism one day, living among friends whose chief thought this was, I went often to the Israeli consulate. Whenever I talked to an official there, he turned up the radio loudly to jam the bugging devices. And every visitor to the consulate was watched and followed by agents, who noted his movements and filed his name for further investigation.

Judith and her family applied for passports. They hoped to reach Israel. The dream of living in freedom made nothing of all the suffering involved in this attempt. There was something very beautiful in this absolute faith of the Jews that some day, somehow, they would be reunited in their ancient homeland. The dream was 2,000 years old, but still the cry was: next year in Jerusalem! They repeated, as it were, the psalm: 'If I forgot thee, O Jerusalem, Let my right hand forget her cunning; If I do not remember thee, Let my tongue cleave to the roof of my mouth.' However often they were rejected, and even though it meant surrendering every last thing they possessed, the Jews clung to this hope. In the case of Judith's family, the chances seemed slender, for they had renounced their passage in 1948. I hoped that Judith, if she remained, would become a Christian; yet I feared for her too, knowing that she would then be doubly persecuted as a Christian and a Jew. I tried to give her the advice I would have given if I had been her brother. She was much younger than me, and she planned to meet Bruno again in Israel. It seemed likely that they would marry.

One afternoon as I was walking home from work, we met in the street. Her face glowed with excitement. I knew at once that the passport had been granted.

'We can leave!' she cried. 'At last! I'm so thrilled!'

I was less so. But for her sake I was glad.

Now she began the exasperating business of arranging the countless formalities of departure from a Communist country. After the money had been paid for your release by Israeli agencies, you still had to find some £80 or more for essential documents. You had to obtain from every public service, water, light, power, etc., and from every public library in Bucharest, written proof that you owed no money and had no books outstanding. All these places charged a fee of 50 or 100 *lei*. Everything was done to make departure as difficult and unpleasant as possible. Sometimes the Rumanians would close the Israeli consulate completely to harass the traffic. (This happened only a few weeks after Judith's departure.)

On a fine sunny morning we went to the station to see the family off. Crowds milled about on the platform and the air was filled with tearful Jewish farewells. The train, which would pass through Hungary to Vienna, was packed. We smiled steadily, made promises to write, to send parcels, not to forget. Judith began to weep.

'It is terrible that you have to stay!' she sobbed. Then: 'I'm so upset at going away!'

The family had a deep love for Rumania, the place of their birth; it was a great wrench to leave. But Communism had spoiled the things they loved most about the country.

The Tesslers got into the carriage. Then the train moved, and we walked along beside it, aunts and uncles and assorted relatives, waving handkerchiefs.

'Goodbye! Goodbye!'

Judith was carried away, smiling and weeping, from the station gloom out into dazzling sunshine.

For months we heard nothing. Then long descriptive letters arrived, marked Urgent, Express, Special Delivery. Then another long silence; then more Urgent letters. This was Judith's way of writing. Israel lived up to expectations. Everyone 'was so free!' The girls wore no bras! Everything worked! Even the ball-point pens. The land, the people, everything was beautiful! We were very envious.

I began going about with a girl named Alina. I thought her

very pretty, and other students made it plain that I was not alone in this thought. She was a romantic young woman who liked to laugh and to be with boys who could make her laugh: gay, fun-loving, not unintelligent, with a vitality that made her very popular. She had her serious side, too; and we went to church together, as well as to parties. But I told her nothing of our Underground Church work. Seeing me often with friends from the medical school, she assumed that I too was a medical student.

We fell in love. I cannot say it made me happy, because I was very sure that it could not last. I seemed fated not to finish whatever I started; yet I hoped against hope that our relationship was not doomed.

Alina loved me, too. But she also saw in me a way out of an *impasse*. She was studying at a polytechnic on a course that would take her into the administrative side of the oil industry. Under Communism, there is absolutely no flexibility in taking jobs: once you are in a line of work, everything is arranged to keep you there. Alina and her fellow students knew that beyond any shadow of doubt they would be posted to some remote factory town, living and sleeping in a workers' village near the oil refineries. There was one escape route: marriage.

'Alina is the same as the rest,' said Werner Brink. 'She wants a husband. There's a cachet about being a medical student. This is her last year of training. It's now or never. Watch out Mihai!'

I said, 'Thanks, but you shouldn't speak badly about someone unless you have genuine proof.'

He looked at me with surprise. 'I didn't know it was like that.'

But Werner was right. You cannot hope for a private life under Communism, the Party's tentacles reach everywhere.

I knew that I had to tell her of my 'unhealthy social origin', my father, and all the rest. But for weeks I delayed the moment. Until one evening, after I had walked with her to her home and we stood on the steps, she asked:

'Why don't you show me over the medical school tomorrow? I've never been there.'

Her arms were around me. We held each other tightly. The moment had come to tell the whole story. I explained that I was no longer a medical student, and why: my expulsion from different schools, my father's sentence, my mother's years in the labour camps.

She moved away from me. There was a long pause.

'I'm sorry,' she said. 'Really sorry.'

A tram went by. Its wheels screeched on the curve.

'Mihai, I can't see you again.'

'Please don't go,' I said. 'It is not so bad. You'll see ...'

She had opened the door.

'When will I see you again?'

'I can't, Mihai. Please don't hate me.'

She was gone.

I never did see her again. There was no call, nothing. And, really, there was nothing to say. That was how things went in a Communist state. I walked home alone through the silent streets.

Once more, I tried to get a little education. At the building site, I felt that my mind was drying up, but saw no way out. Then from my old friend Werner, I heard that the civil engineering school was holding examinations for entrants. There were 5,000 candidates for 150 places.

'What of your father?' asked Werner. 'They will find out about him.'

'But not for a time. My father was freed by state decree in 1956—they said, as it were, that Ana Pauker was to blame for putting innocent men in prison. I need not mention that he is again wrongly in jail. I am not obliged to state, in my autobiography, all the mistakes of the Party!'

We agreed to sit for the exam. together. That night I dreamt that I walked with Werner through snowy mountains. We had to struggle to move our feet. But hands seemed to grip us and push us through the pass until we came down into a sunny valley. It seemed an omen.

A month later, we sat and passed the entrance exam., winning two of the precious places in the hydro-technical faculty.

It meant that we would receive a small grant. It meant goodbye to the building site, the grubby overalls, the coughing cement-mixers, the unfinished blocks of apartments.

I filled in the long questionnaire, avoiding all mention of my parents' past. With luck, I might last a few months.

The college was a sterile grey building in central Bucharest where city planning, road-building, irrigation and so on were studied. Our faculty studied dam-building. Eighty boys and twenty girls were committed here to five years of the most strictly regimented technical training. Attendance of all classes was compulsory. You could not choose your instructor or your subjects. The freedom taken for granted in the West was to us unimaginable.

The faculty was split into working groups of twelve to fifteen, and in each there was a student informer. He or she reported on what we did, said and appeared to think. And though we hated their doings, we knew the pressures they faced.

'I have been called to police headquarters,' warned my fellow-student Ion, a thin, quiet boy. 'They wish to make me an informer. Please say nothing in front of me. I may have to tell them something.'

Our student Party secretary was the worst scholar, but enjoyed the best 'social origin'. His name was Nicolae. He had small black eyes like a bird and he took an immediate dislike to me. He was dull as well as sly. The physics and mathematics we studied were quite beyond him.

He asked, or rather ordered me to solve for him a physics problem we had been set. I excused myself politely. I would not help someone who so methodically harmed my friends. Next he tried to force me to buy a ticket for some Communist Youth entertainment. Again, I refused.

'Don't you know I can make trouble for you, if I want?' He grew red in the face.

'Yes,' I said. 'I know. But did you ever hear the story of the fox and the mouse? The fox found the mouse in a trap and was passing by when the mouse begged his help, saying "One day I may be able to help you!" "You help me!" said the fox, laughing. But he had pity and raised the door of the trap with his paw. Later, the mouse came upon the fox caught under a net. Quickly he called his friends and they gnawed through the ropes in a flash, and set the fox free. So you see everyone has his different ways of helping others. So why not try to be a little polite? It can do no harm.'

Nicolae only became angrier. His little eyes flashed. I walked off and left him.

Years later I found myself once more being questioned by the police, with my dossier open before them. My story of the fox and the mouse was there in full.

In a Communist land, the most trivial slip may be used against you throughout your life. A Westerner can never understand what it means to have no privacy at all; to know that a word, a look, even silence can be betrayed.

A visitor comes to Rumania. What does he see? He sees a carefully prepared façade, a stage set to sell him the success of a People's Republic. He meets an 'average worker'—who is a Party official. The 'worker' tells him he receives a salary three or four times as great as any worker really gets. He will show the visitor—if he is considered sufficiently important—his comfortable apartment. The apartment is a stage set, too: there is in Bucharest a whole block of these places, empty most of the year despite the city's acute housing shortage. When a foreign delegation asks to meet a certain writer or scientist, the poor man is snatched from his cramped room—which he probably shares with others—and deposited for a week in a state apartment. The floors are carpeted, there are private bathrooms, in the walls are the very latest electronic eavesdroppers. Here the visitor is wined, dined and never given a hint that his Rumanian acquaintance does not actually live there. He returns to his native land to praise the splendid treatment given to artists under Communism.

My friend George Popeseu—known to all as Gopo—won a prize at Cannes for his animated cartoon movie which relates the evolution of man. He lived in a squalid single room where the bugs in the wall were the kind that crawled out at night. But when some visiting cineastes asked to meet him, Gopo was whisked off to a luxurious apartment. There he stayed for as long as he was likely to be visited by the foreigners.

Rumania's great poet Radu Gyr was eighteen years in prison. An old friend from his student days came calling on the country's leaders and asked to meet Gyr. Since this old friend was now the Vice-President of India, Dr. Sarvepalli Radhakrishnan, the request could not be refused. Radu Gyr was brought from his cell to eat a meal with the Indian leader, then returned.

To this day U Thant, ex-Secretary General of the United Nations believes he spoke before the law faculty of Bucharest University. In fact, for two days before the event, no student was allowed to enter the hall where U Thant was to speak. He then addressed an audience of security officers and their wives. Real students could not be trusted to make the correct response.

The same thing happened in 1965, when the Archbishop of Canterbury visited Rumania and unwittingly preached a sermon to an audience of officials and secret police. No converts were reported.

While at the Civil Engineering College I met a law student named Alexandru who told a terrifying story of how he had been pressurised into joining the secret police. Certain that he had done well in his university examination, Alexandru was amazed to hear that he had been failed. Now he must go for three years into the army.

But before the call came, he was ordered to secret police H.Q. There he was told that he had been selected for a chance to join the People's Security instead.

'My congratulations!' said the interviewing official. 'Only the best boys, the cream of the cream get such a chance. What a pity you failed that entrance exam. But we have confidence in you ...'

What had happened? They had chosen the brightest boys, the ones who headed the examination lists in different categories. And now they offered them the alternative: join us, or serve three years in the army. Dig ditches and slave on the land with the rest of the troops; or study the 'science of criminology'. They make it sound most attractive. Alexandru, aged seventeen, saw himself as the Sherlock Holmes of the People's Security, tracking down master criminals by their fingerprints. He agreed to join a police school.

The reality was shocking. Before long, their instruction turned to practical application. Alexandru had to attend live classes in how to torture a victim. He attended interrogations that sometimes lasted six hours, with breaks in which the prisoner was beaten up by guards. After a few sessions like this, he could stand no more.

But how to escape?

I told him he must get out, whatever the cost. I told him of the saints who had died rather than compromise with their consciences. Several times we met, and I spoke to him constantly about Christ. I gave him my father's books, we went together to prayer meetings.

He told his superiors that he wished to leave, that he could not stand the sight of blood. They put him in solitary confinement on bread and water for several days. When he insisted that he wanted to resign, an officer took him out for an expensive meal, gave him wine, and used all his persuasive powers to change his mind.

When Alexandru still refused, his mother lost her job as a nurse. Agents called and told her that she would get it back only by influencing her son to remain at the secret police school. Alexandru was sent to a police psychiatrist, who told him that he would never escape. 'I know, because ten years ago I tried to—and here I am.'

In despair, Alexandru swallowed two bottles of sleeping pills. He was found, and his stomach was pumped out.

A second suicide attempt succeeded. He was the only student who ever left the secret police school of his own free will.

I do not consider his death to have been an ordinary suicide, but rather a self-inflicted martyrdom for the holy cause of pure conscience. The Communist world is a world apart: some might go from there to heaven by the way of suicide; or even after shooting someone. Such a thing can happen in defending one's friends, or a stranger, out of love towards Christ. I recalled an episode of my childhood.

A Russian soldier named Marinov came often to our house. I remember him vividly: we were very fond of him. Marinov was a devout Orthodox who, when praying with us, would always finish by making big signs of the Cross and saying, 'For the prayers of your martyrs Lydia, Cyrill and Alexei, Lord Jesus save the Russian people.'

My father knew well the lives of the saints, but of these martyrs he had not heard.

Marinov told us their story. Lydia had been the daughter of a priest. She worked in the Underground Church. Betrayed, Lydia was arrested and tortured for ten days to make her reveal the names of others in her group. She did not yield the secrets. On the eleventh day, she could barely walk. As she was being taken through the subterranean corridors to the torture cell a soldier on duty there reached out his hand to help her as she descended some steps.

'May Christ save you,' she said.

Her words went to this soldier's heart. Cyrill Katiev was his name, and he had heard often enough cries like hers, in those corridors. She was not the first to suffer the ordeal. When he heard her begin to cry out under the torture, Christ entered his heart. He was saved.

He heard the officer shout, 'You think you're in pain now. We haven't begun yet! Why don't you speak?'

'I am not permitted.'

'Who doesn't permit you?'

'God.'

Cyril burst into the cell and shot down two officers; then others filled his body with bullets. Before he died, he called out to Lydia, 'Saint, take me with you!'

'I will,' she answered.

The officer who shot Cyrill Katiev told this story on his deathbed in a wartime hospital to a certain sergeant Alexei Ikonnikov, who was converted and made the facts known to Marinov and others. He was himself executed for this.

The true Orthodox Church which lives on in Russia's underground canonised Lydia, Cyrill and Alexei.

How is it, people sometimes ask, that there has been no rebellion in Rumania, if eighteen millions are so ruthlessly oppressed? The answer is that there has been rebellion. Our prisons have been filled with Lydias and Cyrills who have died resisting oppression. Tens of thousands of peasants who resisted collectivisation were killed. Their stories have gone untold.

Communism rules by fear, today as in the past. In a city of one and a half millions, Bucharest, there are 90,000 secret police. Every spy spies on his fellow spies. Even when a prisoner is interrogated, there must be several officers who must come up with the same result: if they don't, one is in trouble. In a Baptist church whose congregation had been reduced by fear and harassment to twenty-one, four were known informers, each checking his neighbour's story. There is a Party boss for every street with spies in every block. They record every visitor, especially overnight callers. All the information is passed to the secret police.

Acts of defiance towards the police are unknown. Student rebellion? Not when the first critical word against the regime means certain arrest. Not when three people meeting together to grumble about conditions is a 'plot' that may end in torture and death.

A university student we knew belonged to a small circle of friends who sometimes talked about their dreams of escape. One was of course an informer. The student discovered that he was being followed everywhere. His whole future was blighted, his educational career over. He fled from the agents in the street, ran into the French consulate and begged political asylum. They gave him a meal and returned him to the Rumanian authorities within two hours. If all one had to do was to walk into a consulate to reach freedom, there would be mile-long queues outside every legation in the city.

The student was subjected to a public denunciation at a mass rally organised by the university. One after another his friends mounted the podium to mouth their shame at having known him.

In the spring of 1964, as my second year at civil engineering college ended, I had another warning dream. The college buildings had five floors, and our classroom was on the second: I dreamt that all my classmates were hurrying up to the third floor, by walking on the staircase rail, as if on a tightrope. During the examination, I felt absolutely sure that I would fail them all. But the session passed without incident and I found that I had earned such good grades that I was to be named leader of a summer practice group. However, two weeks before this summer course ended, I was summoned to the personnel office. Out of the blue, they told me: you are to be thrown out of school. It was the fourth time this had happened to me, and I was getting used to it. But it still hurt.

Since 1962, Rumania has tried to gain a little independence from Russia. Young gangsters often want to break away from the gang in which they have been brought up. Georghiu Dej wished to industrialise the country against the will of the Kremlin, which intended to keep Rumania as a market garden for Soviet exploitation.

Dej wanted to trade with the West. But, he supposed, the West would not trade with him so long as he maintained a police state that kept tens of thousands in jails and slave camps. He was stupid. The West would have done business with him anyway. Lloyd George said long ago that trade must be done, even with cannibals. Capitalists are so eager for profit that they will sell to Communists the ropes they need to hang all of them.

But Dej overestimated the West, and made some 'liberal' gestures. He ended the jamming of broadcasts from the West. He ended the compulsory teaching of Russian in schools. He released a handful of political prisoners, and rumours of a general amnesty spread.

In the spring of 1964, Aunt Alice was released. Guards had beaten her brutally. All her teeth had been kicked out. Years in damp cells had destroyed her health. Her only crime was to help the children of martyrs. Yet her spirit was not crushed, and with love and care she grew stronger. (In 1970, we successfully brought her to the West.)

Would my father be set free?

The weeks passed, and there were more releases. Thousands were coming out of the jails. Every morning we scanned the Party newspaper for the tiny paragraph at the foot of a page that might tell of new releases.

One morning in June 1964, came a call from Gherla to a neighbour of ours. An old friend had been released from jail there that morning. He wished to tell us that he'd seen my father in the prison yard. He was on the amnesty list!

The day passed in a whirl of excitement. It was almost six years since he had been taken from us for the second time. How would he be changed?

In the evening came another call, this time from Cluj. Mother and I hurried downstairs to our neighbour's flat. She took the receiver. Her face went white, and I saw she was about to faint. I caught her with a chair and took the telephone and heard my father's worried voice.

'Mother's all right!' I said. 'She felt faint. Now she's coming round.'

He was at the home of friends in Cluj. When I had given him some of our news, he said:

'I'm healthy and well. I thought I should find out if I still had a wife and son before returning!'

He would come on the overnight train. Why not at once? Later we found out. He was holding his first Underground Church service in Cluj that evening. We need not have worried: he had not changed.

Faith had kept him alive through fourteen and a half years of prison, had healed lungs riddled with T.B., had mended limbs broken by torture. Later, alone in my room the words of Jesus came into my mind: 'Ye shall know the truth and the truth shall set you free,' free even in prison.

Word spread quickly. At the railway station early next morning there were dozens of friends and brethren, all the women with their arms filled with flowers. The crowd milled around us. Everyone was looking for a loved one. Then down the track came the ancient coal-burning locomotive, its black belly caked with grime. At a carriage window I saw father's face. He stared at the waving, smiling crowd with the armfuls of flowers, and for a moment he could not realise that they were his flock and family. He had not expected this.

His head was shaved and he was terribly thin and his clothes were mere rags. Starvation had stripped every ounce of flesh from his face and body, and only his clear blue eyes were unaltered. He had first been taken from us as a vital handsome man in his thirties, and now he was over fifty.

Weeping we embraced. Someone had a camera and when the first greetings were over, photographs were taken.

My mother is shown in them smiling a smile of great happiness. My father's smile is tinged with a deep sadness.

I look as if I'd seen a ghost.

Father had become a living legend. From every corner of the country people flocked to our cramped attic to meet him, many we had never seen before, many were old friends.

We had to try to protect him. He weighed only ninety pounds, the result of a final attempt to break his spirit through starvation, maltreatment, deprival of sleep and brainwashing. Doctor friends persuaded him to enter a small mountain hospital. But there too, visitors came to see him. He moved to a different sanatorium. Still the crowds came. Police agents complained that he was preaching, and he had to return to Bucharest.

Responsible brethren of the Underground Church advised us to get to the West, if possible, there to publicise the plight of all Christians. Mother and I had desired this ourselves: our first plan was that she or I would try to leave alone, then work to free whoever remained. As far back as 1960 I had applied for a visa. Many times I had gone to the Israeli consulate to see if my name was on the list they received from the Government. The consulate would leak the news to Jews, so that they might have time to sell their property before they left. Months became years and I lost all hope of winning a ticket in the great departure lottery. Then I was granted another premonitory dream.

I was walking with my friend Werner between two high fences of barbed wire, he in front and I behind. Suddenly a gap opened in the wire and I stepped through into freedom. But when I turned to look for Werner, the gap had closed and he was on the other side.

I met Werner the next day and told him of the dream. He also had applied for a visa. It seemed impossible that I should leave before him—he had a clean record, and a wife now, working for his release from abroad.

'You'll see,' I joked. 'I'll be free before you yet.'

'Never!' said he. But so it happened.

Almost one year after my father's release, I went to the consulate: and there on the list was our name. We might all leave! Tears flowed down my face as I walked home.

We were, however, still a long way from freedom. More months went by without any official notification from the state. In any case, I began the formalities of departure, my parents agreeing that I should go on ahead. I have already described the papers and documents you must produce before you can obtain a passport in Communist Rumania. These prove that you have no debts of any kind, that your apartment is in good condition and has been checked by bureaucrats. That you owe no bills to state agencies, of which there are dozens, or to libraries and schools, of which there are scores. That you have been released without disgrace by every employer you ever had ... in all there were some fifty documents requiring seventy different signatures. And on each, a tax had to be paid. The total came to almost 6,000 *lei*. I completed all this in eight weeks—but no word came of the visa.

Meanwhile, my father had been granted a licence to preach—of a kind. He could not speak outside the church of Orsova, where his congregation was restricted to thirty-seven people. One more, and the 'licence' would be withdrawn. It was another little trick in the great deception of religious liberty. Father devoted his efforts to the Underground Church. We feared it was only a matter of time before he again clashed with the secret police. He was watched and followed everywhere.

The little news that now seeped in from the West showed us how incredibly ignorant people there were of the true state of the Church. We could surely help best by telling the free world the truth about our religious oppression.

Mother's great friend, Mrs. Moise, worked tirelessly from Norway to raise the thousands of dollars needed to buy us out. This would be paid through Jewish organisations.

Once again, departure fever gripped Rumania. The amnesty has set thousands free, and we saw once more the scenes of 1948 when Jews first fled the Communist world for Israel. It is said that after Thor Heyerdahl's famous voyage to Easter Island, the Government of that remote spot had to mount a twenty-four hour sea patrol to prevent islanders from imitating his feat, so eager were they to leave. The feeling was similar in Rumania, and the Communist leaders grew alarmed. Suddenly, they stopped all emigration.

What had happened? Rumours flew, but it was months before the truth leaked out: secret policemen and emigration officials of non-Jewish origin had been stealing Jewish passports to enable them to get out of the country. The entire staff of the passport office was purged. It was some months before the sale of Jews to Israel began again.

We filed a fresh joint application to leave. More months passed before I again learnt from the Israeli consulate that we were on the list. Money had been paid over for us. Mrs. Moise, the Norwegian Israel Mission, for which father had formerly worked, the Hebrew Christian Alliance; our family, had found the dollars.

We received our first visitors from the West—the Rev. Stuart Harris and Pastor John Moseley, leaders of European Christian Mission. While they talked with father, I spotted police in the street outside. They hung about until 1 a.m. and only then did we allow the visitors to leave.

Four months after our application for a visa, the secret police came to the door seeking my father. He was absent, preaching in the countryside. They said he must report next day to police headquarters. Unable to contact him in time, I went along myself.

It was a bad half-hour. Why had I drawn up our petition to leave, instead of my father? Why was I constantly trying to leave the country and troubling state offices? He was a heavy man with a red face that grew redder as he talked. I tried to say that I'd been thrown out of every school I'd ever entered, and could work only as a labourer.

'So you despise honest work! You consider yourself superior to the workers?'

The rage in his bullying voice got the better of me: I couldn't stop myself from bursting out: 'Comrade, you head this office—you would not like it if suddenly you were made to carry bricks and mortar eight hours a day, when you felt another calling.'

He trembled with fury. 'Are you telling me my job! I would be glad to do whatever the Party ordered! Think yourself lucky! Scum like you have no right to work anyway!'

I sat silent. I remembered my mother's words: even God does not contradict the silent. At last he ended the tirade by telling me to get out and bring my father to his office immediately.

When father returned to Bucharest, he went along. With him they were more cautious, yet more menacing. After explaining that we had been bought out, they warned that if he spoke in the West against Communism 'we can still reach you'.

On an October morning in 1965 our permission to leave came through. I returned to police headquarters to collect a new set of release documents. Those I had completed before were useless now, and I began the whole process again.

We needed money to leave the country. Expelled—for the last time!—from the civil engineering college, I had returned to work on a construction site. One morning, my superviser was unaccountably nervous.

'Go and work elsewhere, Mihai,' he said. 'I need this room.'

I found another office to work in; and then, for no explicable reason, was ordered to vacate that. I went to the chief engineer—only to find him in a strange mood.

'Go home,' he said abruptly. 'I've nothing for you to do. Take the day off.'

In all my working and student years never had anyone said that. I was baffled.

'But it's only 10.30.'

The boss simply repeated that I should take the day off.

So I returned home. I found my parents absent. I'd hardly closed the door of our attic when I heard a knock.

Outside stood a stranger. He had been sent from Switzerland by friends to bring us something to speed our departure.

'I called several times this morning,' he said. 'I was about to leave without handing it over. My plane goes at noon, and I couldn't give this to anyone else.' He put an envelope in my hand and hurried away.

I opened the envelope and found 300 Swiss francs. Enough to pay off most of our 'taxes'.

Somehow we had been brought together on time. It seemed that we were really going to reach freedom this time. Everything was going right for us.

Then came a new blow. A housing inspector called, took a look at our attic and ruled that we had to pay a further L100 for repairs before leaving. Useless to protest that the place was in better shape than when we'd moved in ten years ago. Or that the state had done nothing in that time towards the upkeep of what it claimed as its property.

We had been helped very generously by our family in France and Israel, and we had paid off everything they demanded. We did not know where to turn to meet this new expense.

But once again, God provided. Our former church had been turned into a film studio, and its head—a man trained at the Moscow film academy—had repeatedly tried to throw us out of our attic. He wanted our tiny attic rooms, too. Now he appeared at the door again, ready for a quarrel.

Mother simply smiled. 'We are leaving,' she said. 'The rooms will be yours soon. And we thank you for not forcing us out sooner . . .'

Suddenly, the man became very polite. We were off to the West? How lucky we were! How he wished he was in our shoes! Could we possibly send him some things from Paris . . .?

Now this man had prevented us from using the bathroom in

the house; he had cut off the water and made us walk a hundred yards to a public restroom in another block and carry buckets of water from a tap. But all that was forgotten: he wanted some special, very costly camera lenses, some perfume for a girl's birthday. If we would agree to send that, he would sign a document saying that the whole house now belonged to the state film industry. Then we would have no obligation to repair it.

That was kind, said my mother.

She would send him what he wanted.

Then a curious thing happened. Tears came into the man's eyes.

'I shall miss you!' he said.

What strange creatures we are!

I collected our visas from police headquarters. The red-faced defender of the working man threw three pieces of paper in front of me, after I'd waited an hour.

'These are travel certificates, valid for passage to Israel and nowhere else,' he said. 'Jews don't get passports.'

He waddled off.

That final week in Rumania was frantic. Every day scores of people came to the attic to say goodbye, and request something from the West. An engineer who wanted me to patent his inventions in London, then buy him out. A boss from a building site, who wanted us to arrange with friends abroad to buy him out. An artist, who wanted us to arrange a show of his work in Paris, and buy him out. A Freemason, who gave us sealed documents for other Western Freemasons, who would buy him out. (They didn't.) Stooges of the Communists within the Church begged: 'Buy us out. We can't bear to play this double game any more.'

Werner gripped my hand. 'Tell the world, Mike!' he said. 'Tell the world!'

My father paid a last visit to Bishop Müller, who gave him a note introducing him as one of Christ's most faithful. 'This will open all doors for you.' So it would have, if all the Western Church leaders whom father had to convince about the

Church's sufferings had also been among Christ's most faithful.

At a friend's home, on the night before our departure, we held a secret prayer meeting. Some seventy brethren were there, and we said our last farewells to many. Some came with us at dawn next day to the airport.

Armed guards and soldiers were everywhere. They take no chances with hijackers in the East. They know that without the most rigid security, half the Communist airlines would by now be in the West. We were shut into a waiting room with guards. There were thirty in our party, nearly all Jews.

A crowd of 200 people had come from all over Rumania to see us off. They had to wait outside, behind heavy barriers, watching through a chain link fence. Some women wept noisily, and I was worried that they might start arresting people, or cancel our flight.

The customs examination, which included a body search, took hours, and two women were discovered to have gold trinkets hidden in their underwear. They were taken off by the police. For the sake of a pair of earrings, they had lost their chance of freedom.

We carried nothing illegal. Bishop Müller's note had left the country already by other means. My mother had some hand embroidery which she was taking as a present. An official said it was not allowed.

We knew it was, but dare not argue.

'If you let me take it,' said mother, 'I'd be most grateful.'

'How grateful?' he asked, rubbing thumb and forefinger together with a wink. In a small ante-room, he haggled with her over the bribe. He relieved her of all that we had in cash—some 150 *lei*—before he would let her go. We remembered all the stories we'd heard of planes stopped on the runway, of families snatched back at the last moment. We hardly dared speak to each other.

At last, after three hours, we were led into the big departure hall and towards the aircraft. A long way off, behind the wire, we saw our hundreds of friends, waving and calling.

We settled into the seat of the old, two-engined Russian

plane. Even when it began to trundle down the runway, I couldn't believe that we would get away.

'Your pilot,' said the hostess, 'is Captain Bănică.'

Then we were in the air. The city fell away below us. Left behind, perhaps forever, were fatherland, friends, brethren in faith, the multitudes of the oppressed, those caught in the tragedy of being oppressors, the many whom I loved.

My thoughts stayed for a long time with some I had known, those most worthy of pity. Those who had become Communists, fanatical Communists, ready to serve to the end because Communism had destroyed the beauty of their life and left them nothing to put in its place. They had been ardent Christians once. Then they had been trampled underfoot, their property confiscated, their families jailed or killed, their own bodies tortured. No help came from anywhere. Worse, they heard on foreign broadcasts pastors who praised those who at that moment were beating Christians in underground cells.

While they had lain in prison, nobody from the World Council of Churches and so many other powerful Christian bodies, had cared for their children. Christians in the West had debated theological problems to which no one had answers. Others had made political agreements and done profitable trade with the torturers.

Did it not mean that all power belonged to evil, that Good was an illusion? Why serve the wicked master out of fear? Why suffer torture, and remorse for breaking under it, when the only order that exists in this world is maleficent and seems willed by God—if God exists? They began to hate sincerely the Americans and the British. They had not moved a finger to help them. The guilty West deserved to be destroyed, and the Communists would do it. So the tortured came to love the torturer.

Potiphar's wife loved Joseph. Joseph refused her love. Then her feeling towards him turned to hatred. She joined with the husband she hated and was glad to see her former beloved thrown into a filthy jail. Rumanians had loved America and Britain. They hoped to be freed by them. Rumanian Christians counted on the solidarity of their Western brethren in faith, and many still do. As a rule, the fighters of the Underground Church took the neglect of duty among their Western brethren with the same love and understanding that enabled them to bear the terror of the Reds. But not all: some Rumanians changed. They became hate-filled. They felt misled by those who had told them that the West was their friend.

Christianity they said, was a fraud. Democracy can do nothing: only despots can rule effectively. Let us swear whole-hearted allegiance to Communism, to wickedness.

These men became the worst Communists. Something of the same kind happened to those who today lead the official Church in Communist countries. Those who head the Baptist Union of the U.S.S.R. for example, have behind them a total of 111 years in prison. Their president, Ivanov, has suffered especially severe tortures. Then they grew tired of suffering.

My last tears were for those defeated in an unequal fight. God cannot forget that they once served him faithfully.

These were some of my thoughts as the plane flew through sunny skies towards our first destination—Rome. I was too restless to sit still for long. I encountered an Italian engineer who had been selling electronic equipment to the Rumanians. He had enjoyed himself: his weeks in the resort hotels along the Black Sea had been pleasant—not as pleasant as his native Italy, of course ... but life under Communism was not so bad, was it?

Not so bad, I said—tourists have it well. He saw no irony in this. I said no more. The plane could still turn back!

We landed at Rome's glittering Leonardo da Vinci airport. The sun sparkled from towers and giant jets. I read the Italian on the signs, and knew that at last I was on free soil.

I turned to the businessman.

'Now that I'm a free man,' I said, and tears began to flow down my cheeks, 'I want to tell you that everything you saw in Rumania was a show—we are as oppressed as you were under Fascism. And if you like, I'll tell you what it's really like to live under Communism.'

But he did not wait to hear. With a startled look, he turned and strode towards passport control.

My uncle and aunt had come especially from Paris to meet us, and wished to fly us on to their home. But we had only travel certificates for Israel, and the representatives of the Jewish Welfare Agency who also met us, were determined that we should go to Israel. Until we explained that we were Hebrew Christians. The Italians said we couldn't fly to Paris with our present documents.

So neither Jews nor Italians wanted us. Soon we heard that the World Council of Churches in Geneva did not want us either. My father sent cables and called them by telephone. It was very mysterious: it seemed that 'the Russians would find out' if he came there and spoke; and on no account must the Communists be offended.

'We'll send you tickets to go to Norway,' they said. Later, we found that warnings had been sent from the top leaders of the Lutheran World Federation to Oslo: we must be kept quiet! We could hardly believe it. We had come to the West for the purpose of speaking.

Father worked around the clock meanwhile, turning out sermons and pleas, cables and letters to Church leaders, drafts of books. I sat behind a typewriter for six days, until finally I had to say: 'Tomorrow we're leaving, and we have scarcely looked at the city. It's time we all saw a little of Rome.' Before we departed, he preached in a Roman church, and we had our first taste of the incredible naïvety and ignorance that prevails in the West about the Underground Church and Communism.

We went on to Paris and Oslo. Every country has its natural beauties. Only Norway is all beauty. Pastor Solheim, father's colleague at the Norwegian Israel mission in Bucharest had often said, 'Norway is the most gorgeous country in the world.' Father objected: 'The Bible says that it is rather Palestine.' (For me also at that time, the scriptures had the last word, even in matters of aesthetics.) Solheim replied, 'Moses had not seen Norway.' Now I understood. I was sorry for Moses.

As beautiful as the country were the souls of those we met. In a bitter winter night they waited hour after hour for our delayed arrival. There were Anutza Moise, mother's faithful friend who had worked for our release; Pastor Talaksen, secretary of the Israel mission; Rechenberg, a Jewish Christian who bore on his arm the number tattooed in Auschwitz. Father's friend Pastor Hedenquist, who first appointed him to work for the World Council of Churches some twenty-five years before, came from Stockholm to see us. We were invited into many homes. Everyone was wonderfully friendly. At last we began to realise that the years of fear were almost over.

We made new friends—Pastor Knutson of the American Lutheran Church in Oslo; the Holbys, in whose home we met the Skard family. Mr. Skard was a university lecturer who had just completed a new translation into Norwegian of the New Testament. Also there we met the Overnyes, journalists. We told our story. The seed for the creation of the first mission to take the Gospel behind the Iron Curtain was born.

The Norwegian Government graciously granted us the status of refugees. Now we had passports and could travel. I returned to Paris, where I entered the Protestant seminary, to take a degree in theology.

What professors really believed there seemed to be that the Bible is the most unworthy book in the world. Why else should they spend all their time in its criticism?

There exists an unchallengeable mathematical proof that every letter of the Bible is inspired by God. Everything in it revolves around the figure seven.

A Biblical scholar, Ivan Panin, spent some twenty years of his life compiling a vast concordance of the Bible based on its numerical values. Any observant reader of the Bible must have noticed that the number seven occurs many times and in many connections. It is a peculiarly holy number. Seven days were needed for the creation of the world. The principal feasts of the Jews lasted seven days; and they refrained from cultivating the ground every seven years. Seven times the conquerors of Jericho marched around the walls, led by seven priests blowing seven trumpets. The candlesticks of the temple had seven branches. In the New Testament we find an equally extraordinary number of references to this number. The Book of

Revelation mentions seven symbols each one in its turn mentioned sevenfold (seven churches, seven candlesticks, seven seals, seven trumpets, seven vials, seven stars, seven thunders). The apostle Paul made his journey to Rome in seven stages.

Panin discovered that even the number of words in certain key passages is a multiple of seven. Even the number of letters and the sum of the value of the Greek letters is found to be a multiple of seven. It is not the place here to enumerate all the hundreds of mathematical phenomena which point to the verbal inspiration of the Bible: that might be left for a later book. It is enough to say here that mathematicians were converted when faced with this intricate structure of the Bible text. Panin's work itself covers more than 80,000 pages. This was the subject of my thesis.

My examiners were aghast. They had not known such a thing was possible, they abhorred the idea; yet they could not disprove it. To contradict was to contradict mathematics. What theological professor had ever heard about the literal trustworthiness of the Bible?

My experience of seminaries, both personal and what I heard from many pastors who had passed through them, makes me feel that the situation has not changed since the time of Giordano Bruno, who called them 'widows of learning'.

There were some teachers in Rumania whom I remember gratefully. But from the majority of seminaries here as in the East, you can graduate without a thorough study of the whole Bible, the fathers of the Church, the great mystics of Christianity and other religions. You take chemistry and you know what formulae represent water and sulphur; but you take theology and you hear nothing of the great metaphysical systems, the Vedantas, the Kabala, or even Kant; you don't study the deep mysteries of the Bible, you learn only to nibble at it. There exist spiritual laws as stringent as those of matter. They are not taught. The doctors of theology cannot tell you what soul, what spirit is; the professors express opinions instead of imparting sure knowledge.

My father's words so impressed Americans whom we met in Europe that they offered to raise money to fly us to the U.S.

From the start it had been our idea to create a mission that would spread the Gospel and aid the Underground Church behind the Iron Curtain; and this could be our first opening.

As stateless refugees, we returned to Paris to await permission to move to America. In France I found fatuous and uninformed acceptance for Communism among students and teachers. But at least I was given a personal reason for remembering Paris with affection.

Judith sent me a letter that filled me with happiness. She had become a Christian. For months the Hebrew Christian congregation with which she worshipped had been praying for father's release and our safe passage to the West. What a shock! Israel is a place where few become Christians. The story of her conversion was fascinating.

Judith had been met in Israel by Bruno, the boy she had planned to marry. There was a happy reunion and they went out together several times. But both had changed. Finally, they parted.

Judith found work, contributed to the family budget and studied at night school. After two years she passed examinations and found a good job as an architectural designer. Her mother urged her continually to get married. In Israel, single girls were considered old maids at twenty.

Then one day she met the Levys, the Christian couple with whom we had spent an afternoon once listening to music in Bucharest. It was at a bus stop. They said she must come and visit them. They lived only streets away in Holon. Now Judith and her family had moved into this small community near Tel Aviv that very day. It was the first of a series of strange coincidences.

At first, Judith put off the promised visit. The Levys were in their fifties, she was very young. She did not want to talk about Rumania: it had been enough to live it.

Still, sometimes they met in the street for a fresh exchange of waves or smiles or promises. Then, one afternoon (it was in August 1965, when we in Bucharest were in despair, having been told by the police that we would never be allowed to leave) she felt a great desire to see the Levys. She was not sure why. More than a year had passed. Yet something compelled her to go.

The Levys are a striking couple: he dark-haired with deep eyes, she warm and eloquent—a gifted poet. Both are intelligent, and Judith discovered that she had more to discuss with them than with Israelis of her own age. A great friendship began.

They told her how they had been baptised in my father's church, twenty-five years previously. Though they made no attempt to convert her, what they recounted of their lives as Christians, and of my father's struggles, had a deep effect on her. The seeds had been planted long before in our Bucharest attic. Now they came to flower. The Levys were a catalyst for the many strains that had been bringing Judith to Christ. After several conversations with them, she realised that she believed, had believed for a long time; and that to acknowledge it now was the only reasonable thing to do.

Think it over, the Levys urged. Do not rush. Do not make a mistake.

At first, they would not even take her to their Christian meetings. But Judith fell into the habit of stopping at their house most mornings to join them in prayer or readings from the Bible. Many of their prayers were for our family.

In December 1965, these prayers were answered. We left Rumania. And then the Levys decided it was time to introduce Judith to their friends of the Hebrew Christian Assembly in Tel Aviv. There were some thirty members—Russians, Poles, Canadians ... and many more. Judith, as the youngest, most recent convert, was everyone's favourite.

She wrote to tell me the news. She could not hide her new happiness. She spoke of Christ to her boss, to friends at work, and some turned against her. But this meant little beside the new meaning that had come into her life. She considered becoming a missionary, and the congregation sent word to one of the great missionary schools in Switzerland. An American from the Hebrew-Christian mission in the U.S., on a visit to Israel, met Judith and offered to pay for her schooling. Everything seemed to be falling into place, as if ordained.

Before she left for Switzerland, she was baptised in the sea at Jaffa, near Tel Aviv. It was sunset, and the voices of the congregation singing a hymn filled the golden air.

From the college in Switzerland, she sent me a postcard. She was ecstatically happy. She only wished we could all meet again. Then I suggested that she come to Paris.

We would soon depart for the U.S. Our papers had been approved. I saw that we might never meet again.

On the great day, I found myself in bed with streaming influenza. The train arrived at 6 a.m., and I failed to meet it.

Judith telephoned the flat.

'I see you haven't changed. You never had any manners. It's just like you to bring me all this way, then leave me at the station.'

'Please, take a taxi,' I said.

'Oh!' She hung up.

When she reached our flat I was still in bed, grumbling about my 'flu.

'It's a pity I came,' she said. 'I should have stayed at my studies.'

But when I saw her, my 'flu vanished as if by miracle. My mother—who was busy packing for our departure—calmed things down.

I took Judith on a bus to the centre of Paris. At a pavement café we bought coffee and croissants. She became more and more puzzled: an hour ago I had been too sick to meet her at the station, and now I was all right. She looked at me indignantly and the sun fell through the glass on her chestnut hair. She looked so beautiful that it seemed to me that I had no choice but to ask her, without any introductory speeches:

'Will you marry me?'

The indignant girl replied without hesitation, 'Yes.'

'Good. I can't guarantee you a good husband, but you have a splendid deal with your in-laws.'

The city of New York lay spread below as the plane tilted above Kennedy Airport. Sunlight flashed on blue water and the glass walls of the incredible towers. The great ribbons of highways wound like crawling streams of steel through the concrete. Then, with a bump and a thud we were down on American soil. The dream was over. Here reality began.

After a triumphant tour through some of the big Lutheran churches in the United States, the synod asked my father to work in its Department of Evangelism, where he could begin his organisation freely. But the American Lutheran Church belongs to the World Council of Churches, which is no longer the relief organisation we knew in Bucharest at the end of the war.

We had to find some other way.

But we did not understand America. It is a big country. Everything in it is big. Big saints, big criminals. Big philanthropists, and big scoundrels. We had the misfortune to meet some uncommendable specimens.

My father preached at a town in the state of Michigan. He was invited to stay at a Christian home. The daughter of the family, a high school student, was excited and asked a friend to come with her to church that Sunday to hear Pastor Wurmbrand speak.

'Wurmbrand!?' said the friend. 'That idiot. We've heard him already, and I've never listened to a stupider sermon. He may have suffered, but he's illiterate, an absolute moron.'

The daughter, in tears, repeated this to her mother. The mother was embarrassed. She did not know how to ask my father politely if he was an idiot.

Father preached on Sunday and he was to speak again on Monday at a businessman's breakfast meeting. But along came the group's chairman, clasping tightly by one arm a stranger.

'I'm sorry,' he said, 'but I have to establish which of you two is Richard Wurmbrand. This gentleman here has been going about preaching in churches, saying that he's the Richard Wurmbrand who spent fourteen years in Communist jails. You say you are the same man. I ask both of you to show your identity papers. Here's a cheque, a gift from a church which he has cashed. Here's his signature, "Richard Wurmbrand".'

Father produced his identity card. The other man could

show nothing. After an altercation, he confessed his real name.

Father asked him, 'Did I ever give you the power to sign my name on cheques?'

The man was not a bit troubled. 'How do you know that I signed your name?'

'But I see it here: Richard Wurmbrand.'

'So what? Are you the only one of that name? I may have signed another Richard Wurmbrand's name.'

Father liked the answer. The girl had been mistaken—this man might be a bad preacher, but he was no idiot. He asked one more question:

'But did this other Richard Wurmbrand authorise you to sign cheques with his name?'

The man replied promptly, 'Sir, did this other Richard Wurmbrand authorise you to investigate me on his behalf?'

Father laughed. 'You're a clever fellow,' he said. 'I hope you'll use your abilities in a better cause in future.'

Another man, seeing how the idea of evangelism behind the Iron Curtain appealed to Christians, started a missionary organisation. He invited my father to join him in this group's work. It couldn't enter father's head that somebody would commercialise religion. He had been a missionary under the Nazis and the Communists, and he knew that from such work you gained nothing but chains. So he was happy to accept and to preach for this organisation. It grew rapidly.

I was less trusting. We asked to see the accounts. What we saw was not to our liking, and we protested. We also objected to the way matters which should have been kept secret, for reasons of security, were published simply for the sake of promoting the organisation's work. It wasn't long before our connection with these people ended.

Although a fine organisation was being run by the Rev. Stuart Harris and the Rev. John Moseley, our British and American visitors that night in Bucharest, its work was confined to Eastern Europe. But Communism covers almost the whole of Asia, it advances in Africa and Latin America. Since we started our mission work in 1967, Zanzibar, Congo Brazzaville, Guinea,

Iraq have gone Communist; Communists share in the ruling of Ceylon and Iceland, Egypt and Algeria have become something like Soviet colonies; Red Chinese 'specialists' are moving in on one black nation after another; Chile has a Marxist regime. Daily we read of the growth of Communism on U.S. campuses.

We had to take a world-view, or we would achieve nothing. The Communists have their all-encompassing world plan. We needed world-wide organisation in all the free countries, to help bring Christ to the whole Communist world. We had little money—but it was more than the Apostles had when they started their mission. The Lord gave them an exceptionally good catch of fish: a hundred and fifty-three fishes at, let's say, ten pence each — about £15. This was the initial capital of the universal Church. And it was not tax exempt. But they had the Holy Spirit. And things worked.

Our mission began.

Father travelled across the nation, preaching. Everywhere, people gave their addresses and asked to be kept informed about the Underground Church. Requests for his book poured in. The first contributions to our newly-formed mission came from poor people. From a shoemaker, who gave $100. From a retired pastor living on a pension. From a lady who earned $300 a month, and supported a sick husband and two boys — she gave her entire savings of $500. 'The boys ask you to take this for the hungry children of persecuted Christians,' she said. 'They say they don't want any Christmas presents this year.'

My father also had luncheons with millionaires. They were very pleasant men. One gave $25.

Since then, three years have passed. Our world-wide organisation exists and flourishes. In America we call it 'Jesus to the Communist World', and its sister groups are at work in thirty lands around the free world.

The books written by my father and mother have sold some two million copies, stirring the interest of Christians everywhere for their persecuted brothers. Tears are shed, nights passed in prayer and sermons preached in Western churches that before never mentioned the martyred Church. Children remember the suffering ones in prayers before they sleep.

Our missions receive moving letters. Here is one from a Swiss Christian:

'Your mission writes prophetically . . . I cannot free myself any more from the thought of the suffering of our brethren. I see them continually, everywhere I am. *When I go to bed, I see bodies of Christians lying on the cold concrete and starving.*'

A letter from Sweden:

'It is time not only to pray, but to make a positive effort for those who suffer and fight for their religious conviction. *Otherwise I fear that the blood of those who die a martyr's death will come upon Western Christianity.*'

Another:

'I have long planned and saved money for a journey to Africa, where my sister and brother-in-law work in a missionary hospital. But all the time I have felt inner unrest, at spending so much time on a pleasure trip. Now I have the answer: no. And I feel light at heart when I send the money directly for printing Bibles.'

One very moving letter came from a prisoner in a U.S. jail:

'I read the message of your mission and found that it shows more clearly than anything else the body of Christ. I am in prison, but for sin . . . Now I have begun to feel the pain of the world and of my brethren and all people in the Communist world. *I am beginning to feel the love which is needed to make an end to this injustice.* You taught me patience. I have no money to help.'

Our sister groups bring the Gospel to the Communist world from Argentina, Denmark, Fiji, France . . . from Japan, Korea, Tanzania and many other countries. When we go to bed in America, our fellow workers on the other side of the globe are rising. In the Soviet Union, a chain of Christians has been formed which prays for us and our missions unceasingly, twenty-four hours a day. We can say, like the Spanish king, that the sun never sets upon our work. The growth of our mission is to me a twentieth-century miracle—one that needs a book to itself, for here I give the barest outline.

A pastor in Norway wrote of my father: 'A man who has suffered much is not trustworthy, he must be biased; the memory of the horrors he has passed through makes his mind incapable of distinguishing truth.' This is the reasoning of an Epicurean. Christians consider a man of sorrows to be the embodiment of truth. Indeed, all the great religions take their inspiration from martyrs. The objection didn't hold water. Yet we knew that my parents' experience of Communism wouldn't, by itself, be sufficient to convince people.

The first task was to gather all the facts we could about the persecution. Wherever possible, this must be from the Communist press itself. Our testimony must be unchallengeable. We found people to read the newspapers of a dozen Communist dominated countries. We tapped the rich mine of printed information that circulates underground in Russia—a truly underground press. We collected facts from refugees from China, Zanzibar, Albania, Korea, Cuba ... And we began to realise how limited our vision had been. Seeing through our narrow east European windows, we had not appreciated the extent and the fury of the persecution.

How do Communists treat prisoners?

On my desk as I write is the story of what happened to a man of Russian birth in China ... Arrested in Shanghai, he was tortured to make him confess imaginary crimes. His legs were broken. He would not 'confess'. Red Chinese secret police went to his home and told his wife that if she refused to sign an accusation against her husband, their child would be killed. She did not believe them, and refused. A woman officer smashed the baby's head against a wall, before the mother's eyes. She snatched up a knife—and the guards shot her dead.

I write the blunt facts in the simplest possible words. No one can diminish or exaggerate or convey exactly what it means to live under the Communist terror at its worst.

Christians in China have had their fingers crushed, ears twisted until they tear, chopsticks jabbed into their necks just beneath the jawbone. How can you put these sufferings into words? They do not hurt: you read, and still your chair is comfortable, soon you will get up and eat something good, soon you will forget what you have read.

Already the world has forgotten that Cardinal Mindszenty was forced to stand and walk, stand and walk for twenty-eight days and nights without sleep before he 'confessed'. After such an ordeal you are prepared not only to confess to any imaginable crime, but you truly believe that your accusers are right. With gratitude you come round, sincerely come round, to the side of the Communist interrogator who shows the great kindness of allowing you two hours' sleep. It is all part of their plan. After years of experimentally torturing dogs and other innocent beasts, their psychologists know how to manipulate human minds to achieve the desired results.

In China, all the churches are closed, the Bible is banned. (It is the same in North Korea and Albania.) Yet God must love the Chinese very much: he has made so many of them—every fourth man in the world is a Chinese. We must help them in this time of savage oppression. We must make sure that the persecuted are not left alone.

How does Communist Russia treat its prisoners?

Natalia Gorbaevslaia is a Russian poet and freedom fighter. She is held in one of the many special asylums which the Soviet Union has for those sick with love of God and His children. In Leningrad, this asylum is at 9 Arsenalnaia Street. It is a big cage for human beings, divided into many little cages of iron bars. The floors are of unevenly spaced wooden planks. Day and night you hear the noise of thousands of people, words, cries, coughs, snores, the flushing of toilets; the screams of men and women who have, indeed, gone mad. Men have been driven insane in this place . . . and men have committed suicide.

Tarsis is a Russian novelist who has been through one of these asylums. His novels are hardly the work of a madman. They are highly intelligent, and filled with the sense of beauty. In one, he tells of a man who began secretly to read the Bible.

He saw quickly why the Communists had banned it; for it exposes the futility of bloody revolution as a cure for the world's ills.

A Christian, Lazuta, was interned in another asylum. He asked the doctor of the secret police: 'What happens if I reject my faith in God, if I attend no more religious meetings, if I cease to pray?' The doctor answered, 'You'll be released. You can go home right away.'

Lazuta was lucky to get such an offer, though he did not take advantage of it. Usually they are not satisfied with a simple change in a man's thoughts: their aim is that you should not think for yourself at all; that you should become an automaton, serving the state machine. Romain Rolland (himself once a Communist) has written: 'Who murders thought is thrice a murderer.'

God knows how many thousands—Catholic, Orthodox, Baptist and more—suffer in such ways for their faith. For twenty-nine years the Baptist preacher Hrapov was in Soviet jails. He was tortured. Set free at last, he resumed his underground work. Now he is back in jail. Brother Hmara had his tongue cut out in prison in 1964. Brother Benderski died under torture in 1971. Time does not change these things.

Any charge is good enough to put a Christian in prison. By reading the Moscow medical journal I discovered recently how lucky I am. I have been baptised, yet I lived through it. But in this journal, doctors reveal that baptism causes not only pneumonia (that a germ is involved is a capitalist lie), but severe stomach ailments. In fact, the mortality rate of baptised people is twice that of those who did not suffer this fate. So Christians are jailed for murder-by-baptism!

The teachings of the Church are widely publicised today in the Soviet press. God, you may read, wishes living sacrifices: they are useful in expiating sin. And this is why, in the town of Neftogorsk, the pastor slit the throat of a child of three during a service, while the whole congregation, including the mother, sang the praises of Jehovah. As for the pastors Iuri Susla and Mikhail Borinski, it seems they constructed stoves of vast dimensions in their churches; and they were on the point of throwing into these stoves two women when the police, getting wind of yet another human sacrifice, appeared in the nick of time to rescue the victims. It is an old, old story, this of ritual murder: in the past it has been the excuse to massacre countless Jews. Revived in our times, it is used to send Christians before the execution squad.

All these things change little from country to Communist country, though they are presently at their worst in China, where innumerable believers are in jail. Let me write only the names of Watchman Nee, Wang Ming Dao, Wen Yuang, Liu Ling Chiu, Chou Ching Tse . . .

In our mission the telephone rings constantly. One moment it is a courier back from a trip smuggling Bibles in eastern Europe; the next, a friend from Korea who is arranging an airdrop of Gospel tracts over the Communist-ruled North. Or maybe it is the *New York Times*: the sea has washed up on U.S. shores a few tightly-sealed plastic bags packed with straw, and Christian booklets. The bulk of the material, tens of thousands of leaflets, has reached Siberia. They would like to know who is behind it? But those responsible prefer to remain 'behind'; they are not much disposed to talk.

We have our opponents, of course. Some try to deny even that there is an Underground Church in the Soviet Union. They cannot imagine a church so totally unlike anything they know, places in which the passion of Christ is preached without passion, where pastors preach that God's miracles are fairy-tales and the Biblical stories all myths, where it is no longer necessary to be re-born and unite the sacrifice of Jesus with one's own life. Some go so far as to say that God is dead. And in the U.S.A. we have pastors who know even how to revive him—by a revolution conducted hand in hand with Communist guerrillas who bomb and kill.

Then where is the true Church? In chapels where abstruse quarrels are conducted over interpretations of Bible texts? (They do not mention two I love: 'Weep with those that weep'; and 'Remember those in bonds as bound with them'.) Or is it in seminaries where students toss about barbarous words — dispensationalism, millennialism, Pelegianism, Sabellianism ... crass dogma which they forget the moment they leave with their degrees? Is this the Church?

That the Underground Church exists in Russia was finally acknowledged by Mitchevici, secretary of the official Baptist Union of the Soviets, at a press conference in Sweden in 1971. He had denied it until then.

But I do not agree even with him.

For me the Church is those many millions of believers of all centuries who sometimes live in peace and sometimes in persecution. But even disorganised, abused and homeless, they know how to love and die for those they love, and to save, as Jesus did.

If you had asked the first generation of Christians in Palestine if they had ever heard of the 'Christian Church', they would have answered 'No'. 'Christian' is a nickname given us by unbelievers. We need no name, not even that of the Underground Church. The Church works openly where it can, even under Communism; and when it must hide—for it is idiocy not to go underground when you risk sentence of death for no reason at all—then it works in secret.

Why does Communism continue to grow? Maybe it is God's judgment on a flabby Church that will not learn from its martyrs.

And how many these are! The couriers I meet on their return from Communist countries tell amazing stories of courage.

A Soviet Christian in a concentration camp was made to dig his grave by guards. They made jokes while he worked. Then they ordered, 'Kneel in it. We'll bury you alive.' But the tractor which was to shovel the earth over him would not start. Yet it worked perfectly a moment before. The driver could find nothing wrong. Time and again, he tried to make it move. It would not budge. The driver saw the victim's shining eyes, and jumped into the grave beside him, crying, 'You are a man of God.' They took the man away. We do not know his fate.

A prisoner named Klassen was ordered to strip. He was to be tortured by being ducked in a bath of boiling water. While he undressed, the interrogators heaped fuel on the blaze. Suddenly, the boiler exploded, killing several of the would-be torturers. Klassen lives still, in a prison in Komi district.

From our sister in Russia, Sloboda, four children were taken away. You may not bring the Gospel to the young. She herself serves four years in prison, witnessing for Christ to her fellow inmates. For this, she was punished by being put for two months in an unheated cell, in winter. The concrete floor was like ice. Her clothes, all but her underthings, were taken away. Her food was bread and water.

Much later she was allowed a visit from relatives. She had felt no cold, Sloboda said. A warmth that had no natural cause had surrounded her all that time.

It is not the only case of its kind. In a book written by a Communist, a non-Christian who suffered under Stalin's purges, is the story of Christians who stood all day as a punishment, barefoot on ice. Not one fell sick. Sceptics can read this eye-witness account in Eugenia Ginzburg's book, *Out of the Whirlwind*.

I live in this world of suffering and heroism and miracle, day by day. The stories I read, the reports before me mean something more than to the average reader. When I see an article in *Uchitelskaia Gazeta* about children taken from their parents, of secret Sunday schools shut down, I know their sorrow and despair. Once I knew the same despair, that almost made me forsake belief in God.

Then I remember that it took the Soviets one day to subdue the Czech revolt. But they have not been able in fifty years to crush the Russian Church, nor the Church in other dominated countries.

Who can prevail against the children of God?

If I don't have much to say about my personal life in the U.S., it's because I don't have much personal life. None of us in the mission have. We are simply too busy. But the reader might find interest in two things about my life. It was, after all, I who had to marry; and I who had to be ordained.

When Judith came to the U.S., I met her in New York.

But we left New York immediately and flew to our Glendale home, where we were married. At the wedding, we talked of our underground work. Judith was thrilled by what we'd done so far. Our honeymoon was beautiful: we worked late into the night in the little mission office.

Over breakfast we discuss the latest arrests; luncheon and dinner the same. Judith, too, has given up her personal life. We read the mission, eat it, sleep it, dream at night of a triumphant Church in the Communist world.

My ordination was in Switzerland, where I'd gone for the first international conference of Christian missions to Communist countries. Black, white, yellow — men from every continent and eighteen lands were there. The conference, three years after we'd started work, was in itself as much a miracle as many of the things that happen in the Communist camp.

I was ordained by Bishop Monrad Norderval, of Tromsö, Norway. He wore the ornate cope that had belonged once to Bishop Berggrav, a famous name in Norway. Berggrav chose prison under the Nazis rather than submission to tyranny. Bishop Norderval was assisted in the ceremony by pastors from Britain, Holland, India, the U.S.A.—and my father.

One of the mission's big tasks is to provide Bibles. Millions of Bibles. The Soviet Union has 122 recognised nationalities within its boundaries. In the languages of more than 100 of these, no part of the scriptures has been translated. In every Communist country Bibles are scarce. In Red China there are almost none at all.

So we became smugglers. East Europe last year had four and a half million tourists, and though searches are often rigorous it isn't possible to check every tyre, every car for secret compartments. Sometimes they try, but in searching the vehicle, perhaps they forget to check our women couriers, who have a remarkable tendency to become pregnant three or four times a year. The delivery is always happy and painless. It's neither a boy nor a girl they carry, but a carefully padded parcel of Gospels.

Couriers also take in relief for the families of imprisoned men and women. One of the happiest days of my life was when our first letter of thanks came from within a Siberian labour camp. It had been smuggled out. Since then we have had so many others. A recent one came from the wife of a Soviet prisoner:

Dear Unknown One—First a greeting of Love. My heart is full of thankfulness and my eyes of tears on receiving today your gift. May the Lord reward you for showing such love from so far away. My eight little children and my husband in chains also thank you. The things you sent are too beautiful for us. My youngest child is four and my oldest is sixteen and for close on five years now my husband has been kept from us. But Our Father cares daily for his children. '*God will not forget all that you did for love of his name, when you served his people, as you still do.*' (Hebrews 6:10). We look forward to a letter from you.

The people who get our Bibles and the relief help us far more than we help them. They renew our faith; and sometimes they show their gratitude in a very tangible way. No Russian home is complete without a samovar, the big old metal urn in which tea is made. It's nothing to a Russian to drink ten cups of tea straight off. They couldn't envisage a world without samovars and they suppose that everyone, everywhere needs one. So the brethren of the Underground Church in the Soviet Union presented us, through a courier, with a samovar, and also a watch. It was a gift of love. It is a Russian watch, and it's stopped running already. But the gift is precious.

They are thankful not so much to us, as to the thousands of humble people whose contributions make our work possible. With this help, miracles come to pass: a New Testament was smuggled into a Siberian camp to become the daily food of a prisoner. He was able to keep it hidden from the guards, even when he was at last released. Then he sent it to us in the West, with the parts which are dearest to him underlined.

We *owe* these Bibles to Christian prisoners in the Communist camp. They pray for us in their cells. While we, keeping busy in our office, find a moment to talk to God only now and then. Then we go back to work, relying on the knowledge that all over Russia and East Europe, in jail and out, people are praying for us.

Couriers need careful instruction and training. They're risking their lives and liberty, and if they are not prepared, they may panic on arrest and betray the names and addresses of contacts. Or they may crack under torture. We explain things we learnt in these situations ourselves.

'Breathe very deeply when you're arrested and the questioning starts,' says my father. 'It adds oxygen to the blood. Stretch and loosen one after the other the muscles of your arms, legs and belly while answering their questions. This also adds oxygen and quickens the blood circulation. It increases your powers of resistance. Do this daily, exercising at home, now.' We can all train ourselves to a certain amount of stoicism. By deliberately inflicting small hurts on yourself while watching your face in a mirror so as to control tremors, you can school yourself slowly to bear more and more pressure. It is like any other form of physical training; and I have known some people to become so expert in this skill that they can put themselves into a state of near-catalepsy, a suspension of almost all bodily feeling, under interrogation. It's equally possible to learn the art of side-tracking an interrogator.

The couriers have had some narrow escapes. They know that the chance of capture and suffering is high. We explain every risk, but few are deterred. In fact, we are constantly employing more and more, and learning new tricks from them. The number of stitches in a pullover can carry an important message to and from the Underground Church. A shirt button, a dot on a piece of paper may be the cover for a microfilm of several pages of the Bible.

One thing that works in our favour is that Russia, which has swallowed so many small nations, has today a huge racial minority problem, far more complex than anything faced by the U.S. With more than 100 languages spoken inside the Soviet Union, internal quarrels are frequent. The Kremlin suppresses news of them—but sometimes it leaks out.

We sent an American of Ukrainian origin back to his homeland with a consignment of Bibles. The guard at the frontier found the cache. But he was a Ukrainian, and Ukrainians hate the Russians.

He said, 'Give me five Bibles for my friends, and you're free to go!'

Our courier did so gladly.

The people of the Baltic Republics feel the same contempt for Communism. They were overrun by Stalin's armies in 1940, and six million people enslaved. Religious oppression there today is especially fierce. But our agents always feel safe, at least relatively, knowing that the people will help them. Local authorities will send back anyone they discover rather than turn him over to Moscow.

Our couriers travel alone, at the height of the tourist season. Many of them are young. They carry detailed maps of every town they visit which show them exactly where to go when they get off the train, which bus to take, how they may recognise a contact. In this way they need talk to nobody. If a contact indicates by a certain sign that he is under surveillance, the courier must leave immediately.

In the past two years, this work has been carried to many new parts of the globe. Here is a report from a courier recently in Cuba:

> I had no trouble contacting A., who has the confidence of the evangelical churches and is in touch secretly with the families of many martyrs in jails and camps. There are a good number of pastors in prison. Others have been kicked out of their churches. They are extremely poor and unable to get decent work or make any living. The brethren received our financial help with great joy. They are terribly poor. I was wise to change most of the money in Europe (the courier reached Cuba via a European country) for gold watches and trinkets. An $80 gold watch can fetch the equivalent of $500 in Cuba. That is a tremendous help to a needy family.
>
> I handed all the gold and money to B., who will distribute over a two-year period to the families of those in prison. It is a very risky business, bringing in watches, but this time the Lord helped us.

We face a problem that is not only religious. When religious freedom goes, every other will follow, sooner or later. If the free peoples of the world forget their responsibilities—and they are doing it — Mao and Kosygin and the rest will take over. The world is frightened, because it thinks there are only two alternatives: appeasing the Communists, or unleashing a nuclear war. But the Communists themselves know a third way. They yield nothing, and they do not start a nuclear war. Their weapon is subversion, and we have to learn it from them.

Our answer is a spiritual struggle—the opposition of Christ to Communism in the lands it has overtaken. Our mission is not only concerned with saving souls: it cannot be. Western Protestants often use the expression 'to take Jesus as a personal saviour'. It is not a Biblical expression. I have other sins beside personal ones, and so a personal Saviour is not enough. The sins of our church, our family, our social group—all these involve us; the sins of all men are in part ours, if we have not done all we can to oppose evil.

So we have to try to unstop the eyes and ears of Western leaders who do not want to know. One believes a lie heard a thousand times more readily than a fact one has never heard before. The Communists repeat endlessly the lie of liberalisation and greater religious freedom. The Western world is easily duped. Nobel prize winner Solzenitsyn tells how Americans, including one 'Mrs. R.' (guess who?), visited a Soviet jail in the fifties. How impressed they were with the beds, the food, the clothing, the library, the ikons of the Virgin, the Bibles supplied to the men—'all Nazi war criminals', they were told. In fact they were in jail for such crimes as talking to an American tourist. But Mrs. R. and friends were convinced. They left, and the inmates went back to their icy, bare cells, the beatings and the bad food. They had no chance to read that Bible.

There is no end to these techniques of deception.

A leading official of the 'Baptist Union' of Russia told the press during a visit to the U.S. that they have thirteen churches in Moscow, each seating between 2,000 and 3,000 people. This was news to our mission, which knows of only one church in the capital: it has to serve not only the Baptists but also an array of other Christian sects. We asked the British Baptist Union, which is on good terms with the Russian officials, for the addresses of these thirteen churches. They replied that the thirteen churches—described, in fact, as 'preaching stations'—were scattered through the Moscow District, an administrative area the size of England, and not in the capital itself. We persisted in asking for the addresses of these 'thirteen preaching stations' but received no answer. Yet this lie, like so many others, continues to confuse well-meaning folk abroad.

Western Church render honour — the tomb of Lenin, a mass-murderer of Christians. None of them has ever left a flower at the grave of our martyrs in Russia. The Underground Church (I use this term because it has become common) is the Church of one third of the world, which cannot worship freely, but I do not know a single seminary in which students are taught about its work. Communism is still spreading from one country to another: the Yemen, Southern Yemen, the Emirates of the Persian Gulf, where soon the Church will have to go underground as well. Yet the pastors have no knowledge of the ways in which they will have to continue their work secretly for Christ.

Deceptive Communist tactics have blinded most people to the spiritual and political potential of the Underground Church as the free world's best ally in the enemy camp. Even though we tell our couriers what to expect of our friends behind the Iron Curtain, they are always impressed by the courage, strength and selflessness they meet with there. They find Christians who travel at the risk of their lives from place to place with short-wave radios to transmit the Gospel, others who print leaflets which are copied by hand and passed on. A group employed by a state publishing house managed to print thousands of copies of a hymnal, bearing a false title: in a few hours they had all been distributed. They have even started a secret Bible Society of their own.

What our mission has been able to do until now can only be a start for the much greater task ahead. After an intense fifty-year campaign to wipe out religion, Russia still has millions of believers. Instead of fading out, religious ferment is growing and these millions must be reached and helped by every means.

Contacts are not easy. Here in the West, cultural groups from Iron Curtain countries are warmly received. Western nations show their latest scientific discoveries, receiving in return shows by singers and folk-dancers, always accompanied by a cohort of 'cultural attachés' who keep the artistes under close surveillance and act as spies.

Our mission tries to give these visitors a Communist-style welcome. We get hold of an advance copy of the programme of the event—which may be a performance by Oistrakh, the Russian violinist, or the Rumanian Folk Ballet—and duplicate its cover. It looks exactly like the other programmes handed out, but opens to reveal in story and pictures the facts about religious persecution. Night after night at Los Angeles' glittering Music Centre and other such places, we put across our message by this ruse, counting on the audiences to spread the leaflets further, as they do. One of the Rumanian dancers we contacted opted to remain in the West; others wanted to but feared reprisals against their families. We gave them all Gospels to take home with them—not one was rejected.

This is a Leninist gambit, to introduce your propaganda in disguise. We have followed it successfully with touring groups from Iron Curtain countries in many Western cities. When some of our young people met a group of Russian students at a welcoming luncheon, they offered each of them a Bible. Nobody wanted 'that obsolete book'. But later, in the privacy of a hotel washroom, we offered the Bibles again. This time, not a single Russian refused.

We adopted 'activist' tactics from Leftist students in the U.S. and found that radicals like a pastor who has the courage of his convictions. Christian students who used to study the Bible in some corner were encouraged to attend Red meetings in the 'free speech' area at Berkeley, the most revolutionary campus of California University. The Communists heckled our speakers, we heckled theirs. They shouted, we shouted louder, having seized their microphones.

We told them how we had seen Communism come to our own country by infiltration, deceit and force, as it has to so many others. 'It can't happen here?' The top Communist thinkers, from Lenin to Mao, have said it can and will. Shouldn't they be listened to, now they have put a third of the world into slavery?

I said that many young people of my own age, or younger, who enjoy their own cars, homes, music and books talk cheerfully of communal sharing and living, and seem to think this is Communism. It isn't. Communism is not just stripping stores and factories from the rich: it means confiscating a one-man barber's shop from its owner, his tractor from the farmer with a few acres. An American rock group has a song, 'They can't take away our music'. They can. Music is one of the most rigidly controlled forms of expression in the Communist world.

Our 'radical' tactics paid off so well that some radical 'free speech' areas are now dominated by Christian speakers. Spurred by our activity and also helped financially, big youth organisations have arisen in America. They are determined that the youth of the free world shall belong to Christ, and not to Satan. The same spirit is being carried around the world, with some striking successes. While touring South Africa my father was angrily heckled at a students' meeting; early next morning he was awakened by his chief adversary, to say he had been converted and come over to our side. Every day brings its challenges: a ship from a Communist country with a crew which must be met, diplomats and newspapermen from Iron Curtain capitals who are willing to talk to us, if secrecy can be secured.

Our chief and most immediate aim is never out of sight. It is to bring some comfort to the hundreds of thousands of people who sit in prison for their faith. We ask our friends in the free world to remember them, to 'weep with those that weep'. Jesus said that we who fail to visit the stranger, naked and ill, in prison are also neglecting Him. 'Inasmuch as ye did it not to the least of these my brethren, ye did it not to me.'

The author welcomes correspondence
and enquiries about the
Underground Church
at this address:

Christian Mission to the Communist World,
P.O. Box 19
Bromley, Kent
BR1 1DJ.

A year in the life of Frankie Dettori

The Champion Jockey in both 1994 and 1995, Lanfranco 'Frankie' Dettori is the most successful jockey in the world today. Riding not just in England but in France, Germany, Italy, America, Australia, Dubai and Hong Kong, Dettori's notable victories include the St Leger, the Oaks, the Breeders' Cup Mile, the Nunthorpe, the Arc de Triomphe, the French 2,000 Guineas, the Queen Elizabeth II Stakes, the Prix L'Abbaye and many more. In 1995 alone, he had 1,000 rides in the UK, with a massive winning total of 215, putting him some 70 wins clear of his nearest rival. He liv Newmarket, Cambridgeshire.

To my mother
Iris Maria Niemen
All my love
Frankie

A year in the life of
Frankie Dettori

FRANKIE DETTORI

Mandarin

A Mandarin Paperback

a year in the life of
frankie dettori

First published in Great Britain 1996
by William Heinemann Ltd
This edition published 1997
by Mandarin Paperbacks
an imprint of Reed International Books Ltd
Michelin House, 81 Fulham Road, London SW3 6RB
and Auckland, Melbourne, Singapore and Toronto

Copyright © 1996 Lanfranco Dettori
The author has asserted his moral rights

Photographs copyright © Clare Bancroft

A CIP catalogue record for this title
is available from the British Library
ISBN 0 7493 2392 2

Printed and bound in Great Britain
by Cox & Wyman Ltd, Reading, Berkshire

Contents

Acknowledgements

My fiancée Catherine Allen
Tony Stafford
Matty Cowing
John Gosden and Rachel Hood
Peter Burrel and Christopher Little
The Maktoum family
Clare Bancroft
Colin and Andy
Gianfranco Dettori
Alessandra Dettori

Preface

Just when I thought I'd finished writing this book, something like that had to happen. I thought I could relax for a while and wind down, but then along came Ascot. It's hard to win the National Lottery, but there is one winner at least nearly every week. My seven out of seven, in all seven races, on the first day of the Festival of British Racing on 28 September 1996 was truly a first.

It seems that never in England, or anywhere else in the world, had a jockey gone through the card in a seven-race programme until my wonderful, brilliant, unbelievable day. And what a day to choose: national television coverage, a big crowd, great racing and the support on the day of most of the people who have helped me so much throughout the years, and whose story you will read in the following pages.

We travelled up to Ascot with a single race on our minds. Mark Of Esteem had given me two of my greatest moments during the topsy-turvy year in which injury and suspension, funnily enough not just for me but for so many of my friends and colleagues in the weighing room, had been as much a factor as big race wins. Walter Swinburn, who was the jockey closest to beating me on one of those Saturday seven stars, had been almost killed in a fall in Hong Kong at the start of the year. Willie Carson, who had won six races out of seven one day at Newcastle in 1990, was still in hospital after his awful accident when he'd been kicked and close to dying in the same Newbury parade ring where I'd broken my elbow back in June and lost any chance of retaining my title. But, as we hoped that Willie's health would get better just as Walter's had, I was reflecting that seven out seven would be better, in the context of my career, than seventy-seven championships. Although don't think I'm going to be satisfied with the two I've had so far.

In the days since that memorable occasion at Ascot, when racing went onto the front pages for the first time for all the right reasons, I have never stopped thinking about the enthusiasm, warmth, kindness and sheer excitement that the 20,000 people at Ascot showed that afternoon. Each win got a better response than the one before. The other jockeys started by being frustrated as I kept on winning, but even Pat Eddery, who I had to beat three times, Mick Kinane, Walter Swinburn, Ray Cochrane and the others actually began to share and enjoy (almost) the atmosphere. They would all rather have won a race, but their chance came on the Sunday.

It might look as though it was my day. But for me it was horse racing's day. The people's day. An occasion to show that a day at the races can be as much fun as any football match, tennis final or golf tournament. We have a great sport in our hands. It's up to us, the people who are identified by the public as the leading players, to fuel that enthusiasm. I loved the responsibility of all the interviews. It's always at the back of your mind that media attention can be cruel, but for once all the exposure was positive and I loved it.

But to come back to Mark Of Esteem. The way he won the Queen Elizabeth II Stakes, Europe's mile championship, against six other top-class horses, gave me the most astonishing feeling I've ever had for a single performance. When we turned for home up the final straight at Ascot, all had been going well, but I knew that in Bosra Sham, the 1,000 Guineas winner, we had a top performer to catch. Pat sent her on by the two-furlong pole but with my horse still going so easily I decided to wait – as I hadn't when he'd won the 2,000 Guineas, when I'd asked him about 100 yards too soon. This time I delayed his challenge until the furlong pole, and the way Mark Of Esteem quickened showed the difference between a great horse like Bosra Sham and a true champion. It was exhilarating and such a joy to come back and meet Sheikh Maktoum and Sheikh Mohammed, whose family's support for me has been so constant and such a great part of my career.

That was the third winner in the royal-blue colours of Godolphin, following the first two races, the Cumberland Lodge Stakes with Wall Street and the Diadem Stakes with Diffident. The Diadem Stakes was probably the one race where I needed a slice of luck. We beat Lucayan Prince by a short head. Walter had not been able to get out for a clear run until it was too late. If he had and had beaten us, I could have spent the rest of my life moaning that David Loder, another of the trainers who has been a great influence on me over the past years, ruined my moment of history.

After the big race and Mark Of Esteem, it was wonderful that John Gosden should get in on the act. John is much more than my boss. He's a friend, a great man and really my mentor. His horse Decorated Hero had top weight in the Tote Festival Handicap. He won so easily. He'd have got there – and from a bad draw in twenty-two out of twenty-six – if he'd carried 10st 13lbs, never mind the actual 9st 13lbs.

And so it went on, Fatefully giving us a fourth Godolphin win in the fillies' handicap and then Lochangel, half-sister to my lovely old friend Lochsong, making all – despite the trainer Ian Balding's instructions to hold her up and give her a chance – to win the Blue Seal Stakes in great style.

So now it was a big field, another top weight and a full two miles of the testing Ascot circuit for Fujiyama Crest, trained by one of the greatest trainers, Michael Stoute. The reception on the way to the start was sensational and, having realised in the morning I would be on a 12–1 chance in that last race, it was a shock to see in the paddock as I waited to get on the horse that he was 2–1 favourite. But, as they say, Fujiyama Crest didn't know he was a 2–1 shot, not until the canter to the start anyway.

As we went past the post on the first circuit, I took the lead and, all the way round, the horse was moving nicely within himself. All the time I was waiting for them to come and swallow me up, but when we got to the straight I was still ahead. Later, Ray Cochrane asked me, 'Did you hear the crowd as we turned for home?' and, thinking about it, he was right. It was incredible. The noise began there and, as we thrust for the line, got louder and louder. I could sense Pat Eddery and Northern Fleet coming up. The crowd knew what they wanted. I'm sure Fujiyama Crest knew, too. He must have read the script the night before as he stood in his stable at Newmarket. Pat and Northern Fleet kept coming, but the crowd and Fujiyama Crest just wouldn't let him go by.

I was there! It was an amazing feeling. The usual cliché from a sportsman is that 'it didn't sink in until …' I'm sure in this case it will never sink in. Certainly, until my first loser the next day it was possible to imagine it never ending. But, as the wonderful people who stood and cheered for so long on the Saturday night discovered, it's like the lottery. It's a once in a lifetime achievement. Unlike the lottery, my seven out of seven was a once in everyone's lifetime achievement.

1 The Young Lanfranco

Well, here I am, twenty-five years old, twice champion jockey in England and it's all flown past me like a fast-running river. Who would have believed that the little Italian boy in Milan would find himself living in England – for the past ten years – and writing a book about some of his experiences in those times?

Writing a book indeed. In my school days I read only one book, *Twenty Thousand Leagues Under The Sea*, by Jules Verne, and now I'm writing one myself, and in English! That wasn't because I was dumb at school. No, I was one of those middle-of-the-road people. I was actually pretty smart, picking things up first time. But all the time I was trying to get away with doing as little as possible, not wanting to be too much of a swot. I found mathematics very easy, thought geography was very interesting, but didn't enjoy the other subjects much.

Apart from that there was football. Always football. We

went to school from eight thirty in the morning until five o'clock. We had our lunch break between twelve-noon and two and were supposed to take between twelve and twelve thirty to eat and digest the food. But of course we gobbled it up as fast as we could and by about five minutes after twelve we were picking the sides for football.

We were always about twenty a side and played for an hour and a half every afternoon in the hot Italian sun. We would rip our jeans and need a new pair of shoes every week, but I must say it was the best time of my life. I was always the one standing on the goal-line, the goal-hanger, waiting for the ball to come to touch it past the goalkeeper. If I didn't score fifteen goals in an afternoon I would be disappointed.

Apart from the size of the teams and the fact there was no offside, our game was different from real football in a more significant way. It's funny that the school only had basketballs because the main sport there was basketball in the hall. So we used a basketball for our games. It was so heavy for a kid – it was like kicking a pot plant around the place.

The football helped take away some of the unhappiness that I always felt at home. My father was a jockey, a very successful one, but there was never much contact between us. Being a jockey is a pressure job, and when things don't go well, you take your losers home. He would always put the paper up, studying the racecard for the next day.

My father was always cold. I remember when I was about six years old, me and my sister, who is six years older than me, might want to play and he would be in a bad mood. We lived in a kind of villa and we could not go out to play in the garden because he would be resting there, preparing for riding the next day. We would kiss him goodnight and go to our room early.

When I was six I was forced to ride a pony for the first time. Me and my friends, whose fathers were also jockeys, used to enjoy going to the races, but only really to play football with the other kids. Funnily enough, most of those boys are also jockeys now. At that time nothing was further from my mind than being a jockey, but it all changed when my sister ran away from home.

My parents had divorced when I was six months old. I stayed with my mum until I was five but then, when it was time to go to school, she suggested: 'Stay with Dad, he's got more money than us.' He did not live far away, so that's what happened.

Life was very strict with my father and stepmother. But without that experience I would never have been able to come to England aged fourteen. My stepmother's toughness on us when we were young made that possible.

I suppose for me there was a lack of love. In those days I was very much into myself and my true character did not really come out until later. It was worse still for my sister, Sandra, though. She had a rejection feeling about our stepmother. There would be tears every night, particularly when my sister knew she was in the wrong. She would fight anyway, just wanting to prove a point. For me, I was quite a little boy, learning all about these things, so I thought, Why fight? Still do what you want but not get caught, not get found out. In other words, I developed a little native cunning.

This went on for a couple of years. All the time we had our duties. I would have to prepare the table for dinner, my sister would clear up after. At eight thirty I would have to go to bed; she was allowed to stay up until nine o'clock, but by eight thirty she would already be in an argument so she would go to bed when I did. Then we would cry together, but while she could not wait to get away, I would still have my toy car to play with, so I was less unhappy than her.

Then, when she was fourteen, she ran away from Dad and went back to Mum. Dad asked her to come back but she didn't want to. Then something happened that would end up changing my life. In all the time we'd been with Dad, he'd never taken me to school. But the day after my sister went away he dropped me at school, for the first and last time! Otherwise, I walked there every day. Soon after, I came out of school and he had come to pick me up – in a horsebox. 'Hey Dad,' I said. 'Jump in,' he said. I jumped in and he was carrying on as usual about how bad my sister was.

Anyway, he took me to a horse farm, owned by one of the Italian owners with horses running at the San Siro track in Milan. I'll never forget it. It seems like yesterday. He said hello to the owner who showed us three ponies in a field. He pointed to the ponies and said: 'Which do you like?' At my age it was like taking an adult to the Ferrari shop and asking, 'Which car you would like?'

There were two bay ponies and one palomino, with four white socks, white tail, mane and face. Of course I took the palomino. We put her in the horsebox and took her home. We stabled her at a local farm, which in those days still kept cows and made their own milk, but it is no longer there. Dad taught me how to muck out, put the bedding on the floor. He gave me a bag with tools and taught me how to clean her and how to use the hoof-pick. He said: 'This is it, your toy. You will look after her. After school, you will come to muck out, feed and ride her.'

Every day, I could not wait to finish school. I'd run home to put on my jodhpurs and my jockey silks in the famous colours of Carlo d'Allessio, and run to the pony, who was about a quarter of a mile away from home.

I would not be able to wait to ride her, so instead of mucking out first, I'd hide the droppings in the corner. I'd sling the saddle on and go straight out and gallop for the hell of it. It was a big circuit all round the outside of the farm. The pony was called Sylvia and soon I would tell all my classmates to come and watch me and Sylvia. Near the farm there was a kind of showjumping ring, very run down and falling to bits. As I rode past the little grandstand there, all my mates would shout: 'Vae Lanfranco!'

From then I always wanted to be a jockey. About a year after my sister left home, when I was nine, all the local ponies were entitled to run in the Pony Derby, staged on the racecourse at San Siro during June. I became a man with a mission. I would get Sylvia ready each day and gallop her in preparation for the Derby. When we got to the race, though, all the ponies were giants compared to Sylvia, all the riders were giants compared to me. My only advantage was that my pony would carry much less weight than the others.

It did help that for years I had been to the track twice a week to watch my dad. The course was made on the jumping track between the last two fences, probably around three furlongs. As we waited for the start, though, I was a nervous wreck and when the flag was dropped I missed the kick and crossed the finish stone last. Sylvia then saw the finishing flag, dug in her toes and I fell over her head and straight into the water jump! I got out dripping wet and jumped back on. My first experience of race riding was hardly an unqualified success!

After about a year the novelty was gone. Of course I loved my pony, but every day after I finished school I was supposed to muck her out and exercise her. By the time the winter came, it was really cold. I suppose I got lazy and if she wasn't exercised one day she would be twice as fresh the next. Once, I left her four days in the box after she'd dropped me but there was no one there to advise me. She definitely had got the better of me. By this time I'd got scared and never had control of her.

Luckily, Dad saw the signs and finally sold the pony, and I went right off racing for a year. But then, just as suddenly, aged around eleven, I became interested again. I began to bet on the races – but I could hardly reach up to the window to place my bets. That was the age when we all began to think we were the business. We would wear trendy jeans but still we'd play football, now with a small ball, between the races. Sometimes we would take branches from the trees and pretend to run our own races, whacking our own legs in time as if hitting a horse to make it go faster.

Then we'd hear the commentator say that the horses were going into the stalls, and run across to the window to place our bets. Usually it would be the minimum stake on a short-priced favourite, say a 2–1 on chance, and we'd be delighted to get our money back. This was when I really got the love of horse-racing. I would go with Dad when he would look round the yards with the trainers. That was when I finally knew I just had to be a jockey.

By the time I was twelve, during the school holidays, it was arranged that I would ride in the d'Allessio stable. For three months I walked and trotted round the roads, and then had to get down for someone else to do a canter. You could hardly say I was learning much.

In those days, starting early was not unusual, unlike now when sixteen is the minimum age. But I began at thirteen and was one of the last to do so. Then it was really a case of: 'You know how to count to ten; how to sign cheques; it's off to the real world!'

Dad sat me down. 'So you want to be a jockey?' To my stepmother, I was just a quiet little boy with no motivation. But really she never gave me a chance to show what I could do. She was too aggressive. When she and my Dad were around I was too scared to be outgoing. They thought there was not enough aggression in me to become a jockey. But at school I was the naughtiest boy in the class!

Dad and me had our first 'man talk'. He told me, 'You might want to become a jockey but it's not easy. For most boys who come into stables, nearly all of them only get to look after their three horses, only one in a thousand makes it as a jockey.'

Despite Dad's pessimism, I started soon after with the d'Allessio stable. Dad had been first jockey there for fifteen years and won nearly everything in Italian racing when Luca Cumani's father, Sergio, was the trainer. I remember going there sometimes on Tuesday mornings, the main work day, before school, when I was about seven or eight years old. Bolkonski, who later came to England to win the 2,000 Guineas, was one of Dad's regular rides for Mr Cumani, as was Wollow.

The first racehorse I ever sat on was an old sprinter called Or Bettelo. I was seven or eight years old and he was about ten. After he'd done his work I would walk him around. He knew so much about racing I'm sure he could read and write! In truth, he walked me around! One day, Mr Cumani gave me some lumps of sugar to give to the horse and then put me on top. Looking down, I could not believe how far the ground was.

By the time I came into racing, Mr Cumani, sadly, had died from cancer, and Mr Botti had taken over. The stable was still the classiest in Italy, a bit like Vincent O'Brien at his peak, with forty horses all Group or Listed class. When

Mr d'Allessio died, the empire collapsed.

With Mr Botti, I was given the same horse to exercise first and second lots, as he took so much work. My first four or five months I didn't learn anything. Dad was too busy, except on Tuesdays for one and a half hours when he would shout and scream at me the whole time: 'Pull your jerks up; put your bum down; lean a bit more forward; do the arch this way.' I'd make a big point to do as he told me but by second lot I'd immediately go back to riding 'cowboy style'. That was my John Wayne impression: left hand holding on to the neck strap, choking the horse; right hand up near the chest; legs out straight in front, like Eddie 'the Eagle' Edwards doing a ski-jump.

I wasn't learning much, but for the first time I had a feeling of being myself. It was like when I was a kid and was able to go out on my bike, that sort of freedom. I felt like a man, as though I was achieving something. At first, when I was working in the stables, I was very slow. It took me half an hour to groom each horse, but at the end of that time, the horse would be really spotless. I loved the work.

One guy I remember especially from that time is Raffaeli Lai. He taught me a few things about horses; how to do them up, generally everything about grooming. He was horse mad and still is. The funny thing was that ten years later I ended up riding his horse, Misil, for him and we finished second in the Coral-Eclipse at Sandown and also ran well in the Prix de l'Arc de Triomphe at Longchamp. Happily for Raffaeli, we won the Gran Premio del Jockey Club at San Siro at the end of 1993. Raffaeli is now married to an English girl, Sandra, and every summer they stay for three weeks with his in-laws and always come to Newmarket to see me.

Apart from Raffaeli, my time in the Botti stable was pretty

unrewarding. For those few months all I had to show was riding the same horse every day. He was so fat, so lazy, I had to push him all the time. We were always at the back of the string when he went out to exercise, never at the front.

Then, when that season was ending in Milan and Rome, Dad was already miles ahead, probably by eighty winners, in the jockeys' title race and already champion. At that stage of the year he would always take a little holiday and then ride abroad in jockeys' championship events around the world. In the season, therefore, I hardly ever saw him because he was busy racing; in the winter he was always away. To me, most of the time, Dad was little more than a ghost.

This autumn, he sat down with my stepmother to decide what I should do. Winters in Milan can be very cold with plenty of snow and the horses training there do nothing. Dad had a good friend from his own wild teenage years called Antonio Verdicchio. Dad knew him as Tonino. He had a stable in Pisa, where the winters are much milder, and Dad called and asked him whether he would take me into the stable to live and work with him. Tonino said he would be delighted to do so, and off I went to Pisa.

Tonino had three daughters, and the move there gave me the first chance to find the real me. This trainer took me on like his own son – the son he'd never had himself, I suppose. Dad had told him, 'Make him work hard, pay him peanuts each month and be sure he does his three.' Antonio kept to the first two parts of Dad's request anyway.

He met me at the station in a big white Mercedes and took me back to change into my jodhpurs – he wore a jacket and trousers – and then we went down to the stables, an L-shaped building containing twenty-five horses. I said to him: 'Tonino, Dad told me you would be giving me my three horses to do.' He tutted and shook his head. He said: 'You start at one end and I'll start at the other. We'll meet in the middle.' We each had a barrow and a fork. That was evening stables à la Tonino!

I found it a bit difficult. By the time I did the first three, he'd done ten. He came to inspect my efforts. 'Don't throw all that straw away,' he said, throwing it back into the boxes. For the little boy used to living at the other end of the scale in racing stables, this was a real culture shock. I was being thrown into the real world where most people are strugglers.

Then the head lad arrived, late and unshaven. He was called Chipola, and by the time he arrived there were only two horses to muck out. He opened the tack room. There was no such thing as a work list for the horses' programme for the following day and the tack would be slung on to anything in the room.

The work riding was done by Tonino, me and Chipola, who must have weighed nearly seventeen stone. The first morning we put the tack on three horses and took them out to the exercise track, which was about six furlongs round and on sand. I was to do a canter on a ten-year-old gelding called Grunland. We went on to the track and started to canter. That was fine, but at the end of the circuit I tried to stop him and couldn't. After the fourth lap I started to scream 'Help!' Tonino shouted out, 'Stop screaming and pull.' He wasn't going very fast by that time, but however hard I pulled he didn't respond. He had a 'wooden' mouth and he eventually only stopped when Tonino got off his horse, held on to him with one hand and stood in the middle of the track with his arms wide open. As soon as he saw Tonino, the old thief stopped in a stride.

I thought to myself: 'I really messed that up. If that had happened in Milan I would have been fired on the spot.' So

I stood there waiting for Tonino to give me a bollocking. All he said was. 'Look, stop screaming. Save your breath and pull!' We rode either seven or eight lots every day, going in and out, slinging the tack on and off. Suddenly, after only riding one horse in Milan, I would be on eight different horses every day. Inevitably, I'd fall off at least once each morning, and we'd work through till about one o'clock. I'd be absolutely knackered, so usually, after lunch, I'd sleep until six, go back for evening stables, then wait for the girls to come back from school.

We'd go out playing in the street with some of the other local kids. On Sundays there was a disco locally for the teenagers and we'd always go there. I was my own man. No one told me when to come home, when to go to bed. Life was beautiful. As for the riding, within a month I was riding shorter than Lester Piggott, confident as anyone on a horse. I knew all the horses and once a week Marco Paganini, one of the top jockeys, who was later to be killed in a riding accident, came to ride work. From being wrapped in cotton wool, here I was finding freedom and my own personality. Tonino gave me everything, never screamed or shouted, and the nice thing was we helped him train a few winners in the months I was there.

When Dad picked me up in Pisa at the end of April, by which time I was fourteen, I had enjoyed the best four months of my career at that stage. I would ride anything, and was fearless, never minding falling off. Of course, when I came back home, I went straight back into my shell, but Dad could not believe his own eyes how much I had improved. As soon as I got back, I was riding fast work with the top jockeys. Final gallops before the races, and I rode short. They put me on hard pullers, anything. In the d'Allessio stable I even led my dad in work at fourteen, and

I was one of the best riding lads in the stable. Once on a horse I felt good and Dad soon saw something in me; saw I could make it one day, so he started planning for my future.

Within a month the brainwashing began. I'm sure he'd already had the plan in his mind, but didn't tell me, I guess. He thought I was young and would not be race-riding for another year, so arranged for me to spend six months with Luca Cumani in England, then six months with Patrick Biancone in Chantilly and be back in Italy at fifteen and a half ready to become a jockey.

He explained it all to me and I said I didn't want to go. We went to the races that day, me in between Dad and my stepmother. He said: 'Lester Piggott and Pat Eddery have aeroplanes, take rides in helicopters and get to ride the best horses in the top races.' By the time we got to the track, between the pair of them they'd managed to brainwash me and soon I was to be off.

The stay in England was meant to be six months, and Dad gave me £366, almost a million lire, all in those big £20 notes. Imagine the young Lanfranco, unable to speak a word of English, due to spend six months in a foreign country. I was meant to leave in the spring, but just before my departure date, I was out riding my moped, slipped on some wet turf and shattered my elbow. I needed two operations and the scar is still visible.

I did not finally leave until early July, dressed like a nice English boy with a suit and tie and carrying a big suitcase. When I got to Luton airport, a taxi driver, holding a sign with 'Lanfranco Dettori' written in large letters, met me and we set off for Newmarket. The journey took about an hour and he turned on the radio, and we heard what I realised was a race commentary. It was the Princess of Wales's Stakes and Petoski won it.

The driver took me to my digs in Bury Road, in Newmarket, but I guess everyone was out at the races. We left my suitcase outside the door, at the driver's suggestion. I was amazed. In Italy if you leave anything like that they'll take it. But the driver said: 'No problem.' He took me down to the stables, and left me in Luca Cumani's office.

In Italy in those days, most trainers' offices would comprise a table, a lamp, the entries, some pens and a telephone. Here, there were computers, two secretaries, trophies and pictures on the wall of all Mr Cumani's big winners. As for the stable itself, my reaction was, 'Wow!' All the doors were in the right place, polished, and there were no dogs, sheep or cats to make things untidy.

So my first memory of England was getting to the office from where the secretary guided me to the stable and introduced me to the head lad (Old Arthur). He grabbed me by the arm, opened a box and slid it open. I didn't understand at first what he wanted, until he put a dandy brush in my hand. I hung my jacket up on the door, and dressed the horse over. At five o'clock, Luca Cumani came. Everyone seemed so frightened of him. It was as though Hitler's come! Everyone panicked, running everywhere like wildcats. I was pretty nervous too, as I'd only met this guy for a few minutes once in Pisa. He had those smouldering eyes which looked at you. Who would have believed that I would stay with him for seven years?

Luca had an Italian assistant, Stefano Ibido. He didn't talk to me much – he didn't want to be a babysitter, I suppose. Each night, the guv'nor would come at five o'clock. You'd stand by, take off the chain and feed the horse. He came into my stall, and you could hear a pin drop; it was like being in a church. He just said: 'Bienvenuto. We pull out at six o'clock,' and moved away. I thought: 'This is gonna be a long six months.' But by the end of that season, I guess they must have liked me – and I became confident enough so that within three months I'd become really cheeky.

I stayed in a bed and breakfast in Bury Road. They really tried hard to make me feel at home. Soon after I got there they served me up a meal with Heinz ravioli, obviously trying to give me a taste of home. It was really kind of them to try that, but I only managed to eat the stuff out of respect for them, not for the food itself. My room was the smallest in the house, only a bed and sink really. The one 'luxury' was a bottle of orange squash which was left for me. I'd never seen it in Italy and didn't realise you had to dilute it with water.

Life then was just work and bed. I earned between £12 and £17 a week and the stable paid for my digs. It got to be like a prison, and the lady whose house it was had two daughters, who took the mickey out of me all the time. Then, suddenly, after three months, when I got my confidence, I started to go out at night. Colin (my best mate) and Andy, who is now my driver, were my first real friends in England and like me were apprentices with Mr Cumani. I was lucky to meet them when I did.

Those early days at Luca's gave me my first experience of the real world as lived by the young stable staff in Newmarket. When I first arrived there I was only fourteen and from the start I felt the eyes of everyone on me. I suppose they saw I was wearing all the flashy gear, and to them I was a rich kid, and my father was a champion jockey. I was always getting hit – not hard – by a lot of the older lads, but I came to see it was a bit of a joke, and not the bullying I feared at the beginning. Then, on Saturday nights, when we all used to go out, I was like the little brother and then they all made sure I was okay and looked after me. There was the usual rivalry between the lads from the different yards and at the end of a Saturday night when a few had had a little too much to drink, it was a big help that there was always someone and usually a few people there to make sure you got home safe.

It was really my first experience of going out regularly, the first time I'd been out for a drink late at night. The regular venue was the Golden Lion in Newmarket High Street. In those days, one of Luca's assistants was an Italian and he gave me some advice: 'If you go out on Saturday night, don't go to the Golden Lion.' After that, where else did I end up but at the Golden Lion? It cost £1 to get in, and the fact I was so young mattered less in Newmarket where everyone is the same size, except the trainers of course! I did look very young, though, especially in the face, but I borrowed a leather jacket which made it appear that I had shoulders like Mike Tyson. Then I would rub the print from a newspaper on top of my lip to make it look (hopefully) that I might just be eighteen. I would go and queue up with the rest of the lads from the yard and, when I got to the door, I tried to put on a deep voice to say, in my best broken English, 'How much is it please?' Then I'd pay the pound and when my age was asked, the other lads would assure them I was eighteen and stick up for me if anyone queried it.

In the event, it was pretty tame. We'd play pool in the back room for most of the night and I would have a couple of vodka and oranges because you couldn't really taste the vodka. I must say I don't really like the taste of alcohol. Then, at the end of the evening, coming up to twelve thirty a.m., the DJ would line up three or four slow records, which was the signal for everyone to try to pair up with someone.

So the cues in the back room would be dropped and we'd run on to the dance floor to look for any available girls. Sometimes you ended up with someone to go home with, or more often there would be fights with people arguing over the women.

The six months flashed by and I went home for ten days in Italy, expecting to leave after that for Mr Biancone. Luca must have said something about me to my Dad, but anyway, ten days later, instead of a trip to France, I was on my way back to England. I'd found myself, and the rest is history!

2 My Apprenticeship

I still used to go back to Italy quite a lot at this stage of my career and, unlike in Britain, where you have to be sixteen to ride in a race, in Italy you can start earlier. I had my first win as a jockey in Turin in late November, a month before my sixteenth birthday. My chance for a first success in England would not come, of course, until the following season, and it was thanks to Mr Cumani that I got my first ride the next year, on a horse trained by Peter Walwyn.

Mr Walwyn had been champion trainer, handling the great champion Grundy back in the 1970s. He was well known for his forthright views. Since then he has been a campaigner for his beloved Lambourn in Berkshire, the training centre where he has been based for so long. He is affectionately known throughout the racing world as Basil Fawlty, because of a sometimes uncanny hint of the John Cleese character in the TV show *Fawlty Towers*. The first ride came because Luca had been telling people that he had a promising young rider in the stable who could ride at 7st 7lb, which was then the minimum weight to be carried in races. Mr Walwyn asked Graham Green, who was then the Press Association representative who compiled the lists of jockeys for races – now it's done through Weatherbys – who would be available for an apprentice race at Kempton at the Easter bank holiday meeting in 1987. Graham suggested me and I got that ride and also ended up on another horse, trained by Reg Akehurst.

As a total unknown, too young to drive, I had to get a lift and it was Lizzy Hare, at the time Luca's secretary, who offered to give up her bank holiday to drive me to the races. Both races were on television and I was so excited as we travelled down from Newmarket. In those days, one of the top apprentices who seemed to be getting all the limelight was Dale Gibson. I didn't know anyone in the weighing room, but suddenly this guy came up to me and announced: 'I'm Dale Gibson.' To say I was surprised is an understatement. He was very tall and really skinny, and to my eyes much too big ever to be a proper jockey. I was overawed by him, but I soon found out he is not only one of the nicest and most talented riders around, but also one of the most intelligent.

You have to realise that at this time my English had not developed much beyond writing out my betting slips in Ladbrokes, but now of course I was a jockey and could not bet any more! If I could, I might have had a pound each way on the first horse, Mustakbil, who was a 33–1 shot for the apprentice race. The horse was owned by Sheikh Hamdan Al-Maktoum and I didn't realise just how privileged I was riding for him on my first mount in England. We finished second, beaten a head by a horse ridden by Dennis McKay, and when I came in I must have been a little too full of myself. Mr Walwyn probably expected a polite 'thank you' and not much more from this raw apprentice and I'm sure now that my post-race comments were not the most sensible. When he asked me how did it go, I said: 'Not fit.' 'What?' came back the answer in best Basil Fawlty style. 'Not fit.' 'Not fit?' he repeated, and by now it was almost as much a comedy as the TV series. 'Not fit, too fat,' I concluded, and with that I took the saddle off and went straight into the jockeys' room. After that exchange, it may not surprise anyone that Peter 'banned' me for a year. My other mount was favourite, but, still excited after my initial 'success', I sent him off five lengths clear in a twenty-horse race and he stopped dead as soon as we got to the home straight.

The next morning, Mr Walwyn rang Luca and said: 'That chicken of an apprentice of yours told me one of my horses was too fat. He'll not ride for me for a year.' He was as good as his word, but a year later at Folkestone he gave me another chance on a sprinter of his. He was quite well fancied, second favourite for a six-furlong maiden race. We jumped out, and three strides out of the gate he whipped round and left me on my backside. I did not get another ride for Peter Walwyn until a few years later, when I rode in the 2,000 Guineas on Sheikh Hamdan Al-Maktoum's Mukaddamah.

It was appropriate that my first winner in England should be on the filly named after Lizzy Hare, my driver to Kempton that day and a lady to whom I owed a lot for all her help while she was Luca's secretary. Colin Rate, now my closest friend and a fellow apprentice in those days, looked after her namesake and rode the filly first time out at Yarmouth, where she finished out the back. Not surprisingly, Luca didn't fancy her chances in the race at Goodwood's evening meeting and Lizzy again drove me to the track. The favourite was a horse of Sheikh Hamdan's, trained by John Dunlop, who had finished very close up in a decent race at Ascot. Lizzy was a 12–1 shot and Colin, of course, led me up. By this time I'd had about ten rides. In the race I was pushing away at the three-furlong pole, on the inside. I came through inside Pat Eddery, my idol Steve Cauthen, and Gary Bardwell and went on to win. What a thrill to beat Steve and Pat, two great champions. Two weeks later, Lizzy Hare went back to Goodwood and won a handicap and she ended up winning the Del Mar Oaks at the beautiful track near San Diego in Southern California which stages top-class racing every summer.

My early wins luckily were noticed by Lester Piggott, who had set up as a trainer after his first retirement following his astonishing riding career. His stable was very well run and the winners soon flowed. One filly of his, Versatile Rose, was a great favourite of mine, and I lost both my 5lb claim on her at Leicester and my 3lb claim at Beverley. Apprentices can claim an allowance of 7lb, then 5lb and finally 3lb when competing against senior jockeys. They lose the claim either by riding a certain number of winners, or when they turn twenty-five. Versatile Rose had a more unfortunate 'fame' later on, though, as she was the horse on which Susan Piggott suffered serious injury when riding her in a gallop during the early days when she held the family's training licence. Lester was always very supportive, and even in the spring of 1996, following his final (who knows?) retirement from the saddle, he still looked a brilliant jockey when I regularly rode work with him for David Loder on the stable's classic candidates. The day after I lost my right to claim I was due to go to Catterick again. Traffic problems cost me my first ride without a riding allowance and naturally the horse won. I did not ride another winner for almost four weeks.

To become a top jockey does not simply involve the ability to ride horses well. Of course, that is the fundamental requirement, but there are plenty of good riders out there who may not have it for one reason or another when it comes to going to the track. Seventy per cent, I feel, is the ability to ride. Then other factors come in, like the ability to communicate with trainers and owners and the temperament to handle the sort of pressures involved in a business where split-second decisions can make a large difference both in financial and prestige terms. It also helps if you can be friendly with people. The man who shows up for work with a grumpy attitude is the first to be overlooked when an opportunity arises. I'm aware of the need to communicate with people, and very few people ever react badly to a smiling face, though, of course, it helps if you mean it.

My first real break, which made my initial spurt from just another jockey to one of the people in the limelight, was soon after I finished my claim. Luca did not have a stable jockey at the time I was going through my claim, but Ray Cochrane was riding quite a bit for him. He'd won the Oaks the year before on Midway Lady for Ben Hanbury and I would say Ray had a big influence on my becoming champion apprentice and always gave me plenty of confidence. Things went well for me for the next season and then in 1989 Ray eventually became stable jockey. One day at Newmarket, where I had the mount in an apprentice race, and Ray was riding Luca's other horses, Luca was trying to sort out his plans for the next day at Haydock. He said, 'Who shall I get to ride at Haydock? Shall I get Pat (Eddery)?' Ray pointed at me and said, 'Let him ride it.' Things like that give you plenty of confidence, especially when there are a lot of potential jockeys in a yard. Ray was always helping me and pushing me forward. While Ray rode all the good horses at the big meetings in the south, I would ride lots of winners in the north and Midlands.

After I lost my claim in the summer of 1989, I had a quiet patch for a month, and then in September the winners started to flow again. Here, fate was to take a hand. Ray had already decided to accept the offer of stable jockey for Guy Harwood in 1990, and I was already champion apprentice-elect. I rode more than 100 winners, equalling the achievement of Lester Piggott, the last apprentice to achieve a century, nearly forty years before. To think we would still be riding work together forty-eight years after his first winner on the racetrack is mind-boggling! Then, Ray was one of the jockeys involved in the terrible incident in the Portland Handicap at the September meeting at Doncaster. Ray was luckier than Paul Cook and Ian Johnson, neither of whom ever rode again, but he had a broken collarbone and had to take some time off and I got to ride all the horses. I'd been getting lots of publicity in the press thanks to my winning run in the days leading up to the accident.

I was lucky enough to be given the ride on Markof-distinction, one of the stable stars, in the Kiveton Park Steel Stakes, the following day at Doncaster. Markofdistinction was a hot favourite and all the senior jockeys had their eyes on the mount, but Gerald Leigh, his owner-breeder, very kindly stuck by me. I think I rode a good race but the ground was much too soft for Markofdistinction, and he finished second to Gold Seam. Happily, I only had to wait another twenty-four hours for my first Group-race win. Races in Britain are divided into seven distinct Classes, A, B, C, D, E, F, and G. The top grade, Class A, is sub-divided into three Groups, 1, 2 and 3. Races like the Derby are Group 1, but any owner's, trainer's or jockey's ambition is to win as many Group races as possible. They are all staged

on the most important tracks, almost all have national television coverage and carry plenty of prize money. My first
Group-race winner was Legal Case, owned by the late Sir
Gordon White, who was the main influence behind Ever
Ready's sponsorship of the Epsom Derby. Sir Gordon
worked closely with Lord Hanson and their Hanson Trust
was the parent company of Ever Ready during the years of
the sponsorship. Sir Gordon, known by everyone as Gordie,
was very popular and charismatic and his death at a relatively early age a couple of years ago was very sad. The St
Leger was postponed for a week that year and switched to
Ayr on the following Sunday. Michelozzo and Steve
Cauthen won it for Charles St George and Henry Cecil, and
even if my first Classic ride on N. C. Owen finished sixth,
the joy of being in that company so unexpectedly was
impossible to restrain.

It seemed that I could do no wrong. Luca's stable was flying, seemingly winning races every day and, with it being
common knowledge that Ray was moving next year, the
better I did, the better the chance the owners would accept
me as Ray's successor. One day Luca called me into the
office. He told me he had spoken to my dad and to the
owners and had decided he would not be employing a stable
jockey. Instead it was agreed that I would ride all the horses
without a retainer, but just a little money to get a car and a
driver. Most of the owners were happy with the arrangement, but apparently the only question mark was the Aga
Khan, for whom Ray had won the Derby in 1988 on
Kahyasi. Naturally, I leapt for joy as I left the office. I'd
travelled from my digs to the yard in a taxi – the little Mazda
I'd bought for £200 to learn in was rusty and you had to
hold the doors shut while driving. I ran home.

At the races that afternoon I did not have a particularly

good day and when I spoke to Gerald Leigh, who is one of the most successful owner-breeders in racing and the breeder of Barathea, who won the Breeders' Cup Mile for me, he said: 'I'm delighted you got the job but it may be a bit early. It could be like picking up a knife. If you grab it by the handle, you're okay: if you pick it up by the blade it can cut you and mark you for life.' Luckily for me, I started my first year – 1990 – in the Cumani job the right way. In a few days, at the two important early meetings at Newmarket and Sandown, I partnered three Group race winners: Mr Leigh's Markofdistinction in the Trusthouse Forté Mile at Sandown and Statoblest (Palace House Stakes) and Dick Hern's Roseate Tern (Jockey Club Stakes) both at Newmarket. It seems to me that I was at the right place at the right time, and took my opportunities when they came to me.

Sometimes in Britain you get the feeling that there is a little jealousy when someone does well. Luckily, in my case, the people I was working with at the Luca Cumani stable were good friends and true friends. They shared the enjoyment right from the first, when Colin Rate led up my first English winner, Lizzy Hare. As I went through my career, Colin, Andy Keates, my driver, and the rest of them were pleased for me and their reaction to me never changed in any way. Andy had a couple of rides without much luck, but he can always have that experience to help him understand what it means to be a jockey. Colin rode a little more, starting with Ben Hanbury, and had a winner or two. For apprentices in a big stable, it is hard to catch the eye of the boss and his leading people. It's hard, too, in England because school-leaving age is sixteen. By the time I was sixteen I'd had two years' experience with horses full time and was already a step ahead, without the help being my father's son obviously contributed. I suppose I was the blue-eyed boy!

Even within a stable, it gets competitive, whether it's on the gallops, where some lads I know treat every ride like the Derby, or, most important for the lads' future enjoyment, the allocation by the trainer of which young horses each lad will look after for the duration of their life in training. Usually, the main qualification is seniority and the senior lads get the best-bred, most expensive yearlings to look after. But the edge which Colin and I had was that, being light – Colin is only eight stone and I can still ride at around 8st 5lb – we were chosen to break in the new yearlings after we had been in the yard for two years. Each yearling you have to look after becomes your baby and each October you welcome your new son and/or daughter. Already, before it comes into the yard, you're dreaming, 'This is my Derby horse.' It's every stable lad's dream and obviously, in those days, it was mine.

Once the yearlings were bought to go into training with Luca, they were sent to his Fittocks stud, near Newmarket. Young racehorses are totally uneducated and the early days are the equivalent of a young person's schooling. The first step is to attach a long rope to the side of their bridle and teach them to travel in a circle. This is called lungeing and is often done in a sand ring. After they prove amenable and willing to run around in a circle, the next step is to put on a shadowroll and then the tack, trying to keep them calm and take them at whatever pace you can through this very traumatic period. We were the rodeo boys as we were light, and with yearlings, who are immature in every way, not least physically, the weight of a human body on their back can only be introduced gradually. We would lean with our stomachs on the horse's back a couple of times in the box, the horse already having been lunged by the other – heavier and stronger – lads for fifteen or twenty minutes so it was already a little tired and not fresh and ready to rear up. The next stage is to go into the ring with the horse. Again you would go and lie across his back and, still on a lunge rope, go a couple of laps like that before gradually getting your legs across him. In England this is always – in the major stables and at those studs which break in their home-breds – done in the proper way. Obviously, the time it takes to finish the process depends on the horse. Some are quick learners and the whole job is done within three or four days; in other cases, with a slow learner, it can take two to three weeks.

In Italy, in some of the places I've seen, the job is done in three days, *whatever*. The first day, you lunge them; the second, you put on the saddle and the rest of the tack; day three, you're on, rodeo style, riding them for your life. Under whichever method, by the time the process is done, the yearling is said to have been 'ridden away' and is (more or less) ready to go into the training yard with its trainer. In England, you let the horse get used to you. You have to be gentle. In those days I was much braver than I am now, and needed to be. I'm sure I could still do the job if need be and some jockeys enjoy breaking yearlings every autumn. I'm less keen on danger myself nowadays.

The trainers, busy at the yard, probably don't have either the personnel or the time themselves to ensure everything goes well, and I must confess that me and Colin were not always entirely professional in breaking yearlings. One winter in particular, at the height of the Pat Eddery–Steve Cauthen rivalry, Colin was a Pat fan, I was always Steve's follower. At Fittocks stud there was a little tack room where we would sit in front of the fire and wait for our time to go out with the horses. You would have two or three each to break every morning and after you had done that, you would then go back and continue the job with those you had broken the day before. On the last day before sending these particular yearlings to the yard, the Cauthen–Eddery rivalry spilt over into little private races with the yearlings. We took them to the paddock and pretended to be our respective heroes. Finally, we saved the two nicest ones for a big Classic race-off. Generally, we had merely trotted around the paddock, doing a Peter O'Sullevan commentary as we rode. With these two nice yearlings, both well behaved and quiet, after a couple of minutes we trotted them to the starting point, I waited for Colin to pair up and then we hacked to the telegraph poles, which acted as the finishing point. My horse had the better speed so I won that time and again the next two times. Then we had a great idea: the Gold Cup! Twice round the paddock, a total of around three furlongs, which after the earlier races was more than enough. We started the first lap at a sedate pace, going into a hack canter passing the line first time. The second time round we went at a nice swinging canter and just as we were finishing, getting close to a gallop, we were spotted by the head lad. The yearlings were blowing like mad, eyes bulging out of their heads. Everything had got a bit out of control. He had us in the tack room, and I still to this day cannot believe we never got the sack. The lucky thing for us was he didn't know this was the fourth race; he thought he caught us first time round! Fortunately, from what I remember, they both made it to the track and won races.

The reward for the lads doing the breaking in is that usually they get to make a choice from those they have been handling. I used to like to watch them when they were turned out in the paddock after being broken to see which ones looked like they wanted to run, and watch their action to see how quick they were. That year I selected a nice filly by the great stallion Danzig, whose sons and daughters were usually very good, out of a filly, Maria Weleska, who'd won the Italian Oaks. I chose her not just for her pedigree, but also because she was owned by Sheikh Mohammed, who, when he came to the stable, always gave the lads a drink. This filly took the maximum three weeks to break in. I rode her in the mornings for six months and she drove me crazy. She was a real neurotic woman and she gave me so much trouble. She drove me mad. Eventually, Mr Cumani took her off me, much to my relief. If those people in racing who are closest to the horses have no idea which is going to turn out okay, what chance have outsiders got? This filly proved that it's not always the good-looking ones that are the best, the ugly brutes can turn out better sometimes – just like people!

When I started riding, Lester Piggott had been the star rider for so many years and the generations around and just after him tried to adapt his style for themselves. Then, when Pat Eddery came to prominence, his style was the one to copy. When Steve Cauthen came to Britain, the second American age of race riding started. During the last century, Tod Sloan and his monkey-on-a-stick style was fashionable, but Steve Cauthen's success was much longer lasting. Strangely, Steve's own style was adapted for British racing; but several of the jockeys here tried to adapt his style for themselves. My father's famous words on the matter were: 'When you ride, always make an effort to look good.' I liked the look of the American style and when I saw videos of myself riding, I thought I looked neat. As it turned out, because other people thought I did look tidy, they never seemed to tell me how strong or otherwise I was in a finish. For the first couple of years riding in my style, I found it difficult, but my dad said if I kept my style, the strength would come later, and in my case it did. I'm fond of the American style. In some ways it's the same thing as riding a moped. On a moped if you want to go faster you crouch down. I suppose it's some sort of aerodynamic theory.

In the early days, if anything, I was trying too hard, crouching down from start to finish, and it's very hard physically. That's fine in America where they go flat out from the start and most of the races are shorter. Here, the pace tends to be slower and the races are longer, so I had to adapt the style. Once again it was Ray Cochrane who gave the crucial input. He would give me a kick up the bum, saying, 'Drop those jerks, you're riding too short.' That proved a really important influence and now I ride my races in two halves. Early in the race, I'm trying to relax my horses and then I'm rather higher in the saddle. Then, in the last half, when I want to go faster, I go into my American crouch. It seems to work and gives the best of both riding styles. Ray's own style is very effective and is based on strength. He is a good race-reader, but sometimes gets a little too opinionated. Like Luca though, he is a very strong character. I owe them both a lot.

For many small boys growing up, all it often takes is the suggestion 'You should try to be a jockey' and a love of animals, which many times they only find out about later, and they join the pilgrimage to one of the big stables. As I said before, even the pretty good riders, simply as riders, cannot be certain of getting more than a ride or two in a race. In ninety-five per cent of cases, the lads who start as apprentices with the ambition of making it as jockeys can only hope to be a senior stable lad. Then at least they stay in the mainstream of racing and training and still have the thrill of riding a powerful, classy thoroughbred, if only on the gallops in the morning, rather than in the Derby or the Breeders' Cup. Without the influx, it would be impossible to train all the horses which enter stables. As I explained earlier, you need the lighter lads to break in the delicate yearlings and ride the faster work with the actual jockeys. There are too many horses to 'work' – gallop fast – each day for there to be enough licensed jockeys to go round. So we tend to be selective, only getting involved in the work of the better horses or to assess a young horse for one of our trainers before its début. Ability, natural light weight, temperament, and the right attitude to work are helpful but do not guarantee success. You also need opportunity, and, if you are at the end of a line of promising boys, determination to succeed is then most important.

The snag for most who fail to make it as jockeys is that usually they have come out of studying at a time when many of their old schoolfriends may have stayed at school to gain qualifications. The experience of being outdoors in all weathers, wonderful as it can be on a nice summer morning, and tolerable at best in winter, plus the enjoyment of working with horses, often makes office work an unattractive prospect. Instead, they stay on as stable lads, work riders or as stud hands. Even though the wages in the industry are below those in many office jobs, it is a lifestyle they find hard to give up.

Throughout the racing business there are men like Gozzie, an old stableman who had a few rides in his apprentice days. He worked for Luca until his time to take retirement aged sixty-five. He was a work rider when I got there, and was just a little way off retiring at the end of my eight years. And to tell you how long he had the job, my dad, who had ridden some horses for Italian owners when Luca had first started training twenty years ago, used to say: 'Is that guy Gozzie still there?'

For Gozzie, every work day was the Derby. Racing needs people like him. Every horse he rode got the same all-action treatment. Not all horses go sweetly along and respond to a light touch. Gozzie pushed all the way and many horses in training need just that encouragement. Most of the Gozzie types are just the same. Small, tough, little weather-beaten men. True men of Newmarket.

3 Overcoming a Crisis

It was during my time with Luca Cumani that I learnt nearly all I know about race-riding. I did have some experience in Italy, not all of it entirely helpful, and obviously the knowledge imparted by my dad was valuable, but when I got to England I was still very rough around the edges. At Luca's I picked up the finer points, and the good thing about the place was that in Stuart Jackson, the head lad, there was never a chance that you would get big-headed. Suppose I had been to the track and ridden a winner, when I got back you could bet your life that Stuart would be waiting out of sight for when I came in for evening stables to do my horses. Suddenly he'd appear and give me a massive kick up the backside to remind me that my job hadn't ended just because I'd been lucky enough to ride a winner, or a 'steering job' that anyone else could have ridden given the chance.

Being at Luca's stable was very good for me professionally.

He moved me up one step at a time. But in some ways it was always a little difficult. Luca is a very strong-minded man, and he was always very much the boss. While I was there, in the early stages of my time in the job, I was still one of the stable workers. I would come in every morning to look after my horses, feed them and ride work and then in the afternoon, go to the races. In some ways it was a help, because it would prevent you getting too big-headed, but as the relationship developed and altered neither I nor Luca knew how to handle it. Eventually, although I had everything I ever wanted, I didn't realise it and wasn't happy and I certainly was not enjoying my job.

By the time I was in my fourth year as stable jockey I felt I was being held back and that other opportunities which might have come my way were being denied me and I felt I was missing out. That was one of the reasons why I decided to accept the offer of a job in Hong Kong. The job carried the promise of a lot of money and at the time that was my reason to myself why I was taking it, but, in reality, the reason was much more the dissatisfaction with my life. I spoke about the offer to my dad, instead of to Luca, who should, I now realise, have been the first to know. When the news came out, Luca heard about it from someone else before I talked to him. I had already decided to leave, and the Hong Kong thing made it easier, but the way it came out left a bad taste. In the long run, the break between Luca and me was the best thing that could have happened at the time, but Luca was very upset and we took a long while to become friends again. For my part, though, I had been with the man, a great trainer, for eight years and learnt a great deal, around ninety per cent of what I believe I needed to become a good jockey. It would be a couple of years before I found the man who could offer that elusive missing ten per cent – John Gosden.

In between, came the most traumatic period of my life. When I left Luca, my entire concentration was on the forthcoming job in Hong Kong, but during autumn 1992 there was a lot of experimenting by young people with drugs. They were freely available in many places and, like many young people at the time, I felt some curiosity and decided to try it. One night, during that winter, I was in a club in London and bought a small quantity of cocaine. You would have to say I was naïve and, in retrospect, the fact that I was searched by the police, who found the drugs on me, was the best thing that could have happened at the time. I was not actually charged with any offence, but Hong Kong and much of the Far East has a very strict public stance on drugtaking, so the fact that I was given a police caution and the massive publicity which my being cautioned caused, was enough for the Hong Kong authorities to revoke the offer of a job there that year. The shock of that decision woke me up, made me realise I was not working at my job and that drugs were not for me. Since then I've always advised anyone who mentions drugs to keep well away from them. I also saw just how distressing that sort of newspaper and media attention can be. If the press are with you it can be great fun and very rewarding. When they want to bring you down, fairly or unfairly – this time the reports were inevitable, I suppose – their power is amazing. People in the public eye have to be whiter than white, and I've had no wish to be anything else from that point on.

During this difficult period, when the papers were doing their best to finish me off, the first person to help me was Barney Curley. I have known Barney since I was about eighteen years old. I saw a television programme and ever since then I have been fascinated by him. He was a guest in a late-night TV show called *After Dark*, on which John McCririck, the racing broadcaster, was also on the panel. The show consisted of several guests sitting round a table, and the subject was 'The Sport of Kings'. For much of the time, Barney sat very quietly, but every time he opened his mouth he made a lot of sense. He made a big impact on me. His character fascinated me. I found when I gradually got to know him that he was a very deep person. He was training about eight horses, and, just to get to know him better, I was glad to ride for him. I rode three or four of the horses, and, almost every time he asked me to ride for him, the horses won.

Barney is well known for being a shrewd operator as a trainer, but to me he was always a very nice person. He always likes to do good things for other people. So when I won a race on one of his horses, I was glad to have achieved something for him, and not let him down. It was never a question of money or even my own success. Then, in the spring of 1993, when I was at my lowest ebb, Barney was tremendously supportive. For a period of a few weeks, I was what you could call 'Zero Man'. I'd lost my confidence and was just drifting into obscurity, I suppose. Then one day Barney gave me a call. Barney is very religious, like me, and maybe that's our first real point of contact. Anyway, I went to his house, and we played snooker. Despite the publicity, I knew he felt I was a nice person.

Then we sat down and he said: 'Look, you have had the good fortune to have a God-given ability to ride horses. You must go out there and just ride. What's done is done.' Those words were the most important I'd ever heard. 'Just go out and ride', and that made me fight on. That year helped me a lot to find myself. Barney said that what happened to me had happened to thousands of other people. He made me understand that I had had too much, too early in my life. Too much achievement and too much money. The thing I thought I was looking for I already had in my hands. In those days, I never really worked at anything. All I wanted to do was wait for the weekend and party. I never worked at any aspect of my job, just went through the motions in the mornings, ate the easiest things whenever I felt hungry and never studied form – I was simply lazy. I suppose in those days, that was my reputation and I deserved it.

Money in those days was something to spend as fast as you made it. Nowadays, for me, money is a vehicle for security. Britain is a good place to live and work. For me, it's the best. No one bothers you, and the tax system, which has a maximum forty per cent deduction on even the highest earners, encourages people to play it straight. In the old days, the racing game was full of people with bags full of cash, or so the old-timers in the weighing room have told me. Now, everything is above board. The money, even presents from a winning owner, go straight into the bank, and into the official accounts. I have enough money for my needs, and now, in many ways, I am rich – not in the financial way of judging it, but now for me being rich is being happy with yourself. I can claim that, and I have the good fortune to love the job I do.

Being a believer in God came easy to a Catholic boy living in Italy. In those days, naturally, I went to church regularly. Now, I am even more sure there has to be a God. How else could the world and everything in it have been created? Different religions believe in slightly different things, but they have one thing in common: a greater being which controls everything. I also believe in life after death, and therefore try to do good in my life, to use the gift I've been given and care for other people. I ride my horses and in the meantime behave like a normal person.

When a person in the public eye is successful, inevitably he will attract attention from people for various commercial reasons. They will try to use his talents and the fact he is well known to give themselves a lift. So they use me as a ladder, just as on my way up I had to find my own ladder. The problem for someone in the public eye is where to draw the line on all the offers that are sure to come your way. Then you need to sort out the time to work, the time to play, and to be normal. Also, as you become well known, the press, which in this country seems very quick to take people up as they become established, are also ready to knock them down at the first opportunity. I believe that the press, remembering how they pushed me down during my troubles, respect me more for getting back on top.

When the door to Hong Kong closed, at least I still had the option to prove myself in the big arena of English racing. This time, though, I had to roll up my sleeves and start again from scratch with no safe job in a big stable to make things easier for me. Luckily, at the start of 1993, I bumped into another young guy who had something to prove. David Loder had just begun training in the Sefton Lodge stables, which had been the base for Charles St George's horses which Henry Cecil trained for him. The St George string operated virtually as a self-contained unit. Sadly, in 1992, Charles St George had died and his brother Edward, who lives in the Bahamas, where he runs the Grand Bahama Port Authority with Sir Jack Hayward, the owner of Wolverhampton Wanderers, took over.

Edward St George decided to operate the stable independently of Henry Cecil, and, in the autumn of 1992, he appointed David Loder, who had been assistant trainer with Geoff Wragg, as trainer of his family horses. David's family had had a long involvement with racing ownership and breeding and his cousin Edmund bred and raced the brilliant fillies Marwell and Marling. Like me, when 1993 started, David had something to prove, and he and I teamed up. Both of us were hungry for winners. To that extent we used each other. The winners began to flow. I was on my way back and David was starting his very quick rise towards the top of the training profession. In spring 1993, too, I had plenty to thank Ian Balding for. Especially his great mare Lochsong, who was making her own strides towards the top of her tree. Gradually, thanks to Ian and David and many other small stables which also helped me, my rehabilitation began and when at the end of the year John Gosden took me on as stable jockey it was pretty much complete.

Apart from his friendship, I will always have a debt to Barney Curley because it was he who first introduced me to John. I did know him slightly, but Barney made me wait for the right time before he introduced us properly. We had a chat and at the end of 1993, I was lucky to be appointed to the job of stable jockey. Even that did not go totally smoothly. We had a brief chat at the end of September, but somehow the news got out. That was unfortunate because at the time Michael (Muis) Roberts was the official jockey for Sheikh Mohammed, having taken over the job when Steve Cauthen had retired from riding and had gone back to America. We hadn't settled anything, but, obviously, John was Sheikh Mohammed's principal trainer, and when it came out that I would be joining John's stable, it was embarrassing for Muis Roberts.

Of all the people I have met in racing, John Gosden is the most straightforward. He is always to the point, and allows you the chance to stretch yourself to the limit. In racing, with many other people it's 'me, me, me' all the time. The difference with John is that he wants you to do well, to achieve something for yourself. If you do well, he's pleased for you. It's only in England, in my experience, that that happens in the jockeys' room. I think it's because racing in England is like a very big pie, and for the leading jockeys there's plenty of pie to go round. In other countries, when someone wins the Derby everyone else hates them as there may be few other big races where they can catch up. The saying goes, 'Racing tames lions', but here I think we jockeys at least share each other's successes and enjoy them.

When I first got the job with John, he told me he wanted me to achieve something; to become champion jockey. He told me he would not tie me down, that if his stable had one horse going to Carlisle and I could ride four outside favourites the same day at Kempton, I could stay in the south. I knew I would need all the help I could get and John said he would not stand in my way in those circumstances. John looks at both sides of the coin and decides what's best for everyone. He's not selfish, so I've been very lucky to work with him.

After the first season, he also helped introduce me to the Godolphin operation of Sheikh Mohammed, which has had such a beneficial effect on my career. Knowing John has given me that extra ten per cent I was looking for, if I had known I was looking for it, that is. Nowadays, I realise that life is not just riding horses. That extra factor is peace of mind, and now, riding good horses and living a rewarding life, I'm the happiest man in the world. I'm in control of my life, and with John as your boss, you are also in control of the horses. He allows you to do what you want on a horse and make the split-second decisions you think will make the difference in riding a race. That freedom in your job is everything for a jockey.

Every day of my life, I had wanted to work for Sheikh Mohammed. He had 450 horses in training, a huge monster of an operation. Steve Cauthen held down the job of stable jockey for two years, Michael Roberts for just one season, and they found dealing with thirty different trainers an impossible situation. I always wondered whether working for Sheikh Mohammed would eat you alive. But John organised things so that while I was Sheikh Mohammed's jockey, the contract was really with his stable. To do things that way, John was putting his head on the line. Look at it from his viewpoint: he was putting up this boy, even though he didn't really know me. Even if he saw that I had changed from how I was a year before, he had everything to lose if things went wrong. But he just said: 'I'll back you up, it's all in your hands.'

His saying that made me more determined to pay him back, to show his confidence in me was not a mistake, that it was the correct decision that he had made. It was just the extra stimulation I needed to prove myself.

At the end of the season, having come second in the jockeys' championship with 149 winners, I took a two-week break in Italy. In the meantime, I'd met Catherine and we were going out together by then, but as part of my preparation for the following year I went on from Italy to Morocco, and didn't take Catherine with me, just a Walkman, ten tapes and went into virtual isolation. I started to listen to my dad. He and my stepmother were also there, but I was so focused, so inside myself, that apart from listening to some excellent advice from him, I was a real loner.

He emphasised just how crucial it would be to get to my

lowest weight before the start of the season. He said, 'If you do that and from the beginning have no weight worries, you can concentrate properly on what you have to do.' He said my mind would be right and that there would be one less thing to worry about.

Talking to Dad and also before the holiday to John, we realised that we could take advantage of what amounted to a loophole. I was very keen to improve on my second place and become champion for the first time. With John and Sheikh Mohammed, as well as my other loyal stables to back me up, I thought I had a chance, and reckoned that if I rode the entire all-weather season in January and February, I could get a big start on Pat Eddery and the other jockeys of the old school who never rode on the sand tracks. I felt I had something to prove to myself, my dad and John.

I would get back from Morocco on 31 December, ready to ride on New Year's Day, and hoping that by working hard I could get a flying start of maybe twenty winners before Pat and the others got going. So back in Morocco I lived the life of a hermit. In the morning I would get up and have a single cup of coffee. In the afternoon I would drink a bottle of Evian water and then every day go to the local market. I'd buy a big fish, grill it and eat it for dinner. Then, at night, I would go out and walk the beach alone with my tapes and my Walkman. I'd talk to myself, hardly at all to my parents. By the end of the time, my weight was down to 8st 1lb, my lightest for more than five years. I had my hair cut short. The whole idea was to create a new image of myself, and with my new look, short hair and gaunt, sun-tanned face, I looked older and meaner, as I had intended. But the image was for myself – for me to see when I looked in the mirror every day – to remind me to do things differently, to behave differently outwardly and inside myself. I was a man with a mission, and the new look would remind me how vital it was I remembered it. We decided, John, my dad and me, that I would not talk to the press, no interviews, just try to prove myself.

At the start of the all-weather, apart from hoping for about twenty winners, I didn't really have a target. I had met Catherine the previous September, and was certain I would eventually marry her. But in January 1994 I had to be brutal and unkind. I said, 'I'm very sorry, let me go out there and work. I'm not trying to be nasty, but I've no time for you. If I do this to the best of my ability, it will make a difference to our lives for the next forty years.' She agreed, and I did 'go out there and just ride', as Barney would have me do, and by the start of the turf season I had fifty-one winners and it was almost wrapped up before we started.

Needless to say, there were people trying to whip up a controversy, saying the winners should not count towards the title. The situation hadn't occurred before because when it was Steve Cauthen or Pat Eddery or Muis Roberts or Willie Carson, none of them ever got involved on the all-weather, which in those days was not so extensive anyway. My view was that I'd earned every one of those fifty-one winners, working my butt off in the freezing cold at Wolverhampton, Southwell and Lingfield. It was bloody hard work, nothing more or less. I was just like the other guys who have to keep going every year on the all-weather, picking up what the big boys leave them. One Saturday, I remember I had five rides in the afternoon at Lingfield, and then had to drive like a maniac for the seven o'clock start at the Wolverhampton floodlit meeting, where I had five more rides. Wolverhampton is great, with its lovely, warm, glass-fronted restaurant where the punters spend a pleasant

Saturday night betting, eating and drinking. Meanwhile, beyond the glass and in the cold, the temperature, including wind-chill, was reckoned to be ten degrees below freezing, and there we were – me, my friend Jason Weaver, Jimmy Quinn, Lindsay Charnock, Tony Clark and the rest of us – all trying to win a percentage of six little £2,000 races.

So right through January and February of 1994, I kept a pledge to myself: to stay hard and lean, to work, and, with the help of Matty, my agent, to get the rides I needed to give me that edge in the race for the title, while Pat Eddery and the others were still enjoying their regular winter break. I was determined also to keep another pledge, and therefore stayed firmly with the idea of not talking to the press. The coverage a year earlier had been so distressing that I wanted to prove a point. Even when the winners started to come, as they did with ever-increasing regularity, I thought, 'Suppose I came off a horse and broke a leg, they would all be calling me a loser again.' I felt that as long as I kept remote and no one could get close, I would be able to get on with it. At the end of the all-weather programme in early March, my dad and stepmother came to stay with me for the whole of the spring and summer.

The fact that they were there was obviously a help. I didn't have to worry much about normal things. The house was looked after and my meals were prepared for me. All I had to do was keep fit and get ready to do my job. It must have been very hard for my parents. Probably, I was trying too hard with my riding and it was not much fun for them. Because my dad was a champion jockey and able to go and watch the races every day in the betting shop in the town, we soon got to analysing every ride. Every race I lost, I felt I had made a mistake and that used to daunt me. I believed that I needed every winner possible if I was to become champion. One lost race could make all the difference. My dad had the same attitude. So, as I said, he would go and watch every one of my rides and, if he reckoned I'd given a horse a bad ride, that night we would argue about it for one and a half hours or more. There was no escape. He was a champion jockey for thirty years and is the one person in the world that I could not bullshit. He was my dad, too.

For all that, the summer came and went, and the parents went back to Italy. All the time I was stretching my lead over Jason Weaver, who had also got going on the all-weather, back in those freezing winter days. By 1 September I had already reached 200 for the year and, with the title already just about guaranteed, there was even talk that I would break Sir Gordon Richards's record of 269 in a year. I knew, however, that this would not be possible, as my winning opportunities were beginning to dry up, and, with very little all-weather racing to come after November, there were just about eight weeks left. So, Sir Gordon was safe, but I did have my eyes on another great champion's record, and this time it was the score of 229.

And the name of this particular record holder? No, it wasn't Piggott, who never actually got to 200 in a season, or Eddery, or Carson. The name was Gianfranco Dettori, multiple champion in Italy. Anyway, with 200 by 1 September it should have been a cinch, but as is liable to happen when the meetings thin out in the early autumn, I hit a really quiet spell. The good rides were harder to come by and it became a question of working even harder, grinding out the winners one at a time. I got to the required figure of 230 by 19 October and by then I knew that the Richards record was well out of reach. It's just as well it was, for by then I was gone, physically and mentally drained. I was going out to the track every day to ride horses because I had to. The relief of getting to 230 and beating the Old Man was immense. I realised straight away that I couldn't manage another step. Already I'd had more than 1,000 rides and wanted to quit there and then.

All year, my dad had been pushing me to the limit. Now I was at the top and couldn't get any further, so I spoke to him. He told me to take a step back, and I decided that because I had a strong book of rides already arranged for the Breeders' Cup meeting in Churchill Downs, Kentucky, the following month, it would be sensible to take a fortnight off, and then go out to the Breeders' Cup a few days early. It turned out to be the best career decision in my life. I arrived in Louisville, Kentucky, birthplace of the great heavyweight boxing champion Muhammad Ali, a few days before the meeting and was able to ride track work on Lochsong, the great sprint mare, Barathea, Only Royale and Belle Genius. They were all great rides and I had taken advantage of my nice rest to be prepared for one big, final effort.

One of the best things to come from the 1994 season was my association with Lochsong. Her trainer Ian Balding had been one of the first, with David Loder, to show his confidence in me the previous year when events had been going against me, and by the following year, when she was a six-year-old, she was assuredly the favourite racehorse in Britain. Considering that the public are generally quicker to appreciate the best jump horses, as they are around for much longer, this affection for Lochsong was unusual. For a sprinter, as far as I can recall, and from what other jockeys and people in racing tell me, this public affection was unique.

It is easy to understand the appeal of Lochsong. She had the most amazing speed and at five furlongs you only had to point her in the direction of the winning post, and, in her prime, at five and six, she would do the rest. At six furlongs, she was vulnerable, especially if, as sometimes happened, she went to post too free. By the time she got to the starting gate, her race would sometimes be run, and on the way back the last furlong would seem like a mile. So she was in some ways a flawed genius, but the flaws were worth putting up with along with the ecstasy of her best days. As I said after one of her best days, 'She's like Linford Christie without the lunch-box.' Sorry, Linford, but she was certainly a gold-medal performer, even if destiny would not smile on her in racing's Olympics, the Breeders' Cup.

By November 1994, though, her fame and prestige could hardly have been higher. She broke the Newmarket five fur-long record by half a second in the Palace House Stakes; easily won Sandown's Temple Stakes, and the King's Stand Stakes at Royal Ascot was virtually a trap-to-line exhibition. The other side of the coin, however, were her 'bolting going to the start' runs in the July Cup at Newmarket and the Nunthorpe at York. By the time we went to Longchamp – she won between the two disappointments at Goodwood – there were those who reckoned she was as temperamental as she was talented. Anyone at Longchamp for the Prix de l'Abbaye that year went home with a different picture. This time, thanks to the co-operation of the understanding French stewards, Lochsong was allowed to walk to the start, saving all that precious energy for the race itself. We exploded from the stalls, came up the middle of the track and the first I saw of any other horse was when we pulled up, apart from a crafty peep which told me we were five lengths clear of the best sprinters in Europe.

And so to Churchill Downs. The test would be severe, in that the Americans go flat out from the start, but also as it was to be on dirt and round a turn, both totally unusual for Lochsong. It was a sporting challenge by Ian and Lochsong's owner-breeder Jeff Smith, and when Lochsong warmed up with her now famous three-furlong work a couple of days before the Breeders' Cup Sprint, she had the locals checking their clocks to see if they had stopped. Lochsong covered that distance around a bend in thirty-three seconds, and when she trailed home in the actual race, finishing tailed off, having chipped a bone in her knee, I had to wonder whether that flying spin had caused it. Still, my other three rides were all good prospects: Barathea, winner of the Irish 2,000 Guineas and the Queen Anne Stakes at Royal Ascot, was going for the Mile; Belle Genius in the Juvenile Fillies had previously won the Moyglare Stakes in Ireland; and Only Royale, who ran in the Turf race, had been just about the easiest winner of the year when she'd run away with the Yorkshire Oaks at York.

They all ran well. Belle Genius, showing that Paul Kelleway, her trainer, knew what it took to challenge the best horses in the world, ran a great third in the Juvenile Fillies race behind the flying pair Flanders and Serena's Song. Injury did not enable Flanders's career to develop but two seasons later Serena's Song was still racking up the dollars in Group 1 company. Only Royale did not disgrace herself, finishing fifth behind Tikkanen in the Turf race, but the best result was her trainer's, Luca Cumani's, other challenger, Barathea. To win the race for Britain and Europe would always be important, but, at that time, European jockeys were getting a bad press in the United States. The owners and trainers there seemed to believe that our jockeys could not match their best riders on their tracks. When you think of it, that made no sense. I would say that American tracks are the easiest to ride. They are all the same shape, oval, and most are little more than a mile round. There is the odd exception, like Belmont Park, New York, where the dirt track is, by American standards, very big. True, things sometimes change when it rains and you get differences in the surface, but, as I said, the tracks over there are easy to ride.

So when Barathea won I was doubly delighted. It is not often that you win a race with a purse of two million dollars and a first prize of more than a million. But it wasn't the prize money or the importance of the occasion which most pleased me. It was the knowledge that I had made a point on behalf of my friends and colleagues in the weighing rooms up and down the country. A country in which the tracks are so different and you have to get to know them all. Their ups and downs; whether they are right- or left-handed. Where the best ground usually is. On which course you can ride a waiting race. On which ones it's better to be up near the leaders or ride from the front. We believe we are the most versatile jockeys in the world, so to win in America you really only need to have the right horse. That year at Churchill Downs I had the tools to do the job and the job got done.

There was also the point for me that for the first time I was going to another country as the champion jockey of the country in which I live and work. I am an Italian, but my home now is England. It's the place I enjoy working in. Ask any of the famous jockeys around the world where they would like to go to prove themselves and if they are being honest they will all tell you 'England'. It's a great country to live in, and horse racing in England has far more prestige than in almost any other country. Television coverage on the major networks is exceptional compared with France, America and even Ireland, and the public in England care as much about the horses as they do about who won and at what odds. After Barathea won there was a whole range of emotions for me, all of them positive. For me, 1994 had been a fantastic year. There was achievement and also the feeling of pride that I had been able to give something back to the people who had shown so much faith in me – especially to John Gosden. But then, of course, we had come to the end of the year of my first championship. To prove it was no fluke, I would have to do it all over again the next year.

4 Champion Jockey

The start of the 1995 season for me was much more relaxed than the previous year. Naturally, I was happy to begin the year as champion, but it soon became obvious that there would be a battle between Jason Weaver and me for the title. We were both ready for action from the start of the all-weather season, and planned to go right down to the wire in November. We had been good friends for a long time and I felt I could always relate to him. We were both at Luca Cumani's as apprentices. He came there a couple of years after me. He's a year younger, but I always believed he was doing all the right things, and I tried to offer him my best advice as we were making it towards the top together.

But in 1995, for the first time, we began to clash. We had always been good friends, but now the media attention on what everyone thought would become a championship battle between us started to have an effect. Friends and parents were pushing us both to the limit and we started to get in each other's way. Like me, he had ridden more than 200 winners the year before, his first year with Mark Johnston's powerful Yorkshire stable, but now he would be in the mainstream in Newmarket.

I suppose our conflict began when Jason got his job riding for David Loder. Like me, when I rode for David's stable in 1993, Jason had no contract, but at the beginning of the year he had the ride on all the horses at Sefton Lodge. Horses that, the year before, I would have been able to ride were now being ridden by Jason, who was pleased to stay in the south and ride at all the big meetings. This suited him much better than the previous year when, it seemed, he often had to travel north from his home in Newmarket when the rest of us were running in big races. You can imagine how disappointed he used to get when he had to go 200 miles north for a couple of rides in small races, when the biggest prizes were on offer a mile or two from his home in Newmarket.

The conflict started on the all-weather. David ran some of his horses as usual in February and Jason made a good start to the season. Like me the year before, he worked very hard and his stables were in good form. So he won plenty of races, and for the first time in his life found himself in front of me, rather than pressing up from behind. I was a little upset about that, I suppose, and Jason started to make a couple of jokes about it. Things went on from that. I see now that I was sour about it and Jason got sour, too. Before that we had a great friendship. Now the sourness, probably made worse by the attitude of everyone around us, especially the press, but also family and friends, spoilt our friendship.

So, to cut a long story short, we had a fall-out. When I look back, I can see I was feeling nasty in a childish way about him. I'd watch out for his rides, whether we were riding together or at different meetings. If he didn't have a winner during the day, I'd think, 'Great.' If he did, I'd be miserable. I was not living my own life. I was living it through him and his successes or failures. For about six weeks I was feeling really hurt. A year later, I was able to look back and had to admit it wasn't Jason's fault. But then it probably wasn't mine either. There was definitely a case of the press wanting to make us jealous of each other. The split between us was totally out of character. Then Jason lost the job with David Loder, and at the same time my stables started to get going. I also got back some of the rides for David.

Without quite matching the score of the previous year, I was able to retain the championship, but when I sat down and thought about the business with Jason I realised how stupid it had been. We sat down together and sorted it out. We agreed we had both been silly. Why had we fallen out? Only for a silly old championship. Friendship is worth more. It was a good lesson for both of us. The price of success.

Friendship means a lot to me. Many of the jockeys are good friends, and with the success I have enjoyed I realise how lucky I am in my life. When I was younger, not working very hard with my job, I had no idea what I wanted. Now I want nothing to change. If anything, I have too much of everything. My job is very satisfying: riding good horses for nice people who understand the animals. And my personal life is marvellous. I am one of those lucky people who knew when I had met the person with whom I wanted to spend the rest of my life.

Catherine, my fiancée, is from a racing family, as her father Twink Allen is an expert in the horse breeding industry. Catherine is reading for her degree but as she has always ridden she also enjoys riding out in the morning. I had noticed her while I was at David Loder's, as she worked there for a couple of months during her holidays. One day, Catherine took a filly to run in a race at Haydock and I was riding the filly. I was not in a good mood as the filly was carrying 8st 4lb, which is my absolute minimum, so I felt quite grumpy. The only thing to cheer me up was seeing Catherine leading up the filly. As she held the filly while I got up in the paddock, I asked her, 'Can I take you out for a date?' She didn't answer, so I said, 'Give me your phone number.' Catherine said, 'You won't remember it anyway.' But she still told me. So we went out for the race and when I came back after the race I repeated the number correctly. So we arranged to go out to the pictures. I must say I was very nervous. It was during the time when I was being most hard on myself, trying to sort things out and I hadn't had a girlfriend for a year. So we went to a cinema in Cambridge. I went to pick her up and Catherine was wearing bright pink lipstick. Outside of racing I'd never met the girl, yet I said, 'I don't like girls with make-up.' She didn't say anything then, but she hasn't worn any make-up since. She says she didn't usually wear any anyway.

I thought it would probably not be easy retaining my championship, but it didn't take long to see that the ammunition I had to call on was going to enable me to win some pretty big races in the 1995 season. The Godolphin team came back to England in brilliant shape, and with Moonshell as my ride in the 1,000 Guineas, I knew she could be anything. Godolphin have their horses in work in Dubai right until the time they fill up the planes to England with the animals, their grooms for the journey, and all the equipment they need. Another part of the stable staff is sent ahead to England to make sure their new accommodation is ready when they step off the planes. It's important that everything is right, because there's no time for any mistakes. Within a day or so of arriving, the 1,000 Guineas is on us and the horses have to be ready.

Some cold winters in England in recent years have left trainers tearing their hair out in frustration. It's a delicate balance to time a horse's preparation for a big race. If on the day the trainer wants to work his horse in a serious Classic gallop it has been raining hard and the ground is too soft, or if winter drags on too long and it leaves the horses with shaggy coats, they will probably not be able to show their best form. Fillies, especially, can suffer in that way in a cold English winter and when the horses came into the paddock for the 1,000 Guineas of 1995 Moonshell's coat, bursting with the healthy sheen that weeks of warm sun had given it, stood out against some of the others. She had raced only once before as a two-year-old for the Henry Cecil stable, and won a maiden race nicely, but it was going to be a big step from a maiden race to a Classic, with a mile probably short of her ideal trip.

Moonshell ran a great race, coming in third. When we came back afterwards, the family – she was in the joint-ownership of Sheikh Maktoum Al-Maktoum, the ruler of Dubai, and Godolphin, run by his brother Sheikh Mohammed – was very happy. Naturally, that was because the winner, Harayir, ridden by Richard Hills, is owned by another brother, Sheikh Hamdan. He rode her because Willie Carson, Sheikh Hamdan's first jockey, chose Aqaarid instead. She was second and that made it a clear sweep for the Maktoum family. We were just as happy as we all knew Moonshell's chance would come when she went a mile and a half for the Oaks. The Godolphin magic, which we'd seen the year before with my great favourite Balanchine, who'd won the Epsom Oaks and Irish Derby, was still working, luckily for me!

I didn't have a ride in the 2,000 Guineas, so missed out on the first two English Classic races of the year, but if I had been able to look into a crystal ball I would not have been able to believe my eyes. I was to win twelve Group 1 races in Europe during the year. Considering there are only seventy-three of these in Europe's major racing countries – Great Britain, France, Ireland, Italy and Germany – this was to be an unbelievable year, especially when, as an English-based jockey, I was to win six of the twenty-five Group 1 races in France. I'd already won my first: I had been delighted when, at Longchamp in late April, the five-year-old, Pelder, had been a very easy winner for his owner, my compatriot Osvaldo Pedroni.

Pelder was originally trained in Italy, but was switched to Newmarket into the care of Paul Kelleway. Some people find Paul's nickname, Pattern-race Paul, amusing, but he earned it with his many wins in major races, despite always having a small team in his yard, a few steps down the road from John Gosden's stable on Bury Road. Pelder is a horse who had to have soft ground, and when he got it he was a match for anything. He got the mud that day in Paris and beat the champion hurdler Alderbrook, by then back with Julie Cecil after his winter with Kim Bailey, by three lengths. Some hot French horses were behind that day and Freedom Cry, a horse I would encounter another day on the same Longchamp track, made the form look very solid.

I had to wait only a week after the two English Guineas races for my next classic, and therefore Group 1 win, and again it was at Longchamp. I was to ride a horse whose name should have given someone the idea of writing a poem, something like:

> A jockey called Frankie Dettori,
> Won a French classic race on Vettori,
> It sounded strange at the time, that their names made
>   a rhyme,
> But I tell you, it is a true story.

Perhaps it's as well that nobody did!

Vettori was not the best Classic winner I'll ever ride, but he took his chance to beat the best horses that the French trainers could put out against him. In the end, we beat Atticus, a horse with a big reputation trained by the brilliant Criquette Head, with the rest nowhere. The Godolphin knack at winning first time out was also still working. John's horses, too, were flying at this stage, and, the same afternoon at Longchamp, we won another Group 1 together, with Flemensfirth, owned by Sheikh Mohammed. John had a great spring, and we were back in France again the weekend before the Epsom Derby meeting, with Flemensfirth once more, this time in the Prix du Jockey Club, the French equivalent of the Derby. This was a tougher test for Flemensfirth and he ran a good race, but was only fifth this time. Still, it wasn't too bad, with the much-hyped Celtic Swing, the champion two-year-old of 1994, winning, Winged Love, next time out the winner of the Irish Derby, in third, and none other than Classic Cliché, of whom more later, in fourth. The day was not unfruitful, though, as we won the Prix Jean Prat over nine furlongs with John's Torrential, another Sheikh Mohammed horse.

My own tally of winners in ordinary races was also going quite nicely by this time, and I was in great shape as I went out to ride Moonshell in the Oaks at Epsom five days later. Willie Carson was again on Aqaarid and she was favourite even though her stamina was less certain than Moonshell's.

In the race it was no contest between them, but the two Michael Stoute fillies Dance A Dream and Pure Grain made us work for the big prize. Moonshell would not be denied and won nicely by a little more than a length. The Maktoum family have an amazing record in the Oaks, but for the relatively small Godolphin team to win for the second time in a row was fantastic. I was delighted to win and delighted for everyone in the team as I came back. Twenty-four hours later, the same mile and a half at Epsom brought a different reaction from me to a Godolphin win. I was glad for them that Lammtarra won, but I'd rather he'd have let Tamure and me stay ahead for the last few yards instead of flying past as he did just when I thought I'd won the Derby.

Some jockeys wait a lifetime for the one big horse. For me, in a few short years, I can point to Lochsong, the fastest horse on four legs in my opinion, and the unbeaten Lammtarra, as horses associated with me. As I just mentioned, Lammtarra had spoiled my Derby party, giving Walter Swinburn another win in England's most important race. The previous year Lammtarra had won his only race as a two-year-old, for the late Alex Scott, so tragically murdered by an employee just when his career was taking off. Lammtarra went to Dubai to join Godolphin and had some niggling problems before coming back to England, where the Derby probably seemed an impossible quest. The first thing I remember about Lammtarra was when Walter Swinburn rode him one morning in a gallop at Newmarket against me on Vettori, my French 2,000 Guineas winner. The gallop was staged two weeks before the 1995 Derby and, while Vettori was a good miler, I thought Lammtarra would need to win by more than a mere neck that day in order to have a chance in the Derby so soon after. I would have called the gallop 'workmanlike', but Sheikh Mohammed, who watched the work, said: 'Run him in the Derby.' I was shocked and thought, 'You're mad.' How could they run in the Derby a horse which had not yet run that season and which had run just once as a two-year-old and then had had a serious health problem during the winter in Dubai and had suffered disruption to his training programme. When it was confirmed Lammtarra would run, I thought: 'They've definitely gone mad.'

As I said earlier, I was on Tamure for John and we were very hopeful that he could win. Tamure was unbeaten until then, having won the Sandown Classic Trial last time out, and we felt he had a really good chance. For me, the race went absolutely to plan, spot-on, and I made my ground exactly where I wanted to. I hit the front in the last 100 yards, only for Lammtarra to catch me fifty yards out and beat me by a length. I shouted 'You bastard', but then immediately thought back to the gallop and Sheikh Mohammed. 'The Boss is always right – that's one thing you have to learn in life,' I said to myself, and it's not far from the truth. The result was very hard for me to swallow, though, but you never know what can happen, and little did I expect that next time out it would be me that had the good fortune to get the ride on him.

At the time it was offered, of course, it was a nice feeling to get the ride, and when I was asked, I accepted like a shot. But then when I thought about it, I reckoned I was in a no-win situation. I thought, 'What if he gets beat, they will all be saying "Walter would have won on him".' Luckily for me, when the news that I had the ride was announced, I was having a four-day break in Sardinia. I came back on the Friday, the day before the race, and until the race I hadn't sat on him. Because of the way he'd won at Epsom, many people were regarding Lammtarra as a speed horse, but I had been studying the video of the Derby and reckoned he needed a couple of furlongs to wind up and get into his stride. I thought that Ascot's short straight and the horse's inexperience might be a problem, but, as everyone knows, Lammtarra won.

Everyone in racing, especially in English racing, has the same ambition. There are three races to win, the Epsom Derby, the King George and the Arc – and Lammtarra achieved all three before I did! At Ascot we were drawn on the outside. The King George is a race where it's easy to find trouble, especially on the rails, but from our position we were able to keep galloping. I decided to make my move at the three-furlong pole. Lammtarra was one of the first off the bridle but then I had just got him going when I could feel this monster coming through – that great buzz. I'd been rowing away and then I got a bump and was knocked wide. Just for a second I even forgot about Pentire, but then I looked to my left and saw him. Just as a racing car driver looks at the line at the end of every lap trying to cut a few milliseconds from his time, entering the straight I tried to pinch a few inches.

I looked at the reins on Pentire and saw they were really tight. I thought, 'I have to get him off the bridle', so I asked him to give me another gear. Then Michael Hills had to ask Pentire to go as a response and he got a neck in front. But then Lammtarra fought back and showed that determination which sets the champion apart. The race was like a boxing match, Lammtarra being the true prize fighter. Unlike some of the other talented horses you get to ride, Lammtarra could take a punch and then come back with his own knock-out blow.

And so to the Arc and the final challenge. In my mind,

until the Arc I had only paid back half of the hurt which losing the Derby had meant to me. The Arc would complete the consolation for me. Catherine does not come away racing with me very often but this time we spent a long weekend in Paris. I had a couple of rides at Longchamp on the Saturday and Lammtarra was to be the highlight on the Sunday, Arc day. I rode two Group-race winners, Flemensfirth in the Prix Dollar for John and Grey Shot (Prix de Lutece) for Ian Balding, from my three rides on the Saturday and we were all in a great mood when we went back early to the Georges V, a beautiful old-fashioned hotel right in the centre of town. That night, rather than stay in the hotel, we decided to go out and see the show at the Crazy Horse, where we had dinner.

The next morning I got up at nine o'clock and started getting ready at nine thirty. I knew the traffic is always bad in Paris on Arc day and I was anxious not to be late. By the time Catherine was organised, at eleven, I was 'walking the box', and I insisted we went then. On the way to the Bois de Boulogne there was hardly a car in sight, and when we arrived at eleven thirty, not even the gatemen were in place. You can tell I was not my normal pleasant self when I admit that when Catherine asked me to get her a badge, I said: 'Get your own badge, I'm working!' I can understand why she might not have been that delighted with me while she waited the three hours for the first race after that performance from me.

For me, though, the early arrival at Longchamp was just the thing I needed to take away my nerves. In the jockeys' room I at last began to relax. I had a couple of races to ride in before the Arc and that also helped. When we went out for the big race all I needed to do was to remind myself that Longchamp can be a very difficult track to ride. My requirement was to make sure I kept out of trouble. The Godolphin–Sheikh Mohammed team planned everything to perfection, and in Luso, owned by the Sheikh's great friend Saeed Manana, they shrewdly found the perfect pacemaker. More importantly, nobody else was entirely aware that Luso was fulfilling that role. I was able to take a prominent position behind Luso as Lammtarra jumped off well from out of the gate. Everything went to plan and I waited to let him see the straight and what he had to do. Then I got hold of him, and said, 'Let's go.' I wanted to kill them off. In the paddock beforehand, Sheikh Mohammed had said, 'Be handy. It's up to you to make the most of it.' By then I'd ridden Lammtarra a few times, at home as well as at Ascot, and knew that he stayed really well and was a great fighter. So when we kicked I knew that the others would have to use their speed to get to me. Then, when they did get to my quarters, they had to try to contend with his fighting spirit. I remember seeing Freedom Cry coming up to my horse's quarters and wondering whether we had enough petrol left in the tank. We did and Lammtarra was going away again at the line. It was to be the last race of his career, and he therefore remained unbeaten, the first European champion to do so since Ribot, a horse from the 1950s that was a great favourite of my father's, as he was Italian owned, trained and bred.

As we crossed the line, everything seemed to stop and to my mind it all went dark. It was the reaction of being able to ease off and stop concentrating, I suppose, but I remember standing up on the horse and looking across at the huge, packed grandstands. For a few seconds I was in a kind of shock, almost trance-like, but then, just as quickly, woke up to the enormity of the moment. I came back and jumped off the horse, in my then-normal Angel Cordero style, and participated in the presentation in front of the winning post. Sheikh Mohammed and his family and friends were all there and when it came to my turn to collect my own trophy it was a wonderful moment.

When the presentation finished, I could not contain myself any longer and, holding the cup in my left hand, ran right along the front of the grandstands at top speed and into the exit from the track to the paddock, doing high (or in my case, quite low) fives to every hand that was presented to me. On either side of the exit the crowds were lined, tightly packed, and by this time I was more like a dervish than a jockey. Starting on the right, I slapped all the hands I could reach, still galloping at Lammtarra pace, and then halfway through it, changed the cup to my right hand, and veered across to the left before going into the paddock for the post-race interviews. The funniest thing for me during the presentation was the sound of the British national anthem being played to salute the success of a horse bred in the United States, trained and owned by Dubaians and ridden by an Italian. If nothing else, it showed how international racing in Britain has become.

As I was saying before I was so rudely (at first) and then so beautifully (the next two times) interrupted by Lammtarra, the Oaks was great for me. To win the classic again for the team showed we were doing everything right. Sheikh Mohammed wanted to win the big ones with Godolphin and we were doing it. I had a nice win in the King's Stand Stakes on Godolphin's So Factual, who came late and fast to catch Lake Coniston, then reckoned to be the next champion sprinter. Unfortunately, the King's Stand, while still the top sprint race at Royal Ascot, is no longer a Group 1, and is now a Group 2 race. Lammtarra's King George was my next Group 1 win, but before I got another there was the pain and shock of that terrible fall at Haydock in early August when we lost a faithful old servant of John's, Wainwright.

That accident killed Wainwright and I was laid out on the track for quite a while. Happily for me, I was able to make a pretty quick comeback at the big York meeting, and again it was So Factual who kept my run going, with an easy win in the Nunthorpe Stakes.

In recent years, the Maktoum family have been having a number of horses trained in Germany, and one horse I rode with some success in that country was Germany, a four-year-old trained by Bruno Schutz, and owned by Mr Jaber Abdullah, one of the close friends of the family. He won two Group 1s, first in Munich, and then the Grosser Preis von Baden at the pretty track of Baden-Baden, which stages some great racing, especially in late summer. The ground was soft that day at Baden-Baden and Germany was able to show himself a high-class performer, winning by five lengths. There were some good English horses a long way behind that day.

Now, though, it was back home with thoughts of another Classic win, as I had been looking forward to riding John's nice horse Presenting in the St Leger, the last Classic race of the season. Presenting was the ante-post favourite, but it began to look as if I would be snookered anyway, as Godolphin were planning to let Classic Cliché take his chance in the race, which meant I would be claimed to ride him. Unluckily for John and Presenting's owner George Strawbridge, who breeds some lovely horses in the USA, the rain started to come down at Doncaster and there was no option but to withdraw Presenting, who must have fast ground to show his best form. Luckily for me, though, I had Classic Cliché to ride. He had been running well in some top races over a mile and a half, just getting outpaced at the crucial time by Pentire in the King Edward at Royal Ascot, and then in the Irish Derby where he was a close fifth. Both times, though, he was running on and while lots of people were asking, 'How can a horse by Salse win a St Leger?' I was in no doubt he'd stay the trip well.

I didn't realise when I went to Doncaster that day that I needed two wins to reach my 1,000 winners in England. The race before the St Leger made it 999, as I won on a nice handicapper of Bryan McMahon's called Band On The Run. Then it was the big race and the possibility that I had timed it to win my thousandth race in a Classic. In the race I rode the horse as I believed he should be ridden, never doubting his stamina. From the start we were always going easily, and early in the straight we went on. I asked for his effort two out and we went clear, galloping really strongly. We'd won another Classic, the fourth in a row for Godolphin and my third of the year in England, and the reception as I came in was tremendous. Like a great big party. The St Leger, which is the oldest Classic race, has an added attraction for the winning jockey and the public: the famous hat with St Leger written on it, which is placed on the winning jockey's head. I'd wanted to win that ever since I'd come to England, and now it's the most treasured item in my trophy cabinet. When they gave me that it was a bit like getting an international cap for football. As the hat was presented, I saw a bottle of champagne which had been left on the table. I quickly opened the bottle, and sprayed everyone around with it. Now I know what it's like to win a Grand Prix race!

So I'd got to 1,000 winners and won three classic races in England in a single season and was still only twenty-four. But then I still had a few to go to catch my dad. Around 2,800, I think!

Meanwhile, John was still flying, especially where major races were concerned, and only a week after the St Leger another day trip to Longchamp brought another big double. John's two-year-old Lord Of Men had been going well as he'd gained experience and won a couple of nice races at home. John decided it was time for him to step up in grade and aimed him at the Prix de la Salamandre, one of the three most important races in the French calendar. André Fabre's Barricade was the favourite and we were pretty unfancied by the betting public as 6–1 fifth favourite in a field of seven. But Lord Of Men put up a great show and won by a length from With Fascination. On the same card, Tamure had his first race since his great effort in the Derby, in the Group 3 mile and a quarter Prix du Prince d'Orange. The race developed into a sprint, and the fact that he was able to hold the very talented Spectrum, a mile and a quarter specialist, and on the soft ground that Spectrum prefers, was brilliant. There was still time for more big wins on Mons, for Luca Cumani in the Royal Lodge (Group 2) at Ascot, and on Flemensfirth in the Group 2 Prix Dollar at Longchamp before all the excitement of Lammtarra in the Arc. Lammtarra's absence from the Breeders' Cup and Halling's inability to cope with the dirt track and Cigar at Belmont Park, New York, made that meeting an anti-climax for me and Godolphin. I did have rather better luck on a trip across the Atlantic two weeks before, though, when the great Irish filly Timarida easily won the Group 2 E. P. Taylor Stakes at the Woodbine track in Toronto, Canada. Ten months later, Timarida made another raid on dollars, US this time, and won the Beverley D Stakes at the beautiful Arlington Park track in Chicago.

By the time the season ended in Britain, I had clocked up 217 winners, amazing considering I'd not been so aggressive on the all-weather at the start of the year and my summer injury at Haydock. I'd also ridden abroad a fair bit, admittedly in most cases on Sunday, but to get within sixteen of the score I'd made the year before was something. I understand that Fred Archer, the best jockey of the last century, and Sir Gordon Richards, by far the most dominant personality of the pre-war and immediate post-war era before Lester Piggott took centre stage, were the only others to get 200 wins more than once. I know there are more opportunities now with the all-weather, night meetings, Sunday racing and above all the chance to fly between meetings, but to think that Lester, Pat Eddery and Willie Carson never managed it once, while only Jason and Muis Roberts of the others have done it at all, makes me proud of my achievement.

5 A Typical Season

The knowledge that I had won the jockeys' championship twice in succession gave me a good feeling as I contemplated the winter when my time would be split between riding and a couple of short holiday breaks. The first time I won the title it came as a great relief. The second championship was much different. I really enjoyed it. As I approached the end of the year, everything seemed really set up for a third title. I was sure of one thing: I would be going all out for the hat-trick. And with John Gosden and Godolphin, as well as David Loder, Ian Balding and Luca Cumani backing me up, I had to feel I had a favourite's chance.

I had been attached to John Gosden's stable for two years and we were looking forward to a good time with his three-year-olds which had shown so much promise in their first season. Godolphin, the brainchild of Sheikh Mohammed, was also going to make a major contribution to my season, luck permitting. The Godolphin team consisted of the

Sheikh, his racing manager Simon Crisford, trainer Saeed bin Suroor and his new assistant Tom Albertrani.

For a top jockey, the racing year goes on for all 365 days, however the domestic title race is arranged, and unless you are careful it can sweep you up. At the end of the 1995 season I did manage some time off, but I was pleased to get the chance to ride again in Hong Kong at the big December meeting, where they stage three valuable international races over various distances.

So on 15 December I was back in the colony, two and a half years after I'd had my contract to ride there for a season cancelled. I was due to ride Needle Gun for Clive Brittain and Triarius for Godolphin. I was happy to be there as it gave me a chance to meet up with my good friend Davie Wong, but the day before the races, I received the worst news imaginable.

For some time I had been grateful for the advice and help that Barney Curley, the racehorse trainer, had given me, and I had got to know all his family, especially his young son Charlie, or Chuck, as everyone in Newmarket knew him. Chuck was the sweetest guy in the world, and the news came through from John Gosden that Chuck had been killed in a car crash in Newmarket that morning. It had been a frosty morning and on his way to work he'd skidded on some black ice, had gone into a ditch and been killed outright.

From the time I heard, until the races, it played on my mind and I couldn't have been on the top of my game when Needle Gun ran. Needle Gun was beaten by a neck in his race and, looking back, I'm sure it was partly because I was a bit under the weather.

It was a difficult time. I flew back straight after the races for Chuck's funeral in Newmarket. I'd never been to a

The two great loves of my life.

My great friend, John Gosden, at breakfast.

Another early morning start.

Two key players in the Dettori team:
my valet, Dave Curry (above),
and my agent, Matty Cowing (below).

Mark Of Esteem winning the 2,000 Guineas.

Victory!

Swain winning the Coronation Stakes.

With Mr and Mrs John Peett, directors of Vodafone,
who sponsor the Coronation Stakes.

At Stanley House Stables.

Schooling a David Loder filly at Newmarket.

Derek Thompson cracks a joke at Sandown.

Collecting money for the Centre of Riding Therapy from
Peter Walwyn, Lady Howard de Walden and Lord Howard de Walden.

Riding out.

Relaxing at home with Catherine.

funeral before and it was not a comfortable experience for me. All you could do was be there. As I said, I'd been quite close to Barney for a while and it had hit him very very hard.

I was asked to be one of the coffin-bearers from out of the church. The most poignant moment was seeing the effect it had on Chuck's girlfriend. That day was also coincidentally her sixteenth birthday and her grief put everything in perspective for me. She stood there so bravely, so strong. You might lose a race or a ride in a big race and be upset . . . but death is so final, so unforgiving and, in Chuck's case, seemingly such a waste of a good, young life.

It was a very cold, dark midwinter day. I stayed until late afternoon and there were a lot of people there sharing Barney's and his family's grief. One person for whom it was also difficult was Neil Foreman, a pilot who flies a small plane. Most of his work is to do with taking some of the jockeys and trainers to the races up and down the country and he is my regular pilot. Barney often comes along with us if he is interested in going to a meeting in the north of England and he usually takes the mickey out of Neil the whole time. It was after the funeral service at the church that Neil came to Barney's house. I noticed that Barney was looking at Neil quite a lot, but hardly said a word to anyone all day. Then, suddenly, he said to Neil, 'There's no joking now.' He burst into tears and looked so bleak.

I took the night flight back to Hong Kong as I had left Catherine there with Davie Wong and his wife Virginia. I had flown to England, a thirteen-hour flight, straight from the races, went to the funeral and then flew back out again, another thirteen hours, so that by the time I arrived I was exhausted.

Catherine and I stayed in Hong Kong for two days before going away to Phuket to start our holiday. We were there for ten days and had a lovely time, although Christmas in Thailand did not seem quite the same. Still, it was a good rest and we got back on the twenty-eighth, still conscious of the sadness of Chuck's death, but rested and ready for a solid year's work.

Before starting to ride on the all-weather in February, I had organised a two-week skiing holiday for Catherine and me and my best friend Colin Rate and his fiancée Alex. I own a small ski chalet in Mejève in France. The accommodation is very limited – just one bed, a couch and two bunk beds – but we had a great time.

Catherine and Colin had never been skiing before, so I appointed myself as the teacher. The first day I made them go right up to the top of the difficult runs and it took two hours to get down. They walked most of the way and told me I was crazy to take them there. But by the fourth day Colin was getting braver and followed me everywhere. Unfortunately, during the day he fell over and hurt his leg so badly that six months later he was still limping. For the last week while we were there, we had to do our best to keep him entertained. It was a good job we had a Monopoly set.

It is great to take a holiday to recharge the batteries. During the racing season at home, the days are very long, especially when the night meetings come along. You can be on the gallops at six thirty in the morning, ride four or five horses, travel to one race meeting late in the morning, fly on to another, and if the last race is very late, possibly have to drive home the last leg to Newmarket, sometimes not getting home before midnight.

But for me, a holiday is often the start of a worrying time. When we got back from skiing, I was 9st 2lb, 11lb more than my minimum riding weight. Luckily, I had a few weeks before I was due to start to ride on the all-weather, and because the jockeys had decided unanimously to revert to a March to November season to calculate the jockeys' championship in 1996, I was able to pick and choose when, where and how often I would ride, a big change from the two previous years, when I was flat out from 1 January.

So, straight away, I was back on my diet. To be frank, I'd pigged everything in France and enjoyed the food and also the chance to relax and eat the wrong things for once. Some jockeys can eat anything and never have to sweat. For instance, my father had shoulders like a miniature Mike Tyson, had boxed and done weights in his younger days and yet never needed to watch his weight. He is just five feet tall, and I'm taller, without the shoulders, but I have a different metabolism. When I was an apprentice growing up in England, I ate all the wrong food, all the junk food from the various fast-food outlets in town. In that respect, I was no different from most of the stable lads in the town. In the early days, when money was a factor, you just rushed the first thing down you, but as I grew and began to gain weight the question of my diet became not just a factor, but the most compelling factor in my life. At eighteen most people thought I had a weight problem, and I did, but when you think how Ray Cochrane, whose natural weight is nearer 10st than 8st, manages to ride somewhere near that weight, you can see that controlling weight can be achieved.

The question of diet for a jockey is something he can learn to cope with only through experience. Early in my apprenticeship I did not get many rides, and in those days I was totally undedicated. I ate lots of ice-cream, junk food and lots of sweet things. At the same time I hardly ever ate a proper meal. Once I started to get more rides, going to the races and actually being there more with the jockeys helped me start controlling things.

Most jockeys who do have a weight struggle try a few things before settling on the right method, which in all honesty can only be eating sensibly and watching the calories. One thing I tried was using laxatives. At first one or two tablets would have the desired effect, emptying the stomach quite efficiently. But as my body got used to the tablets, I needed to take more and more, so that it took four or five to make things work. That was an unpleasant method, to say the least.

For a while I used to play squash wearing quite a heavy sweatsuit, and another old-fashioned and drastic method was to travel to the races in midsummer wearing warm clothes, keeping the windows shut, with the heater full on. When you got to the track, you felt you'd had half a dozen rides already and it was hardly the ideal preparation for a race.

Many racecourses have a sauna, and most of the top jockeys also have one at home, and if you are, say, a pound and a half too heavy for a ride, spending a little time in the track's sauna usually gets rid of the final necessary ounces.

You soon learn as a jockey that weight is the perennial worry. If you control your weight, you are in control of your life. Sometimes there is a temptation to try to get below your normal minimum for a special fancied ride, but it rarely pays off and often can harm the jockey's health in the short-term, especially in the summer when you are losing a lot of liquid anyway.

The least wise and least successful method I tried, happily for just a couple of weeks, happened when I first went to ride in the United States in the winter of 1990. One day, I was in the jockeys' room when one of the local riders gave me a small tablet about the size of a Tic-tac sweet, rather smaller than a Smartie. It was a Lasix tablet. Lasix is primarily used in racing in America to prevent horses bursting blood vessels. Its use is outlawed in Europe but a majority of States in the US allow it. In fact, most tracks, with their long meetings of up to 365 consecutive days, could not keep the show on the road without Lasix and Bute, which is a painkiller.

The weights are lower for the jockeys in the United States than here and obviously some of the jockeys need to find extra help from somewhere to keep their rides. So, anyway, I took one Lasix tablet and within an hour I'd lost four pounds. But then came the side effects: after one ride my calves cramped up, my eyes felt as though they were in the back of my head. I felt terrible. After I had been taking the Lasix on and off for two weeks, I finally gave up, and I blew up like a balloon.

Over the next couple of years, I continued in the same way, doing well enough and riding plenty of winners for Luca and other trainers who liked to use me on their horses. But, eventually, during a personal crisis, I had to look for more reliable methods of controlling my weight and so, and really for the first time in my professional life, I turned to my dad for advice. He made me realise that for years I had been getting by on my talent, without any dedication to my job. I had been lazy, not thinking about where I was and not happy in myself and what I had achieved. He had been a jockey for thirty-five years and, as I've said, was lucky that he could eat what he wanted and keep a steady weight. If I allowed my weight to stay at its natural level, I'd probably be around 9st 4lb. During the season, however, I have to have a body weight of 8st 3lb to be able to ride at 8st 5lb on my lightest saddle. Dad told me that the key was always to start the season at your lightest so you would be free to think about the rest of the job without having the constant battle with the scales.

Even when a jockey is comfortable and managing his weight well, he always jumps on the scales at home every morning. All the calls to his agent about the forthcoming rides concentrate on whether he is 'doing light' – his minimum – weight, and then the minor sacrifices have to be made.

On a normal day I would have a cup of coffee and maybe a biscuit in the morning. During the summer when the weather is hot, a Diet Coke is not harmful calorie-wise and I like the taste, too. At the races, the tracks all provide sandwiches in the weighing room, and sometimes when you feel hungry, you grab a bite or two. Most people seem to think it's easy keeping your weight down when it's hot, but I find the cold weather better. However tough it gets, though, I insist on eating a meal at night, however late I might get back from an evening meeting. Catherine is a good cook and she's building up a good range of recipes which are not too high in calories. Luckily, I do not really like beef, which is high in fat and therefore calories, so I normally eat either chicken or fish. Catherine has one particular recipe for chicken with salad, where she cuts the chicken meat into small cubes and puts it in with the salad and some fresh Parmesan cheese. I could eat that for dinner – and lunch while I was injured – every day.

The midsummer part of the year provides plenty of exercise to keep the weight down. Riding work early in the morning, maybe up to ten rides at two meetings during the day, is hard work. But when there's a little less of a hectic schedule I sometimes go for a run in the morning, or for a swim at the pool in the Bedford Lodge Hotel in Newmarket.

I mentioned earlier that most days during the height of

the racing season are long and arduous for jockeys, that once you start the treadmill in the spring you cannot really jump off from what has become for many of us a seven-day week until November at the earliest, unless you make a special effort to take time off. Of course, an injury, like the one I had in 1996, or a ban by kind permission of the stewards, another of my 1996 'privileges', will mean you get a less welcome period 'off the treadmill'.

The racing season for the top flat-race jockeys, and even for those lower down the scale, can be divided into three parts and the 'normal' day will vary accordingly. The spring, summer and autumn phases of the season are different as the length of the days and therefore the amount of time available for work in the morning and extra race meetings in the evening alters as the year moves on.

Spring

When I come back to England each year, the important thing is my own fitness. Race riding requires an extra edge and after a layoff, like the one with my broken elbow in the summer of 1996, the first few rides back are tough, just as it's hard for a footballer who has been injured or on a summer's break. It's tough until you get into the swim. That's where I find the all-weather racing helps. I think the ideal starting point is early February. David Loder usually starts to have a few runners on the all-weather tracks, and his strike-rate is very high. So it's nice to know that while it's getting you fit, you can clock up a winner or two. Wherever and whenever they come, winners are always welcome, and when it's for a small owner who has just one horse, and he's pleased you've ridden for him, it gives you an extra buzz. Coming back in February gives me a month before March, which is the starting point for the serious work for the horses with Classic potential. That month also gives you the chance to show the lads who have been stuck here through all the cold weather of December and January that you have some respect for them. At this part of the year, you join them in the mornings riding the horses out from the yard.

First lot is a little later at this time, and it's just as well, for Newmarket in midwinter, when there's nothing to stop the cold winds coming from Siberia other than you, can be pretty bleak. At least the lads see you show your face, and they then get a little respect for you too, seeing you pulling your finger out to get out of bed on a cold morning. That time of year is important. John Gosden takes the opportunity to get me to ride many of the horses, and in a big yard like Stanley House, which can have up to 200 horses in training, that takes a while. I think I'm lucky that, when I sit on a horse, in a few seconds I'm able to tell most things about him. It's a technique you develop when you ride every day. You have an affinity, perhaps it's something some people are born with, or it might be taught along the way. The obvious things I believe I can detect are the horse's temperament, which is most important; the way he looks – Is he alert?; his walk and trot. Some horses you can sit on for two seconds without doing anything and know 'he's a good racehorse'. He might be light on his feet, very sharp and full of himself. Others are merely slobs and feel like they have a refrigerator on each foot.

So, at this time, you ride a different horse each day, and at this stage they are not doing much, just a little canter maybe, building up to more exertion later in the spring. You're very aware of how each horse works, and John, like any top trainer, is anxious for me to see and get acquainted with the horses he thinks are going to do the business for the yard. At this stage I'm making a mental list of between perhaps five or ten horses which will be pulling much of the weight for the entire string in the early part of the season. Then once they are identified, one or two of the dark horses can be expected to come along midway through the season, and not always the obvious ones. When I first get back, I expect to get up around six a.m. and go out from the yard at around seven a.m. The walk to the cantering ground takes a while, and after their exercise you walk back, so first lot may not be over until eight thirty when the lads go in to breakfast. I'll normally have my breakfast with John and his wife Rachel, usually just a cup of coffee and a piece of toast, before going home.

By March the days are getting longer, and gradually a little warmer, and the work is a little more serious, stepping up half a gear. One day it's 28 February and winter, and there's not much happening. But go forward just twenty-four hours to 1 March and all of a sudden it's spring – in racing's clock if not in the weather. There's a big difference: everyone's ears are pricked, maybe the bookmakers will open a book on the Lincoln handicap at the end of the month, and the Warren Hill canter, a four-furlong grass gallop up Warren Hill, opens. Now the grass gallops are open, and even though flat racing on grass is not due to start for another three weeks, the trainers have their own very private race, and they are immediately off and running. It's the 'Who Can Get to the Gallops First Stakes' and however early anyone else starts in the mornings, there's only ever one winner. Clive Brittain has done many amazing things in his career, being one of the few British trainers to win a Breeders' Cup race, as he did with Pebbles, and the first to win the Japan Cup, with Jupiter Island. But Clive is even better at being first string out every morning. There's just no betting: it's like Manchester United being in the Vauxhall Conference. But even for the 'normal stables' the start is earlier. Instead of pulling out at seven a.m. the teams go out half an hour earlier and then another two weeks later it'll be at six.

It might seem a silly race, but, with the number of horses in training there, even the large area of gallops at Newmarket can soon get chewed up with all the horses going over them, especially in a wet spring. So we get a Premier League of teams following Clive out. Godolphin are always early; so is John, and David Loder and Luca Cumani are not far behind. Of the top stables, Henry Cecil is normally last out, but it's simply the trainer's mentality which governs when they go out, and clearly the end results probably do not get affected much.

In my time with Luca Cumani I never had much money and wanted to make a little extra. I had noticed that when we were on our way to work we nearly always used to see Clive's horses on their way back. Rae Guest was one of Luca's jockeys – he is now a very skilful trainer in his own right – and he said I should have a word with Clive if I wanted extra work. So I went to Carlburg Stables and spoke to Clive, who said, 'Yes, sure. We pull out at four thirty.' In those days I had a Vespa moped, which had gears which you had to wrestle with manually. The idea was that I would meet Clive's horses on the Limekilns, one of the main galloping grounds north of the town, but I had to use my moped to get there and leave it where I jumped on the horse I was riding work.

Very few of Clive's lads knew how to ride a moped, or anything else, so, while I was doing the work up the hill on the horse, the lad whose horse I was working had to push this awkward little machine up after me in order to hand the bike over to me again at the top. You can imagine how popular I was with Clive's lads. I managed to keep going to ride out there for three months, by which time I couldn't sleep and was simply exhausted. One thing my exertions did achieve was my first Royal Ascot mount, which was on Clive's filly Merle, on whom I did 7st 6lb in the Royal Hunt Cup. After the three months I told Clive that I'd have to stop coming as Luca's string had started going out a bit earlier and I would not be able to get back in time. I'm sure Clive saw through that excuse.

Like the horses, the jockeys have to get used to the new routine. So I have six weeks to adjust to the earlier starts, while the horses are building up for more important days ahead. In March, first lot will take around one and a half hours. First the horses will walk around a ring for twenty minutes to stretch their legs. Then they will have a little jog or warm up to check whether they are sound. That's the time when the lad riding the horse can tell the trainer if there is a problem, at which point the horse would probably be taken back to his box. The others will go off to the walking grounds, and then have a warm-up canter. Then they will take their turns to work, in the early days working a short distance before walking home again. People wonder why having a horse in training is such an expensive luxury. With an hour and a half out each morning, plus all the grooming and feeding back in the yard, the lad will spend upwards of twenty hours a week with each of his three horses. Even with the modest rates of pay which stable lads receive, and then with the costs of feeding, veterinary and shoeing bills, racehorses are obviously a costly proposition.

As March continues, gradually my riding out days from the yard finish. It is more important as the racing gets ever nearer for the stables to assess the progress of the horses.

Now, on the main work days – Tuesday, Wednesday, Friday and Saturday – there will be fast work and trials to be carried out for various trainers. Most horses ready to race are given fast work once a week and the jockeys go to the gallops by car to meet the horses which they are to partner in the fast workouts. The lad who looks after the horse jumps off and the jockey jumps on. That way he can ride a number of horses on any work morning, getting to know them in good time for when they race. He can also tell the trainer his opinion of how they are progressing. At this time, I spread myself around in order to find some more business. That's when I slot in work for David Loder and Luca Cumani.

The days of each week differ, too. Monday is an easy day for the horses, who usually need to get started again after what for most has been an easy Sunday. The exception, of course, is when they have a race in a few days' time and so also need to have a workout on Sunday. Staff, too, like their weekends off, but the big stables are used to sending runners overseas in the season, and now there's Sunday racing here, too. It's like planning a military operation, running a stable like John's.

For me, Monday is usually my chance to take the morning off to catch up with some sleep. The four work days are invariably busy, with a five forty-five start as the season begins. There's just time for a quick wash and my mandatory cup of coffee before getting to the gallops by six fifteen or, if I'm lucky, six thirty to meet John's first lot. At that time of year, we'll probably be on Racecourse Side, where the gallop runs parallel with the Rowley Mile racecourse. I'll jump up and give a little canter to see that the horse is all right and then, depending on what the trainer wants me to do – that's why he's the trainer – I'll ride according to instructions. All the time I'm building up a store of information about the horses I will be riding in the coming weeks, and hopefully a store of rides on 'outside' horses with chances of winning races. Like Monday, Thursday is a quiet day for most stables and another chance for a little rest.

By the middle of the month, the first Doncaster runners are already in trim for their races and for me, I can't wait to get up in the mornings. Good or bad, every day you find out something new. Before this time, you have learnt seventy per cent about your horses. Now you'll discover another twenty per cent, and while you may be pretty sure of what they can do, it's not until they get to the track and operate under race conditions that the final ten per cent becomes clear. Sometimes there's great news, sometimes disaster, but it's a new year and another chance to get a big horse for the owners, the trainer, the lads and the stable jockey. Everyone has that hope. When you swap over the horses with the lads in the morning they want to see you come back and tell them their horse finished in front in the gallop. Their attitude is so refreshing. Then, once the races start towards the end of the month, it becomes even busier.

You have to carry on with everything else, but when I go back for breakfast with John, that's when I'll be looking through the racing papers to have a glance at the races I'll be riding in. Then I'll go home, and I always try to get an hour in bed before travelling off to the races. It's a kind of routine and seems to help relax me at a time when it's beneficial. That's my best sleep of the day and it's not surprising I need it, getting up so early. When I wake up, I have a more detailed look at the races for that day, trying to get a clue how each race will be run and what tactics I'll need to get the best out of my rides.

Getting ready for the track, one thing I really enjoy is putting on a tie and a suit. It makes me feel smart and makes me feel good. I think a champion in any sport should behave like a champion and be an example to his colleagues. Depending on whether I need to lose a pound or so, I might have a sauna for half an hour. Other mornings, I could even have the luxury of a lie in, although in the busy part of the spring that doesn't happen too often. When it's time to go, Andy Keates, my driver, will arrive. He's never late and in the six years he's been with me he's never missed a day through illness. As we travel, I'll have another look at the papers and then probably make a few calls to trainers and my agent Matty Cowing before grabbing around twenty minutes' sleep.

Summer

A different tempo and different objectives compared with the spring. By summer, all the early hopes in the major three-year-old races will have been decided one way or the other. It's amazing how quickly we get through the classic trials in the spring and into the two summer classics, the Derby and the Oaks at Epsom, before another short step to Royal Ascot. By now the evening meetings are in full swing, and the schedule gets ever more hectic. Luckily, John appreciates how busy my life is and only needs me to ride out four times a week, and ride work only two mornings, Wednesday and Saturday. The work-day gallops get even earlier and now it's a case of up at five, breakfast at seven till seven thirty, and back home for a proper look at the day's racing, which is now always a double-header except on Tuesdays, more calls to Matty and any trainers I need to speak to, and then the customary hour in bed.

The motorways of Britain have finished off more jockeys than anything else. Jockeys like George Duffield and his younger counterpart Jimmy Quinn have travelled many thousands of miles in the quest for a winner. Pat Eddery, Willie Carson and Walter Swinburn all realised that the use of a plane, despite the cost, is a great help in staving off the exhaustion which can hit a jockey at any time. In the summer, the roads are crowded with traffic, and Fridays spent travelling north up the M6 are a recipe for madness. I met Neil Foreman a few years ago, when he was flying Michael Roberts during the season when he won more than 200 races and won the title. I had a chat with Neil and said that I would be going for the title myself and expected to be a lot busier, and asked whether he would fly me around. Now I fly as often as I can and the benefit, apart from getting to the track much more quickly, is the extra time I get to relax at home in the mornings. There's no question that since I've been going to the races by plane, I last the year out longer. Instead of six hours a day in a car, I take just a fraction of that time if I fly. It doesn't come cheap, though. Jockeys are expected to pay all their own expenses out of their riding fees and prize money percentage, and on average it costs £150 a day to fly. Over three months that's a lot of money, but we usually share, and jockeys like Willie Ryan and Jimmy Quinn, who've got fed up with the motorways like me, are regulars, as, for some of the big meetings, are Barney Curley and David Loder. We're all founder members of the unofficial Newmarket Flyers' Club. We have a verbal agreement. Neil needed the business and I needed the plane. It's a great arrangement for both of us. And because I get to ride in most of the races at the meetings I attend, I rarely have to wait for anyone else to finish before flying off. They have to wait for me!

To pay for the massive expenses, my agent Matty Cowing has to work even harder than would otherwise be the case. When he books a ride he checks with Neil whether I would need to leave an afternoon meeting, say, a race earlier to make the first ride at the evening meeting. That creates lots of problems for Matty and Neil to sort out. There are only a few tracks where you can land on the middle of the course. Newmarket, Newbury and Haydock all allow planes to land; Newmarket has a strip at the end of the July course and the other two have a strip in the middle of the track. In other instances, taxis have to be laid on from the nearest airfield, which, almost invariably, is a grass strip, often in some pretty out-of-the-way place. All those arrangements are made by Neil, a former policeman in the CID in Hackney, East London, and therefore capable of looking after himself.

For a jockey to take the mount in a race he needs to be fully dressed in his colours, and on the scale with his saddle at least fifteen minutes before the advertised time of the race, and if he's not there in time – fourteen minutes forty-five seconds is just too late – there will be a queue of his colleagues ready to take the bread out of his mouth. Usually, a couple of times a year you are held up going for what turns out to be a winning ride and when you arrive someone will be there warming up the colours for you. If the stewards decide you have not allowed enough time, they will fine you, but as long as Matty and Neil do their job, that doesn't happen and the stewards are understanding.

If Neil is important to me in the summer, Matty is my right hand all year round. He is one of the members of Newmarket's most exclusive club, Ladbrokes betting shop regulars society, of which Dave Shippy Ellis, who is agent for Gary Carter among others, and Blue Duster's famous lad, Billy, who is a great expert on the dog racing from Walthamstow, are also valued members. When I was fifteen, I spent every afternoon in the betting shop, and got to know Matty. He has been my agent ever since and helps enormously.

People outside racing think a jockey leads a glamorous life, where champagne and caviar are the staple foods. But it is only the top three or four who get a good living, and for the past few years I have been lucky to get into that group. For most of the middle-rank riders, however, the expenses are killing. To be able to get to the track, they have to run a reliable car. That is expensive in relation to their income, and then, what with running it, and the cost of petrol and the infinitely higher costs of servicing a car that does 80,000 miles a year, they live from hand to mouth in most cases. The car's value soon drops and as your life gets so intense you have to pay someone to drive you to the track or you would be falling asleep at the wheel. Suppose a jockey gets one booked ride at Edinburgh. He has to drive all the way from Newmarket and spend £200 getting there and all he gets if the horse is unplaced is his £61 riding fee. He's out of pocket by £140. When I fly to the races, I have to think of my first three or four rides, if they are out of the money, as just paying the expenses before I start earning, and that's someone who is doing okay. The less fortunate jockeys have to cut corners and costs, sharing lifts when possible. That's why I never mind giving a lift to a young jockey if there's room.

Racing here is definitely underfunded. At a lot of meetings there's not even a prize for fourth. It's hard on the owners, the trainers who depend on their share of the prize money to make up what a lot of them lose through subsidising training fees, and on the jockeys, too. If there was a fourth prize, even just £300, the paltry extra £20 the jockey would earn would at least go a little way towards helping him meet his costs. It would also help form in the less valuable races to be more reliable. If there were worthwhile fourth places available, all the jockeys would ride out properly for fourth instead of not bothering. As things are now, if a jockey does ride out properly for fourth where there is no prize money for that placing, the owner and trainer are more likely to be furious with him, saying that if he had allowed the horse to coast the last 100 yards, he would have got a better handicap mark the next time.

Some days are made even more tiring for me because the time of my last ride at the evening meeting means that we cannot reach the Newmarket strip before dark. Neil is a good pilot and daring enough to trust his skill on what is a beautifully maintained strip, but the regulations do not allow him or us to risk it. So, even if we fly to the night meeting, Andy will often have to drive there himself to get me back home. On those occasions we will often have extra passengers, but I try to remember to remind myself of all the lifts I got when I needed them when I was a struggling apprentice.

Whatever my day, good or bad, I always like to eat a meal, however late it is. Most times, my lovely fiancée Catherine will have made me a salad and left it ready for me. I'll have had a packet of crisps and a Diet Coke in the car coming home, and then I'll take half an hour to get over the day before eating. Then, five minutes later, it's bed and back on the treadmill again in the morning, a procedure we follow for three months, when we're constantly living on adrenalin.

Autumn

By the time of the York Ebor meeting in August, and from then until the St Leger meeting at Doncaster in early September, most of the jockeys who have had a clear run will be going around like zombies. In 1996, my various absences through suspension and then injury meant that I was fresh while everyone else wanted a break, but normally we are all in the same boat. At this time, all of a sudden, the evening meetings finish and we're back to a similar schedule to the spring with one meeting a day and a maximum of five or six rides. You revert to a more normal life, and the past exertions catch up on you. For the whole of that fortnight most jockeys spend almost every spare minute catching up on the sleep they have gone without for so long. Your body, whose complaints you have been ignoring for the whole of the past three months, finally gets the message through that you need to sleep, and now you can finally listen.

York and Doncaster are two meetings I always enjoy. Both tracks are great to ride, Doncaster a true test of stamina, while the Ebor meeting, on the beautiful, manicured York track, features so many good races and top-class horses. By now the activity at home is settling down again, till it's almost as it was in the spring, although the emphasis now, instead of being on the Classic generation of three-year-olds, is on next year's stars. The dream in all the stables at this time is that those young horses, so carefully broken in the year before, and gently brought along all summer, will show something to say they will be the following year's stars. You might have a major candidate for the St Leger, Arc or Champion Stakes in September and October. Their training will be carefully monitored. Meanwhile the better-class two-year-olds are being lined up, either for the important back-end juvenile races, or for one of the maiden events on the major tracks, which are normally won by horses with a big future.

By now, with the days closing in, the top jockeys are also lining things up. Either a new job for a big stable for the following year, or a winter contract, preferably in one of the overseas countries, such as Hong Kong or Japan, where the pay can be very rewarding. Keeping busy then can put the whole year's work on a sound commercial basis. For me, I love the thought and anticipation of travelling round the world. As the days get colder in England, the idea of warm weather is very tempting. By October, you are invariably tired, having worked your butt off all year.

The attractions and warmth of some of the world's beauty spots in winter cannot alter the appeal of Newmarket. Although Italian, I think now of Newmarket as my home. My fiancée is from there and my work and home are there. Of course, when the east winds blow, Newmarket can be pretty bleak, but I find it more beautiful in winter than in summer. Of course, the trees have no leaves, but on most mornings the trees and grass are covered with frost which gives a dreamy atmosphere. On a lovely clear morning I enjoy seeing the horses (and the lads, if they are sensible) wrapped up warmly against the cold, and to see the breath from their nostrils turn to steam as it meets the cold air. Italy is reckoned to be warmer than England, but winters are just as cold in my original home town, Milan, as they are here in England. Nowadays, there's plenty of good thermal equipment. In winter I wear skiing thermals, top and bottom, made of silk. Above them, I have a thick pair of jodhpurs and then a top layer of a thick pair of riding-out waterproofs. The only inconvenience with looking like the Michelin Man is that all the clothing restricts freedom of movement, but at that time of year you don't have to do anything too serious on a horse. I don't think you ever really get used to the cold, and one area for which I haven't really found an effective remedy is in the hand department. You can't really ride out in boxing gloves, after all. If someone could find a light glove which could keep you warm in the cold weather I'd pay him a big bonus.

I'm very pleased to live in Newmarket. I find it nice to escape into the freedom of the countryside, which you find all around the town. In London, the life is enjoyable, but the place is too mean and for me and there would never be any escape. How can you say Hyde Park would be an escape? It's nice to have the freedom which the Newmarket area gives you.

As a training centre, Newmarket is as good as anywhere in the world. The variety of the gallops and their quality is the best in the world, and enables the trainers to do an excellent job. The popularity of Newmarket means that sometimes there can be a little congestion when hundreds of horses are preparing to go up a particular gallop at the same time. The one improvement I would like to see would be the addition of an American-style oval dirt track.

6 The Start of the 1996 Season

The start of the 1996 season brought about a welcome change for me and all the jockeys who felt that riding twelve months a year was unwise. Before the advent of all-weather racing, the flat in Britain began at Doncaster at the end of March and ended back at Doncaster in early November. That had been the format for many years. All-weather racing began not because anyone felt a need to prolong the flat-race season. Originally, it was brought in to compensate for the lost jumping fixtures in the worst of the winter, which, in practice, is usually January and February. So while Lingfield's first meeting on their new all-weather track was on the flat, the main reason behind it had been to provide a more reliable surface in cold weather on which to stage jump races while the turf tracks might be frozen or covered with snow. It soon became obvious that the artificial surfaces at Lingfield and Southwell, the other all-weather track, were not ideal for jumping, and the number of injuries to horses led to a campaign against all-weather jumping after a couple of seasons.

Racing in Britain is funded through a levy on betting and, with the failure of all-weather jumping, the authorities quickly introduced more and more all-weather flat racing to make up for it. So the original idea, to give alternative chances for jump owners, trainers and jockeys, was lost. Perhaps that's why they now have a programme of summer jumping.

People think we flat jockeys are over-paid but whatever they pay the jump boys cannot be enough, and they do, I admit, earn less than us, what with time out through falls. If a flat jockey is unlucky, like I was with Shawanni at Newbury, he can have an unexpected fall and be out for weeks, or even months as in my case. But those guys: when they go out they know that every so often they'll be falling, probably at a great big fence. I rode in only one hurdle race, an invitation event at Chepstow between the flat and jump jockeys, and I was absolutely terrified. They must be mad. No wonder Ray Cochrane and John Williams concentrated on getting their weight right and going back on the flat. Even Lester used to ride jumping winners before he learnt to live on a cigar and a glass of champagne forty years or more ago. The bravery and skill of people like Richard Dunwoody and Peter Scudamore amazes me. Okay, they don't have to worry about the kind of skin burns they used to get when falling on an all-weather track. Now they can bump their heads on the hard summer turf instead.

But to return to us pampered flat-racing boys. Whereas Jason Weaver and me had both gone flat out on the sand tracks, to which has now been added Wolverhampton and its trend-setting floodlights, Pat Eddery, Willie Carson, John Reid, Walter Swinburn and Richard Quinn had all stayed away, perhaps with the exception of the odd ride when it suited John and Richard. There had been a feeling for a couple of years that something had to be done, that it was an artificial situation when someone, as I had a couple of years before, got fifty-one winners on the board before Pat had started polishing his riding boots in time for Doncaster.

Even Jason and me were aware something needed to be done. In a year we were clocking up not just 1,000 rides, but 200,000 miles in planes, cars and helicopters in a season which went unbroken from 1 January until November. In both our cases, that could not have been possible without the great help of our agents. Jason is looked after by the journalist Terry Norman, but my agent, Matty Cowing, is one of the celebrities of Newmarket. He started as agent to Bruce Raymond and took me on after refusing to sign me up for some time. Every day we will talk by telephone, in the mornings after first lot, and then, through the day, as he compiles my list of rides for the coming days. As I have become more successful, his skill has become more important, as he sifts the best chance from those mounts offered by trainers and owners hoping to get me on their horses. In the weighing room after a race you will often hear a jockey picking up his mobile phone and calling his agent to ask why he wasn't on a certain winner which he considers should have been his ride. It is rare that I reckon Matty has made that kind of mistake, and when he does, there's usually a good reason for accepting another ride instead.

I'm lucky in several ways with Matty. He's been doing the job of an agent for quite a few years now. As a 'face' in Newmarket he already knew a lot of the trainers when he took me on as an apprentice. He works for me and me alone, and that way – and I'm fortunate in that respect – I only have to compete with other jockeys and different agents for rides. I don't think it can be so easy to stop jealousies arising when an agent gets a ride for one of his jockeys that another of his guys thinks should be his. Matty watches almost every race each day in the local Ladbrokes in Newmarket. He gets to know from trainers and also work riders which horses are in form. All of that knowledge, plus many hours' working over the form book, gives him, and therefore me, an edge in what is an increasingly competitive business. Matty knows the form backwards, upside-down and inside-out. His spade work and my own input, either about horses I've ridden or seen in races I've ridden in, plus horses I've ridden on the gallops or heard about, adds to the overall picture. We're a team, just as John and me or Godolphin and me are a team. My first loyalty has to be to either John or Godolphin and when one or the other has a runner in a race at a track I'm going to then there's no question of my taking an outside ride. When they are not involved, then David Loder, Ian Balding or Luca Cumani are the next in line. It's great to have so many good stables on your side wanting to use you. Matty manages to keep them all pretty happy for much of the time, but sometimes of course the clashes are impossible to avoid. Matty's like a favourite uncle, good-natured and great fun. He likes nothing better than backing a winner – except backing a winner I've ridden. Then he gets paid twice – by Weatherbys and Ladbrokes!

When you are involved in racing every day, in some cases from morning till night, the question of studying form is really like the situation in any full-time job. Form means all the races that are run every day. Of course, when you ride for the major stables on the top tracks, you won't be too bothered about the selling races on minor tracks in the north. With more than 4,000 flat races being run every year, you need to be selective. An average field through the season is around ten runners, so multiplying that by 4,000, form involves a total of around 40,000 performances. Just by riding in the 1,000 races I have in my busiest season, I will be aware first-hand of a quarter of everything, and in my case the most significant quarter. In his betting shop, Matty will see a lot of the stuff I miss, but if I'm at home the Racing Channel, which started recently, also helps keep me informed. Jockeys are much less likely to worry about pounds and lengths when assessing the horses in a race. I think it's more important to take the overall picture of a horse – Is he keen? Will he battle? Must he lead? If so, will he be taken on by other front-runners? And so on. From on a horse's back, if you keep your mind clear, you can pick up a lot about the horses others are riding. Just as in a job, it's a matter of experience, and you learn something new every day, if only the fact that, however much you think you know, there is never a real certainty until it crosses the line!

As far as the jockeys are concerned, it is a relief that racing's authorities have not yet organised much all-weather in November and December – but a couple of very cold early winters may even get them looking in that direction. The year before we decided to alter the championship, all the boys in the weighing room were asked when they wanted to run from, but on that occasion nothing was changed. This time there was a free vote and there was a majority of four to one in favour of going back to the old-style championship, based on wins between the start of turf racing at Doncaster and the final day, which for some strange reason now goes on until Folkestone on the Monday after the Doncaster November Handicap, which surely is a much more satisfactory and significant cut-off point.

Riding on the all-weather tracks is very different to riding on grass. I think of it as being a bit like speedway racing. First you must try to make a good break from the gate, and, then, during the race, try to get a smooth run on your horse. That's the most important thing. The reason is that, unlike on turf, when a horse can often quicken in a few strides, on the all-weather it usually takes a horse a furlong to build up to full speed. It's because the top part of the sand is loose to a depth of about three inches and underneath there's much harder sand. So, when galloping, the horse doesn't get such a good grip as he does with turf. Therefore, if a jockey fails to maintain a smooth run and gets checked, he will lose momentum, take that furlong to get going again, by which time the race will be over, for him anyway. When you watch races on dirt in America, or on all-weather here, you immediately are struck by the difference. They race up to five or six wide, all looking for that smooth run, and also to avoid the kick-back which is unpleasant for horses and jockeys. There's nothing worse than swallowing a mouthful of sand while you're trying to ride a race. There's much less weaving around between horses, and, rather than trying to be tactical, all the jockeys are concentrating on not getting stopped in their runs. They don't interfere with anyone else; they are simply doing the best for their own horse. It is very unusual, too, in a dirt race in England or the United States, for a horse which has made the early running, only to be passed in mid-race and drop back, ever to rally and win, unlike on turf where this is much more common. Because the element of luck in running is less of a factor, American horses on the dirt can compile longer winning sequences than the turf horses. It's true Cigar is a star performer and had to be tough and talented to set a sequence of sixteen wins in a row, but the task would have been much harder to achieve on turf. Here, racing is so competitive, it's rare for a horse to win even six times in a row. He needs to be a star to do that, whereas even in the short time of all-weather racing we've had several horses winning many times. In my view, the dirt specialist will win on dirt, and the grass horse of a similar quality will win the argument on turf, just like a Wimbledon champion on the grass courts would have trouble on the different artificial surfaces in Paris, Australia and New York. The Triple Crown in British racing is as elusive as the Grand Slam in men's tennis and the clean sweep of golf's four majors.

The all-weather will no doubt continue to expand and it's great for some of the less fashionable jockeys that their skills can be appreciated. The all-weather season in 1996 proved a great boost for Ray Cochrane, as it had been for me in the two previous years, and both he and Gay Kelleway, who is showing so much promise as a trainer, took advantage of the opportunities. Another jockey who works hard, probably harder than anyone, is Jimmy Quinn. Jimmy is a latter-day George Duffield, going thousands of miles up and down the motorways in search of rides and winners. He's a regular on the sand tracks and I'm delighted that he's getting chances to ride good horses, like Merit, on whom he won the Chester Cup.

When people talk about jockeys and the amount of riding they do, the temptation to compare Britain with America or France is hard to avoid. American jockeys ride many more races than we do, but the top jockeys, apart from flying from one side of America to the other for a special ride in a big race, will stay in their own location. Chris McCarron is based in California. He'll rotate between Hollywood Park and Santa Anita, both in the Los Angeles area, for the whole year, with a break in August when he will be in Del Mar, the track in Southern California right by the ocean, which is

California's answer to Deauville in France, or Saratoga, for the New York riders. We have the odd day at Yarmouth or Brighton, so why should we complain?

The American meetings at some tracks continue for the entire year. The seasons at Santa Anita, the principal Californian track, and Hollywood last for a couple of months or more, and for the jockeys it gets to be rather like going to the office. They ride track work in the mornings, go home for a rest, and then it's back to the track for the afternoon. So they might ride in up to ten or eleven races every day, but they have none of the travel wear and tear that we have here.

The French tracks for the top jockeys are all in the Paris region, although with the imminent closure of Evry, a really nice track on the outskirts of Paris, they will be making more use of tracks like Lyon-Parilly. In August, they all move down to Normandy for a very pleasant month at Deauville, when the locals are likely to bump into Cash Asmussen, Thierry Jarnet or Olivier Peslier in one of the many popular racing cafés in the seaside town.

Here, though, it could be Pontefract on Monday, Bath on Tuesday, Sandown on Wednesday, a day at Yarmouth and then a couple of afternoons at Haydock. Sometimes, with all the travelling, you might just start to think how lucky those Americans are knowing that they will be based in the same place for months at a time, apart from the occasional flight for one of the big races out of town. However, because, as far as my riding education is concerned, I have been brought up in England, I believe that if I were to ride regularly in the United States for any length of time, I'd soon find it boring. It would probably become a question of doing the same thing every day, like going to work at the office: saying 'Goodbye, darling' to my fiancée, as I leave in the morning, and staying shut away in the jockeys' room under the stands every afternoon. The same environment, the same people, and on the ordinary days when even the good American tracks offer ordinary races, the same horses, too.

Here, it's much different. All through the season we have big meetings to look forward to on different tracks, which all pose their own particular problems to the riders. There's the Guineas meeting at Newmarket, Epsom for the Derby and Oaks; Royal Ascot; Goodwood; York; and the St Leger at Doncaster. For good measure, some of us are lucky enough to make regular trips over to France and Ireland for the major races there. Even with all the travelling, the variety makes life tolerable. There's a light at the end of the darkest tunnel – if you are lucky, that is.

The tracks offer variety and a number of different challenges. The hardest to ride is Longchamp. It takes a long time to master France's premier racecourse, with its false straight which is really still some way from the finishing part of the action. In some ways, I think I've rewritten the way to ride the track, where for so long the only correct way of riding there was to follow the pattern of the great French jockey Yves Saint-Martin. He, of course, was the French counterpart and international rival of Lester Piggott for many years and his style at Longchamp reflected the way the French train their horses. In England, the emphasis in training is on stamina and the races are accordingly run at a decent pace. In France, speed and more speed is the emphasis and the races have traditionally been run at a much steadier pace, with all the jockeys coming with a flying late run. I have found that if you take an English horse to run in France and try to play the French jockeys' way, they will swamp you for speed in the last furlong. So to counter this you have to be really bold. I learnt over three or four years that if you go there with even half a query in your mind, you'll get beaten. Boldness pays, and I always try to make sure I ride that way when I go there for any race, but especially a big one.

When I got back to England after my skiing holiday in February 1996, I had arranged to ride a few horses, mainly for David Loder and Reg Hollinshead, on the all-weather tracks. The winners – and I rode nine – might not count for the championship any more, but the riding helped get me back into shape and ready for my first big challenge of 1996, far away in the Arabian desert.

The rise in importance of Arab owners over the past twenty years in racing has been steady and spectacular. The Maktoum family from Dubai, one of the emirates which form the United Arab Emirates, has become easily the most important owning group in the world, and their love of horses is not just a modern development. The breed of the thoroughbred developed from the importation almost 300 years ago of a number of stallions from Arabia. Three of them, the Byerley Turk, the Godolphin Barb or Arabian, and the Darley Arabian are the forerunners of all the present representatives of the breed nowadays known as 'thorough-bred'. It is significant that the family, and Sheikh Mohammed in particular, who is Crown Prince in Dubai, should use the names Darley and, more recently, Godolphin for the two distinct portions of his wide bloodstock interests.

Darley Stud Management is the name under which Sheikh Mohammed's horses, which run in his name and in that of his younger brother Sheikh Ahmed, and horses owned by friends and relatives such as Saeed Manana, are managed from Newmarket. Darley Stud controls up to

1,000 horses in training, and Anthony Stroud is its racing manager. The smaller Godolphin Management is run by Simon Crisford, a former racing journalist who first worked for Sheikh Mohammed as Anthony Stroud's assistant. He spends half the year in Dubai, the rest in Newmarket, where the horses managed by Godolphin are trained under the banner of Saeed bin Suroor. In the last few years, Sheikh Mohammed has concentrated much of his energy on developing a fine racecourse in Dubai, and the fruition of his grand design (after a couple of years, when an international jockeys' series was staged) was the 1996 Dubai World Cup.

As stable jockey for John Gosden and for Godolphin, which in both cases meant riding mainly for Sheikh Mohammed, the enormous project of the Dubai World Cup meant a lot to me, as it did to everyone connected with the Maktoum family. Their involvement in British racing has been immense and I have been very lucky to ride some of the best horses to be trained here in recent years. Lammtarra, Balanchine, Moonshell and Halling will always be high up on my list of the best horses I have ridden however long I am a jockey, and I have to thank John for giving me the chance to prove myself, and the Boss, as everyone in Dubai calls Sheikh Mohammed, for the opportunity to ride for Godolphin.

Any race, whether it has astronomical prize money or not, needs a special kick to get it established, and the Dubai World Cup, even allowing for the fact that there was $4 million on offer, needed to attract a true star to give it credibility. I remember what the critics and cynics said when news of the Dubai World Cup was first released in England: A race in Dubai in late spring on a sand track? It'll only benefit the Maktoum horses who've been preparing in the desert from the autumn. They'll have all the advantages. The English and the Americans might as well not bother – they'll just be there to make the Dubai horses look good.

Sheikh Mohammed, while hoping that the horses originally selected from his and his brothers' strings with such care and trained close to his home in Dubai by Saeed bin Suroor would make a good showing, was more intent on attracting world-class opposition. When owner Allen Paulson agreed to bring Cigar to Dubai, the future of the race was pretty secure. Mr Paulson had been the original owner of Arazi, the flying machine who'd won the Breeders' Cup and in whom Sheikh Mohammed had bought a half-share. Since then the two men had become well acquainted and Mr Paulson's willingness to put his horse's reputation on the line in a race so far away was commendable. Everyone thought the Dubai horses would have an advantage.

I have to say that Sheikh Mohammed did everything possible to get the organisation of the big day right and the whole thing went like clockwork. I was hopeful of going close. After all, Halling, the horse I eventually chose to ride, had won races on the dirt in Dubai the previous winter and had looked a top-class horse when he'd won the Eclipse Stakes and the International at York the previous summer. True, he'd been nowhere when Cigar had won the Breeders' Cup Classic in New York in 1995 but there'd obviously been something wrong with him then. When he won his warm-up race in Dubai a couple of weeks before the World Cup, we were ready.

As it turned out, if we had all looked at things a little more realistically, the true situation might have occurred to us. Halling and the other Dubai horses had, like Pentire who had come over from England, been reared and trained to race on English turf. The fact that Halling had already done well in Dubai was irrelevant. He had been beating other turf horses on sand. Cigar and the other two American horses showed that a specialist is needed. Cigar had been hopeless on turf and had not begun his record-breaking run until they'd switched him back to dirt tracks. While hoping for a good run from Halling, we had to admit that, in our opinion, Cigar was nearly unbeatable. He won the Dubai World Cup, showing the kind of guts that only a top-class performer can pull out when it's most needed. The Americans were 1–2–3 and the World Cup was a success, as all the many visitors, especially the Americans, many of them there for the first time, agreed. Pentire, in fourth, was giving a nice compliment to his old rival Lammtarra.

The timing of the World Cup, just a few days after the start of the turf season, and then the fact that there is very little good racing in England until the Craven meeting at Newmarket, meant that Doncaster became a little episode of its own. When we go back to Doncaster each year, it's always nice to see all the faces, which in many cases you haven't seen much of since the previous autumn. We all use the three days at Doncaster to catch up on all the news from the winter: where everyone has been riding or on holiday, how they like their new jobs and that sort of thing. The jockeys are basically one big family. They spend more time in each other's company in the weighing room during the year than they do at home. Between the races, until we get changed when we've finished, we just sit and talk together, or watch races from the other meetings. But in March 1996, there was one big difference for me: Walter Swinburn's peg was empty. I usually sit next to Wally, but he had had a terrible fall from an unraced horse in Hong Kong during the winter and had suffered major injuries, of which the worst was to his head. For a while he was on the critical list in intensive care in one of Hong Kong's best hospitals. Happily, he made a complete recovery and the public were able to appreciate his skills again in the summer. In my opinion, Wally has more natural talent than any jockey riding today.

The atmosphere in the jockeys' room can be manic at times, with everyone rushing here and there, but it might surprise people to know that very few of us have nicknames, at least not ones which people are prepared to say to your face. Walter is known, largely because of some pressmen, as The Choirboy, but to us he's simply Wally. One unkind name for a jockey I daren't mention is By-pass, because of the number of times he's been overlooked for a top job. There was a lot more humour in the weighing room when Richard Fox was still riding. Foxy was funny, however well or badly he was doing. Nowadays, though, most of the boys are busy speaking to their agents between rides.

Whereas the jump jockeys go out on the track knowing they will have some falls and can therefore sometimes take action to minimise the consequences, falls on the flat tend to be unexpected. Watching Lester Piggott on two occasions when he did fall from horses revealed just what a great horseman he was. In the Breeders' Cup, the year after his brilliant win on Royal Academy in the first few days of his comeback, Lester came down off the sprinter Mr Brooks. The horse lost his footing, his legs went from under him, but I remember seeing Lester still perfectly balanced as the horse went down. Then, another time, at Goodwood, riding a two-year-old of Richard Hannon's, the saddle came right off, but Lester, cool as ever, stayed on until the last minute, and when he fell he still managed to curl up like a jump jockey before he hit the ground. His injuries, bad enough for a man then already well into his fifties, were nothing compared to what he would have suffered without the knowledge, gained over almost half a century in the saddle, of what to do.

Apart from my latest bad fall in the paddock at Newbury, my worst and most dramatic fall had come at Haydock the previous year. The horse in question was a great favourite of mine. Wainwright was the stable pet at John Gosden's. A tough six-year-old, he was a fine big horse, but had terrible feet and John and his staff did a great job ever getting him on to the track. Anyway, he went to Haydock in August for a Group 3, a race which would probably be his last appearance on the track. It was hoped that if he won or went very close, there might be a job for him somewhere overseas as a stallion, but otherwise there was talk that maybe he could be sold to me so I could give him to Catherine as a riding horse.

The race went well at first, but suddenly, after we turned into the straight, I remember hearing a bang and seeing the ground. Then I can just remember a few flashes, and me being in an ambulance. I felt a terrible pain in my back. Then in hospital afterwards, I kept waking up for a few minutes, but then drifting away again. Before the fall the thought of not being champion would have been as bad as not being able to live. Now, I thought, 'Jesus, what does being champion matter?' At that point it didn't mean anything to me. Here I was in bed with a drip, with a terrible headache and a painful back. I was given two tablets, elephant-sized, probably morphine or something, and I felt as right as rain. After three or four days my head was okay and soon my back was fine, too. It's amazing to think you can fall at that speed and come out of it all right. I've had maybe seven or eight falls like that. Obviously, at first it is a knock to your confidence. For the first two to three weeks you have to worry whether you will feel the same about riding. Some jockeys never truly recover from a bad fall, but in most cases time is a great healer.

Richard Hills and I flew out to Dubai straight after the Kempton bank holiday meeting to ride some of the Godolphin hopefuls. Almost as soon as we arrived, after just a couple of hours' sleep, we were out at the Al Quoz stables, riding horse after horse in fact-finding gallops. By the time we'd finished we were dripping with sweat as, even though it was still very early in the morning, the day was warming up quickly. As I said when describing the Dubai World Cup, not all the horses at Sheikh Mohammed's stables, which are situated just behind the office he uses in his palace, are suited to the sand track. But I was interested to see Mark Of Esteem, who looked in tremendous condition, his coat, like those of many of the other horses there, gleaming with health, and quite a contrast to the majority of horses I'd seen struggling with the continuing cold weather at Newmarket. Another horse which looked in great shape was Mick's Love, which had been bought out of Mark Johnston's stable the previous autumn.

We returned to England for the Craven meeting. The gap between the Doncaster March meeting and the Craven meeting in April seems abnormally long. Even with the Dubai World Cup and the Grand National which follows it, the racegoers in England do not have much to interest them. The fixtures look very unappetising until you get to the Craven meeting and the re-opening of Newmarket. In 1996, in England, the winter went on and on, and by the time the Craven meeting came round, we were wondering if the weather would ever get any better.

For me, the Craven meeting is the most nerve-racking

of the entire year. For everyone in the top stables, all the hopes and expectations of the previous six months are about to be tested. It is hard to over-emphasise just how crucial this time of the year is. The first four of the five English Classics are settled within just over five weeks from the beginning of May to the end of the first week in June, with only the St Leger, far off in September, to come. Yet really the season doesn't get going until the Craven meeting and that is barely two weeks before the two Guineas races.

The trainers all hope their horses will be ready to go well in their trial races and then graduate to the Guineas, or in the case of the more staying types, the Derby and the Oaks. The spring of 1996 was a frustrating one for John Gosden's stable, which, with the Godolphin horses still in Dubai, was taking most of my attention at this stage.

At the end of 1995, John and I believed there were several horses with real Classic chances, especially Lord Of Men, who had won his last three races as a two-year-old, culminating with a fine performance in the Group 1 Prix de la Salamandre. Then, coming into Craven week, we had Pommard, who had won his only race as a two-year-old, Sacho, Santillana and the unraced Shantou backing him up.

By the end of Craven week, Pommard had been well beaten in the Craven Stakes and had fallen out of contention for the Classics; Sacho had been narrowly beaten in his maiden race at Newmarket and was found to have suffered a training problem; and, worst of all, Lord Of Men had sustained quite a serious injury which meant he would be out until autumn at the earliest.

If it is bad for the owner, trainer and jockey, I often wonder how earth-shattering defeat for a Classic hope is for the horse's lad. The trainer will see each horse for a few minutes each day, monitor the horse's work with his lad and then take special notice of the horse on the days he goes to the races. The lad, on the other hand, lives with the horse for as long as the horse is in the stable. Arriving early in the morning, he will muck him out, groom and feed him; he'll encourage him on the gallops and report on his progress each day to the trainer. All his hopes for a good year depend on the horses (usually no more than three) that he looks after. He becomes each horse's nurse, teacher, psychiatrist and biggest defender when other people criticise the horse's ability or honesty. At the start of the year, many of the well-bred horses in the major stables will have their lads dreaming of Epsom and June, and leading in the Derby winner. Sadly, for so many modestly paid, dedicated people, it can only become reality for one.

When Sacho was beaten in the maiden race at Newmarket, I spent two hours that night walking up and down in my kitchen. I could not believe it. We'd already had to accept that Lord Of Men was going to miss the bulk of the season. Now Sacho. I'd been very pleased with his work and was shocked that he could lose, albeit in the best, maiden company. Pommard had probably been a little too inexperienced to cope with the best of last year's two-year-olds in the Craven Stakes, but events in the next couple of months showed that Beauchamp King, Alhaarth and Rio Duvida, three of the other four runners, were all less impressive as three-year-olds, and only Polaris Flight, who was a place ahead of Pommard in the Craven Stakes and later second in the French and Irish Derbys, had really trained on.

The disappointment with John's horses made this a most unhappy week for me, added to which Ian Balding and David Loder, the other two big stables for which I regularly ride, were also not yet in great form. I felt particularly sorry for David who had been so hopeful that Blue Duster would continue with her unbeaten form which had made her the champion two-year-old filly of 1995. She had a problem and was sent to Dubai in early summer to take advantage of the fine medical facilities which Sheikh Mohammed has developed there.

All the time, I had the feeling that the very cold weather, which went on right until the end of May, was one of the main reasons for the problems in many stables. Horses were simply not thriving as they normally do in a warm spring. Those stables which did hit form early tended to keep it. Those that were out of luck simply had to wait for things to improve.

Usually, though, when you are at your lowest, thinking nothing will happen for you, one horse comes through to save the day. At Stanley House stables, John's head lad Rodney is one of life's great optimists. Every horse he rides is somewhere between Nijinsky and Pegasus, the flying horse, but after a number of times hearing him say to me, 'Have a sit on Santillana, he's a good horse', I finally took him up on it. Santillana had won a little race at Edinburgh, now known as Musselburgh, at the November meeting, hardly the time or the place to look for Classic clues, but when I sat on him I had to agree he was a nice type.

I was in Dubai when Santillana made his three-year-old début in a small race at Ripon. He won it with a little to spare and, even though he didn't have the Derby engagement, John let him take his chance in the Sandown Classic Trial. Although on his ratings he was miles behind the others on form, several of John's lads were more than hopeful. I have to admit I was surprised when he beat Glory Of Dancer, a Group 1 winner in Italy as a two-year-old, and Luca Cumani's Mons, one of the best of the previous year's juveniles, although time was beginning to show them as a moderate bunch. Then, just when we had something to be happy about, Santillana joined the team on the sidelines.

John Gosden can therefore look back on the first half of what should have been his best year since returning to England after a great career training in California as his unluckiest. So I felt it was unfair when an article written by David Ashforth appeared in *Sporting Life* rubbishing John as a trainer. Ashforth was merely putting into print some of the ideas of the whispering types who create so much jealousy and discontent in racing. There's always someone telling an owner to move his horse down the road, where the grass, as they say, is greener. In John's case he was supposed to have had unlimited chances and achieved nothing. As someone perhaps better qualified, seeing the horses every day, I would have to disagree. The middle-of-the-road horses in every stable are hard to win with. When your best half-dozen candidates all go wrong through no one's fault, it's hard to salvage much, but I'm sure John will be back to silence even the most unfair critics. He has won plenty of major Group races, especially in France, and he'll win plenty more.

7 The 2,000 Guineas

With the Guineas meeting next on the agenda, my thoughts inevitably turned to the imminent return of the big blue team from Dubai. Godolphin had been the sensation of 1995, winning the three biggest races of the European season – the Epsom Derby, the King George VI and Queen Elizabeth Diamond Stakes at Ascot and the Prix de l'Arc de Triomphe at Longchamp – with the same horse, Lammtarra, rightly regarded as Horse of the Year and now retired unbeaten to stud, a status restricted to very few top racehorses.

The Godolphin idea had been conceived of entirely by Sheikh Mohammed, the third of four brothers who rule the Emirate of Dubai. Most people find it hard enough to hold down a single job. Sheikh Mohammed, as well as heading two major racing entities, Darley Stud Management and Godolphin, has another time-consuming occupation: he is Defence Minister of the UAE. His duties commit him to the same round of visits and talks, conferences and worries as any other Minister of a Gulf nation. So, in an attempt to combine his two major responsibilities, Sheikh Mohammed set up Godolphin. The idea grew from his belief that it would be beneficial to the development of some young, very promising animals to be sheltered from the cold winters in Europe and to winter instead in the warmth of the Gulf. In this way, for six months each year, he could also, when in Dubai and not on overseas duty, monitor his horses' progress on a daily basis. As he says, 'I am the owner. I want to see my horses and have a say in how they are trained.' As a horseman with great experience in endurance races, and a man whose people bred the animals which were the fore-runners of the present thoroughbreds, it is hard to imagine anyone better qualified to help with his own horses' training.

For Godolphin, he would provide the best staff, facilities and medical treatment. The entire programme would be based on conditioning to prepare the horses for the demands of the European season. In 1995, the major wins extended also to Japan and the United States. The Sheikh believes that Dubai is a strategic point from which to send horses east and west in the quest for major triumphs.

After Lammtarra's Arc, the news had come that one of Godolphin's major influences would be leaving. Jeremy Noseda had decided to try his luck as a trainer in California, and he made a fine start there with a very good strike-rate of winners to runners. In his place Sheikh Mohammed and his team recruited Tom Albertrani, an American who had been associated with the Cigar stable of Bill Mott in New York. Tom's wife Fonda was the regular work rider for Cigar, and it was a bitter-sweet moment for the Albertranis when they watched Cigar win the Dubai World Cup. I have since got to know them better and they are a hard-working, knowledgeable couple who have fitted in well.

The Godolphin team is very tight-knit, loyal to their boss and to each other. The normal arrangement with horses and their running plans is that the trainer will suggest a race to the owner, and, within reason, expect him to approve the plan. Godolphin works to a different system. From the Boss, Sheikh Mohammed, down to the lads who ride the work, including the jockeys, all opinions are important. True, Sheikh Mohammed has the final say, but everyone else has the chance to offer their opinion and in some cases change the Boss's mind.

As one of the world's leading owners, and a noted horseman in his home country, Sheikh Mohammed has a wide knowledge of horses as individuals, and a vast experience in the selective area of thoroughbred breeding and racing. He has put together, with the help of his advisers, a wonderful band of mares and now he can rely on a greater proportion of home-bred horses. His idea to winter his young horses in Dubai was so different from anything attempted before it was viewed as unrealistic by many traditional racing people in Britain. The results, though, with such horses as Lammtarra, Moonshell, Balanchine, Mark Of Esteem and Halling, to name the best five advertisements for his visionary idea, have been spectacular. As the person lucky enough to ride them, I'd say the idea was brilliant. The care and skill with which it has been carried out, under the Boss's direction, by the Godolphin staff, has been mind-boggling.

Saeed bin Suroor looks more like a doctor or lawyer than a racehorse trainer, and when his appointment as Godolphin's new trainer was announced at the start of 1995 few could have expected the results to be as sensational as they proved. First, with Jeremy Noseda's and more recently with Tom Albertrani's help, Saeed has rapidly found his feet and has made an amazing impact. Saeed and Simon Crisford, once an assistant trainer to Sir Mark Prescott, form the main link with the Boss.

With three weeks to go to the Guineas, and knowing just how skilful the training team of Godolphin were at timing their horses' big-race preparation, I could not wait for them to arrive at Newmarket. They flew in from Dubai a few days before the Guineas meeting, and the press reaction was almost one of, 'Here they are, nobody else gets a chance. They'll win everything again.' Those of us closer to the team knew that this attitude was stupid and unrealistic. No Group 1 race is easily won. To win a Classic you need the best horse, in absolutely top shape, and we were still aware that the best colts from last year, Alhaarth and Beauchamp King, the horse who had recently surprised Mark Of Esteem in the Craven Stakes, would not be easily beaten in the 2,000 Guineas. As for the 1,000 Guineas, our top hope was Bint Shadayid and we never thought that she could beat Bosra Sham, the unbeaten filly of Henry Cecil's who had won her comeback race in the Fred Darling Stakes at Newbury with such style. We didn't have long to wait to find out.

The two horses which I had been most impressed with in Dubai, Mark Of Esteem and Mick's Love, were among the first of the Godolphin team to run, pretty much straight off the plane and almost before they had settled into the Moulton Paddocks stables where they and the rest of the team were to spend their summer. With four runners, two in one race, on the first day of the three-day Guineas meeting, the team had little time to spare. Mick's Love was first to run in the Newmarket Stakes and this looked quite a tough race. There was Henry Cecil's Clever Cliché, a good maiden winner at Nottingham and an intended Epsom Derby runner, and David Loder's Bahamian Knight, a horse David had always regarded highly. I had ridden plenty of winners both for David and Bahamian Knight's owner Edward St George and it was slightly ironic for me that, at the end of a tough race, Mick's Love beat Bahamian Knight in a photo-finish.

Again the cries came – 'Godolphin are doing it all over again' – but we did not make the winner's circle with our three other runners, Fatefully doing best with a second to Ta Rib in the fillies' maiden race. We were disappointed, especially to be beaten by five lengths, but when Ta Rib came out next time to win the French 1,000 Guineas, the Newmarket result was a little easier to accept. Still, with the big one to come, I was very happy about my chances in the 2,000 Guineas. Mark Of Esteem was clearly in great shape and I had been happy with his work in Dubai. But several questions remained. Did he have a turn of foot? If he did, how long would he be able to sustain it? Does he lengthen, and for how long? He had raced only twice before, finishing just behind Alhaarth at Newmarket the previous July, and then easily won a maiden race at Goodwood. We would have to find out everything else about him in the 2,000 Guineas.

I have ridden in plenty of dramatic races, but few which matched this 2,000 Guineas, which, for its unpredictability, the tightness of the finish, the controversy about the watering and another more personal controversy, was unique. There had been much talk, as before any big race, about where the best draw would be. Despite the cold weather in the spring there had been hardly any rain for a long time before the Guineas meeting. But whereas the ground for the trials meeting had been allowed to be very fast, it was decided to water quite heavily for the meeting two weeks later. In the event, many of the best-fancied horses were drawn middle to high, including Alhaarth, the hot favourite, Storm Trooper and Danehill Dancer, winners of two other trial races, and the very fast Royal Applause, who had been unbeaten as a two-year-old and had won the Middle Park Stakes.

I was drawn one off the rail in stall two and was happy to track the leader, World Premier, on that side, but he was already being outpaced by Royal Applause who went at 100 miles an hour up the middle of the track. All the time I felt I was going very easily, and had only to wait for a gap at the right moment to go on and win. At the two-furlong pole, I looked to my right, and noticed Beauchamp King and Alhaarth were almost in line with me, and that Royal Applause, just a few horse widths across, had already weakened. At this stage, Bijou d'Inde and Jason Weaver had just taken the lead and I noticed Even Top beginning a challenge on my outside.

When I got to the furlong pole I asked Mark Of Esteem for his effort, and he quickened far better than any other horse in the race. But then I had to ride him all the way to the line, and the others were coming back after him. All the jockeys on the front three horses were soon riding at full throttle and, at the line, Mark Of Esteem and Even Top were very close, just ahead of Bijou d'Inde with the rest a long way behind. Philip Robinson was convinced he had won. I was not sure, but as I'd hit the line I'd felt that I'd just held on. Because there was a new rule in operation we were made to stay out on the track instead of going back to unsaddle. We were out there for a long time, walking

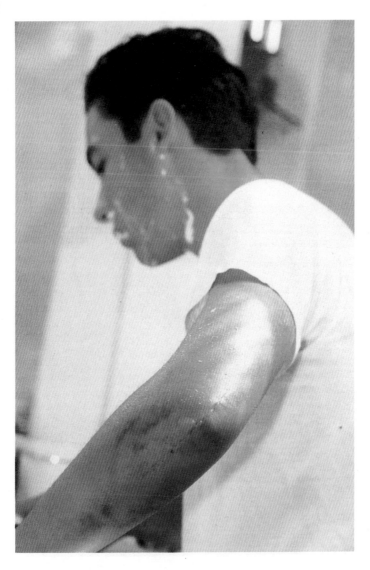

My injured elbow.

Recovering on holiday with my dad.

The great Gianfranco Dettori.

Champion!

All dressed up for Royal Ascot.

Getting fit.

With Sheikh Mohammed and his trainer, saeed bin Suroor, in the background.

Halling winning the International Juddmonte Stakes at York.

Back in the limelight.

Indiscreet winning in the style of a Group horse for '97.

around for ages while a second print was scrutinised. It was strangely quiet, and then the announcement came: 'Result of the photo-finish.' Before the words came out, I quickly checked my number cloth – I was number seven. 'First, number seven.' We had won. On the spur of the moment I did a repeat of my Angel Cordero jump, which had been such a cause of enjoyment for everyone at the Arc when Lammtarra had won. The only trouble was, I simply hopped into the arms of John Davies, Godolphin's travelling head lad. John said, 'You'd better get back on.' I was chuffed to bits, and thought, 'Great, I've finally won the one race I've always wanted to win, the 2,000 Guineas.' It was the race my dad had won on Bolkonski and Wollow all those years ago and the first 2,000 Guineas for Godolphin.

It was then that people started to realise that, technically, a rule of racing had been broken. No jockey is allowed to dismount and come into contact with anyone before entering the unsaddling enclosure. But I was only in that position because they had made us stay out on the track. I believe that action could have been dangerous for the welfare of both horses, and the tension that being in an unaccustomed place caused us added to the difficulties. The 'no-contact' rule was originally framed in the days when cameras and television were still many years off. A jockey could ride in a race without some of the required weight and have it slipped back to him as he returned to the weighing room to weigh in. But, nowadays, to slip someone a big piece of lead, enough to make a difference in a photo-finish, is not a very practical idea.

I was very surprised when Mark Tompkins, the trainer of Even Top, went on television the following day and said that I was unprofessional. He admitted that he would not be appealing the result, but said that he reckoned he had grounds for doing so, suggesting by implication that it was only because he was such a good sport that he did not intend appealing. Amid all the controversy, I was reassured when Mr David Pipe, the Jockey Club's Director of Publicity, declared that in his view racing should be fun and that my action in jumping off had shown just how delighted I had been. I was only showing my excitement, pleasure for the Godolphin people, especially Sheikh Mohammed, and my relief that I had not been beaten in a tight finish in a third Guineas after Grand Lodge and Balanchine.

That flying Angel Cordero leap cost me a lecture in the stewards' room and a £500 fine, but that was nothing compared to the treatment given to all three jockeys who had tried so hard to win the first Classic of the year, and to give the owners and trainers the great distinction and commercial advantage of collecting a Classic race. We were all found guilty by the stewards of excessive use of the whip. Jason was banned for two days, Philip for four and I got an eight-day ban, to my absolute amazement. I'd had to ride all the way to the line. This was a Classic race. I am not known as a jockey hard on his horses, and in order to keep him going, I did exceed the official maximum of ten strokes with the whip. I understand it was supposed to be sixteen, and the stewards said that I had hit the horse out of time with his action. When you hit a horse quickly, as I did, you do not make as hard a contact as someone hitting every three or four strides with full force. I used the whip to encourage him to keep going. I may have given him a stroke too many, but the fact was that at the end of one mile of Newmarket we had won by less than an inch. I felt I deserved credit. Instead, I was banned for eight days for having tried too hard. Add to that the criticism by Mark Tompkins that I had been 'most unprofessional' and you will understand why my fifth Classic win seemed to have exploded in my face, especially when it seems that non-trying jockeys get away with a small fine. In my case, an eight-day ban can cost me a lot of money. It did.

The next day I got up at seven a.m. to rush down for the papers. Normally, on a Sunday, the racing papers are not published, but this was 1,000 Guineas day, so I couldn't wait to read about my 2,000 Guineas win, one of the dream days of my career so far. But instead of great headlines about what I believed was one of my best big-race rides, the stories were all about my riding ban for use of the whip, and about jumping off and the chance of there being an objection about my flying jump. Then they talked about the bans for the first three jockeys and it was as if we were butchers. I cannot imagine winning a big race and having so much disappointment afterwards.

So, for me, one of the best wins of this or any year was spoilt by some petty stories in the press and the remarks of Mark Tompkins. I was not trying to cheat the system, merely showing my happiness at winning. It seemed a lot of people jumped on the band-waggon. When Mark Tompkins was interviewed on Channel 4 the next day, I did understand how he must have felt at missing the 2,000 Guineas by such a small margin. I felt nothing against him but did feel that it was a little below the belt when he said I should go and work in Chipperfield's Circus. What he probably didn't know was that my mother came from a circus family. He also said I was less professional than most apprentices.

All those remarks really hurt me. I am employed by Sheikh Mohammed and John Gosden and if anyone should complain of my actions, when I jump off a horse, for example, it should be them. If they disapproved I am sure they would have told me by now. What Mark Tompkins seemed to forget was that most of the top jockeys spend almost as much time on horses as they do with their feet on the ground. They feel for the horses, and I reckon I know which horse it is safe to try the jump from, and from which it is not.

When things turn against you, it is important that the people you work for are on your side. I am lucky that John Gosden has become not just a boss, but a good friend, and Sheikh Mohammed and the rest of the Godolphin people are also always there for me. After reading the papers on the Sunday morning of the Guineas meeting, I went to the track in a terrible frame of mind. I was very sour and felt that my skill and maybe even my integrity were being questioned. As a jockey you can only try to the best of your ability. Later in the summer, Mick Kinane made the wrong choice about which horse to ride in the Irish Derby. Zagreb, the horse he could have ridden for his own stable, won by six lengths. Mick had preferred to take an outside ride on Dr Massini, the horse who had been favourite for Epsom before going wrong. I know I would find it very hard to take any outside ride rather than stay with Godolphin, or John, and, if they are not involved, Ian Balding or David Loder, if they wanted me. Matty Cowing my agent believes you have to stay with your people, and I go along with that. You have to be loyal to your people. They stand by you when you need them most, and in my case I want to use my skills for the benefit of those people who use me.

People often use Lester Piggott as an example of someone whose loyalty was questionable. Sometimes, of course, he made unpopular decisions and his search for the best possible Derby ride in the days when he dominated the race occasionally put someone's nose out of joint. But the example of his split with Sir Noël Murless, which led to his association with Vincent O'Brien which lasted until the end of the two men's careers, was more about the rights of jockeys than loyalty. Lester is very loyal to the people he values and while I was just starting on my career he gave me many opportunities.

After the 1996 Irish Derby, the press were full of sympathy for Mick Kinane and almost made more of his bad luck than the brilliant win of Zagreb and the great training achievement of Dermot Weld, who has had Mick as his stable jockey for eleven years. I'd hate to think I'd have missed a winner like that, but if you do you just shrug your shoulders and go on to the next race. Mick's a pro and knew that later in the year he'd be back on Zagreb again.

I haven't been with John Gosden anywhere near as long as eleven years. Indeed, I had not even made that first trip to England when Mick and Dermot began their partnership, but I have known John long enough to be glad to call him my friend and happy to tell everyone else, if not him, that he is my hero. He's the first person I would go to for advice about anything concerning all walks of life, not just racing and riding but personal things, too.

Anyway, I arrived at the track on 1,000 Guineas day in a bad mood. I was riding Bint Shadayid in the big race. With Bosra Sham under a cloud because she had been treated for a bruised foot almost right up to the time of the race, we were hoping for the best. But Bosra Sham, thanks to her trainer Henry Cecil and probably just as much to the stable blacksmith, kept her unbeaten record with a brave effort. We ran on to finish third, a good achievement with Bint Shadayid, who is a bit of a nervous filly. I hardly spoke to anyone that day, and when Tony Stafford of the *Daily Telegraph* suggested we do a small piece together for the paper under a contract I have with them, I left him in no doubt that I had other things on my mind. Not a good day. But then it isn't surprising as I'm not a robot, but an individual with feelings and emotions. I work hard, but I can get upset. I'm just myself. Luckily, time heals, and nothing heals you quicker than the anticipation of a big win later in the year.

As I left Newmarket to go home after the 1,000 Guineas, apart from the satisfaction of finishing placed in another Classic race there was also one good win to enjoy. In the race before the 1,000 Guineas, the Pretty Polly Stakes, I rode a filly called Pricket. She had been unimpressive on the sand in Dubai, but the Godolphin team were hoping she would still show herself useful when she got back to England, as she had won her only race at Sandown the previous August very nicely. We thought she would have needed to improve to win this Listed race as she was meeting Magnificient Style, a stable-companion of Bosra Sham. Magnificient Style, owned by Mr Fustok, had won her maiden race at Kempton by six lengths from a decent animal of Luca Cumani's, Migwar, so it was hardly surprising that she started favourite at Newmarket. The race, however, proved no contest. I was always cantering on Pricket, let her take the lead at the furlong pole and, once she went clear, I never saw another horse. She had plenty in hand at the finish, where she was five lengths clear of Faraway Waters. Magnificient Style was only third. When Magnificient Style easily won York's Musidora Stakes from Sil Sila – who later won the French Oaks – it became clear that Pricket was the one to beat in the Oaks at Epsom.

Of course, after my ban I would not be in York for the spring meeting, which is often such a good guide to the Epsom Classics. The Dante Stakes, and the Glasgow Stakes, which are both over ten and a half furlongs, are especially good guides to the Epsom Derby. While the other jockeys were building up their book of rides for York, I had a couple of days' action at Chester and then went away to Amalfi, in Southern Italy, for a few days' holiday with Catherine. We stayed there for four days, and it was great to get out in some warm sunshine, instead of the endlessly cold spring back in England. The holiday did not start too well. We missed our flight by two minutes. The lady from British Airways told us the flight was closed, but there was still half an hour before take-off time. So instead of going direct to Naples we had to fly from Gatwick to Paris, take another flight from Paris to Rome and a third local flight from Rome to Naples. We finally got there at eight p.m. about ten hours later than we had expected. For most of the four days, I took the chance to rest, sleeping for up to fifteen hours a day.

I returned home relaxed and recharged for the rest of the season. Back in England, I found that Peter Burrell, my marketing manager, had arranged for me to help promote the Vodafone Derby meeting. The racecourse at Epsom and the race sponsors were anxious for the race to get as much coverage in the press and broadcasting media as possible, as it was facing strong competition from the Euro '96 soccer championships. With England's first game in the championships starting at Wembley ten minutes after the off-time at Epsom, the course's worries were understandable, but with, I hope, some help from me, the race attracted a crowd of 56,000.

As part of my round of visits to radio stations and other media appointments around the country, I was pleased to call in on the England football team's training base at Bisham Abbey for a photo call. I did a few pictures with my friend David Platt, whom I have known for some time as he is married to the sister of Nicky Vaughan, John Gosden's travelling head lad. I was delighted when in 1995 David signed for my team, Arsenal, and he and the England squad did a great job in Euro '96.

I reckon that the Derby crowd was pretty good in the circumstances, and that the decision to retain Saturday as Derby day for the immediate future is probably the right one. A Saturday Derby means that people who have to work during the week can attend. Also, children will not have to be in school. I know that when young people get the chance to attend major events they are likely to become enthusiasts. There is no question that if the race reverted to the traditional date there would be fewer young people and families attending. With an entry fee of £10 for a car on the Downs in the middle of the course, the Derby is an inexpensive weekend venue for ordinary families.

I was not under tremendous pressure at the Derby because I was riding an outsider, Shantou. He is a well-bred horse and I knew he would last the mile and a half. He had run a good race at Newmarket on his reappearance and had then gone on to win a mile maiden at Sandown. On Derby day itself his odds came down from 40–1 to 25–1, so obviously a few people fancied him. It was definitely a pretty open contest. Shantou ran a hell of a race, putting in his best right at the end and came in third. I was delighted.

Before the race, I had held out higher hopes for Pricket in the Oaks. She had come to Epsom as favourite after winning the Pretty Polly Stakes at Newmarket in very impressive style. I must say I thought I had an excellent chance of winning my third Oaks in a row. It was not to be. Pricket never fired, and although she came second, she was beaten by nine lengths by the Henry Cecil-trained Lady Carla, with Geoff Wragg's Mezzogiorno third. Pricket did not give her best that day. Oh well, that's the luck of racing!

8 Injury

The Chinese, I'm told, have a saying, 'the bigger the front, the bigger the back'. I suppose that means the greater the success you are enjoying, the bigger the fall is likely to be. For me, two days in June 1996 certainly showed the truth of that. It all started so quietly. A morning of riding work, starting very early with Godolphin, getting some of the Royal Ascot horses ready, and then the prospect of about nine or ten rides, split between Yarmouth in the afternoon and Kempton in the evening. Because of the distance from Yarmouth to Kempton I'd have to catch a plane and as I would be riding the next day at Newbury, I'd arranged to stay that night at the Kingsclere stables with trainer Ian Balding so that I would not have to go back late that night to Newmarket and re-trace my steps back to Newbury the next day. Ian was another of my regular trainers to be suffering. With the awful winter, Ian's stables simply hadn't fired. At the time, Ian had won only four races. You had to sympathise with him.

Tony Stafford of the *Daily Telegraph* was going to Yarmouth, and he broke his journey from Hertfordshire to pick me up. We went through a few things, talking about the Derby of the week before, and Tony was keen to find out what I thought about my rides for the day, in case I could give him a winner. I'd had a look in the paper when I'd got back from the work and before taking a quick nap and I thought the best chance I had at Yarmouth was probably Brian Gubby's horse Easy Dollar, who was going in a three-horse race over six furlongs. They say jockeys are not the greatest tipsters in the world, although I don't really agree with that as some of the newspaper guys must make their readers broke. This time, though, I was a little off the mark. Easy Dollar, 6–4 joint-favourite, trailed home last of three. My other three rides at Yarmouth all won, and to make Tony's day, I had three more at Kempton that night. It was the first time I'd ridden six winners in a day: my best before had been five.

With six wins in a day behind me, I was on top of the world. People might think it's nothing special, and that it's the horses that do the work. But the fact is you have to go out there, often encouraging a horse, who might not be too keen, to do his best and get as near to winning as possible, for the sake of his owner and trainer who invest so much time and money into his welfare.

So, leaving Kempton that night, I allowed myself just a little smile of satisfaction. What with my big suspension after the 2,000 Guineas win on Mark Of Esteem and one or two other setbacks, I had been trailing Pat Eddery, who had been going really well since coming back fresh for the fight at the start of the turf season. His agent and brother-in-law, Terry Ellis, had been his usual busy self, keeping Pat's name in the trainers' minds, and Pat as ever did the business. But now, with John Gosden coming into form, David Loder's team showing signs of getting going and Godolphin also warming up some nice two-year-olds to go with their established stars, I was hoping to cut into Pat's lead.

Ten rides in a day, following an early start on the gallops, is quite draining, so I wasn't sorry when Ian allowed me to miss first lot and let me lie in. Ever since Ian stood by me in those dark days three years ago, I've enjoyed my occasional visits to Kingsclere even though each time I have to sit through yet another playing of the Mill Reef video, which must be wearing out by now, with all the times Ian plays it. Still, no wonder he's so proud of that great horse. Ian's wife, Emma, son Andrew and daughter Clare, who now does such a good job in the Sports Department of BBC Radio Five Live, are all very knowledgeable and great company. Matty knows that even if one of Ian's horses might not have the most obvious chance in a race and we've been offered other rides, I'd rather be on Ian's horse. Loyalty deserves to be repaid.

Ian woke me with the papers at around eight thirty a.m. I enjoyed reading about 'Frankie's six-timer' and then we went out with the horses for second lot. It was a beautiful summer's day and I wore a T-shirt, jeans and my racing boots, as I hadn't brought any of my own riding-out gear. I rode four of Ian's nicer two-year-olds. I was pleased to see that they all seemed to be coming into form and looking quite well just when it was needed. It was good to see Ian looking a little happier. After riding out, we went back to the house to change for the races. I was very hopeful as I had some nice rides booked.

Going into the paddock before the Listed race for fillies I remember feeling very happy. I was very philosophical that day, in relaxed mode. As I got to the paddock I remember seeing Damien Oliver. It was a surprise to see him there. He's Australian and about my age. He's the jockey sensation of the moment in Australia and rides incredibly well. I told him I'd have a chat with him in the weighing room after the race. I was riding a grey filly, Shawanni, for the Godolphin team. I'd ridden her before and she hadn't been too bad, but she's one of those fillies you wouldn't like to upset. She's one of those girls, she could be anything, she's gonna be trouble!

When I got on her she froze and would not go anywhere. I took my feet out of the irons and told her lad to take a half-turn behind one of the other horses as she did not seem to want to be in front by herself. So the lad took the half-turn and she froze again. The next minute she reared up. Normally, when a horse freezes you have one or two seconds to decide whether you want to jump off. She went straight over on to her back with me on top.

At that stage I had only one thought: 'She's going to squash me.' Shawanni just veered off a little to the left, though, and landed to my right. I was lucky, otherwise she would have smashed my pelvis. As I landed, I felt a tremendous pain. In that moment I couldn't really pick out where the pain was coming from. But I felt really faint. Within fifteen seconds I'd come to terms with the situation, realising I could not move my left arm. The first thing I discovered was that I could move my fingers, which was a great relief, but when I tried to move my elbow, I was in real pain. I had landed on the tarmac and because, before, I'd broken my right elbow, I knew straight away that the other elbow was broken. A few people came over straight away and they all stood there. I was in pain and obviously in shock. Jane Chapple-Hyam, the wife of Peter Chapple-Hyam, who trains at Manton for Robert Sangster, asked them to take

the pin out of my collar. Jockeys usually wear a pin and Jane
was worried it might stop my breathing properly.

Hardly anyone realised that I'd done some serious
damage. Even the doctor came and said it was probably
'only severe bruising'. I just said: 'I broke my elbow.'
Eventually, the ambulance people put me onto a stretcher
and were going to take me into the medical room. I said,
'Take me straight to hospital', but still we couldn't leave
until another ambulance was sent for. We waited half an
hour for the ambulance to come, and it took another half-
hour to get to Reading District Hospital. Typically, when I
got to the Casualty Department, I was not the only person
waiting to be seen. Everyone in the Reading area seemed to
have chosen that afternoon to get an injury of some sort
and it was an hour and a half before I was seen.

In that time I was in such pain that I thought I would
pass out. To forget the pain I tried to go to sleep.
Eventually, I was taken for an X-ray and only then, when
the doctor saw my X-ray, which showed the main bone
forcing down and right through the joint, did he say, 'Give
that man an injection.' I was wheeled down to a nice
private ward with a TV. Richard Dodds was the consultant
looking after me. He said that, if I was happy, he would
operate on me in the morning. Apart from my family, the
closest people to me in England are John Gosden and
Barney Curley. I spoke to John and he arranged everything.
Catherine came down later with Andy, my driver. They
stayed in a nearby bed and breakfast, which the nurses
found for them, and came to see me in the morning. John
was there, too.

Operations scare me, especially the anaesthetic, when
you never know if you are going to wake up afterwards.
When John came in he looked very worried and pale.

Probably, he was more worried than me. I was told everything would be all right and I was reassured when I saw the anaesthetist. I had played football with him in a charity match a year earlier. He put the anaesthetic in my arm, and I felt myself go. It must have been just before I fell asleep when I remember saying: 'I love you all.'

I woke up at around four p.m. and my arm really hurt. I was disoriented, because of the painkillers, I suppose. Barney came to see me, with Catherine and Andy. John stayed until nine to see Richard Dodds, who told him everything had gone okay. The whole thing at the hospital impressed me, and one aspect I hadn't really expected was just how nice the nurses were. What they have to go through, working with fifty people in the ward all with different problems, yet always they seem to have a smile on their faces. When I got home, I sent them a signed picture.

Because I had had a broken elbow before, I realised it would take a long time, probably three to four months, for me to recover properly. It could not have come at a worse time, with Royal Ascot the following week. When I got home on the Monday I had to come to terms with the fact that I would be out for a while. I had a bad night and, the next morning, the only thing I had to look forward to was watching Italy play West Germany in the Euro '96 football championships later that day.

It was the first day of Royal Ascot and Colin Rate, my best friend, came to watch the meeting on TV with me, and other people kept popping in to see how I was. I said that if some of my horses won at Ascot I wouldn't get up. Well, the first race came on TV and Charnwood Forest, who I would have ridden, bolted in. It was such a shock. It was like when something suddenly hits you in the stomach. We had a late lunch and everyone really took the mickey out of me. At first it was hard to digest – all I could do was glance at my arm and think 'You'll live'. I was disappointed for a different reason later in the meeting when Mark Of Esteem ran so badly. The St James's Palace Stakes was for me the race of the meeting and so it proved with Bijou d'Inde getting back under a great ride from Jason to beat Ashkalani.

That night, Catherine had invited her friends Katie and Julian for dinner, so I was to have my cooking hat on. I called my sister to ask her for a special pasta recipe. I cooked the pasta and made a sauce with sausage, onion, bacon and tomato, and served it with lots of Parmesan. The food was great, but Italy only managed a 0–0 draw. Once everyone realised Italy had been eliminated from the championships, the phone started to ring with so-called friends offering plenty of abuse. Italy were out and Charnwood Forest had won at Ascot. No wonder I got up and went to bed early!

The Wednesday at Royal Ascot had never held great promise for me, but I had been meant to ride the French-trained filly Tulipa for Sheikh Mohammed in the Ribblesdale Stakes in the first race on Gold Cup day. When she won for the André Fabre stable that was disappointment enough, and then, of course, came the race I had been looking forward to for a long time. The Gold Cup might be over two and a half miles, but it is Royal Ascot's own special 'Classic' race. I have always enjoyed riding in the Gold Cup, and won it twice on Drum Taps for Lord Huntingdon. Few horses stay two and a half miles, and for Godolphin's Classic Cliché to win he would not only need to last out the trip, but have too much class for Double Trigger, the previous year's Gold Cup winner. I was pretty confident Classic Cliché would stay the distance, as he is such a relaxed horse, and as a St Leger winner I was certain he'd have the better finishing speed, but, at the same time, I knew the fast ground was not ideal for him.

Of course, Classic Cliché just sat on the tail of Double Trigger, who made the running, and, when Mick Kinane asked Classic Cliché, he won well. I was already feeling very sorry for myself. Once the TV transmission ended, I went to a local bookmaker to see the last two races. Godolphin won the Chesham Stakes, too, with the newcomer Shamikh, so that meant I'd missed three winners in a single day at Ascot. I had been thinking for some time that I'd have a great chance of winning the trophy for top jockey at the meeting. Three wins in a day would almost certainly (as it turned out they would) have meant that I and not Mick Kinane would have won the London Clubs (formerly Ritz Club) Trophy for the first time at Royal Ascot. To win any trophy at one of the major meetings is rewarding, and I've twice been top jockey at the Glorious Goodwood summer meeting. So to miss this trophy and the prestige that goes with it hit me more than the loss of income.

I knew there would be plenty more chances to win races at Royal Ascot and fulfil that ambition, but I still felt very sorry for myself. Poor Catherine, she was being so nice to me, but I thought, 'There's only one man for this job', and called Barney, asking him to come round for half an hour to help get my head right.

On the Friday morning, the newspapers all agreed once more on the main topic. It was not so much how well Classic Cliché had done to win the Gold Cup; instead most of them seemed to be saying that Jason had not gone fast enough on Double Trigger. When it comes to running against a class horse like Classic Cliché, I believe that if Jason had gone any faster, it would have made no difference to the winner, but Double Trigger could have finished a lot further behind.

After reading the papers with all the Ascot coverage, I had a sudden thought. It looked a very nice day and as I had been a pain in the ass ever since I'd got back from hospital, I thought Catherine deserved a break from me telling her 'Do this, do that'. It occurred to me that it would be good to go racing, to help support John Gosden with Shantou. He, after all, had been third for me in the Epsom Derby only thirteen days before. John had been so good after the accident, I wanted to show him that I still considered myself part of the team. Then I thought that, if I was going to Royal Ascot, I'd like to wear a morning suit. As a jockey at Ascot you come in, ride in some races and then leave, so all the jockeys just wear normal suits. I tried to think who might be able to lend me a morning suit and immediately thought of my good friend Bruce Raymond, who I reckoned was a similar height and size to me, and likely to have a suitable outfit.

I called Bruce and asked him if he was going to Ascot that day and was relieved when he said he wasn't. Then I asked if I could borrow his suit and, when he agreed, I had it collected and tried it on. It was a perfect fit all over. We cut an arm off one of my shirts and it wasn't too bad getting changed, even though it was awkward dressing with the arm in plaster. Ever since the accident Catherine had stopped being a fiancée and had become a nurse, something which she knows about as her sister is a nurse. She had to wash me, dress me and everything. I was like a little boy being dressed by his mother for his first day at school. Once I was dressed, I really got quite excited. I was going to a big race meeting for the first time purely as a spectator.

I went in the car with John and his wife Rachel. Even

travelling there had a different feeling. Normally, while I am being driven to the track for Royal Ascot I would be looking at the papers, scanning the races from A to Z, looking for clues as to how to get the best results from my rides, noting which horses I thought might make the running, which would be the ones to follow in the big fields. Now I simply closed my eyes and slept, without a care in the world.

I was looking forward to another unusual treat: lunch at the races. John and Rachel had been invited to lunch with Grant Pritchard-Gordon, the racing manager for the big Saudi Arabian owner Prince Khalid Abdulla, who has quite a few horses with John, and I gate-crashed lunch with them. Luckily, there was plenty of room around the table and it was a good way to escape the crush of a very big crowd. The most enjoyable thing was that I just had lunch and was one of the public in my top hat and tails. I felt that everyone was staring at me; a few of them must have spotted who I was. The one difficult thing was when I went to the toilet and was trying to unzip my trousers with my one free hand, someone tapped me on the shoulder. I hope he didn't think I was being rude when I couldn't shake his hand.

It was a great joy going to the races, especially once we started moving around the track and I realised how many people wanted to talk to me and wish me well. Popularity may be something which you can be lucky enough to have for a short time, but I did feel that day that people were happy to see me. I went in to the weighing room of course and realised, perhaps for the first time, what a rush it is for everyone. No one had much time to talk to me; they were all concentrating on getting ready for their next ride. I did feel a bit of an outsider. It was strange, but the atmosphere was pretty good just the same. I stayed most of the day with John and I was grabbed at one stage by Julian Wilson to have a small interview for BBC TV. I told him all about the accident and said that Royal Ascot is our own Olympics, with its tradition, passion and professionalism; and with the Royal family also there the whole time. After what I had read in the morning about Jason I told Julian I thought he had ridden the best race of his life on Bijou d'Inde in the St James's Palace Stakes on Tuesday. Yet just two days later they are criticising him, when all that happened was that he was beaten by a better horse. I was glad I stood up for him on TV.

While I was at Ascot I bumped into one of John's new owners, Ronnie Wood, who is one of the legends of pop music, having played with the Rolling Stones. I have never met anyone so enthusiastic about racing. He's experienced so much success, but because I had done well in another activity in which he is starting to get involved, he was looking up to me. It was a strange feeling. Then we were in the paddock with Shantou. I wanted him to do well in the King Edward VII Stakes, as he is one of my babies and my ride when I come back. That's something I could relate to. I must say it was more nerve-racking watching him run than being out there riding him. There was nothing I could do to help him.

I bumped into Sheikh Mohammed. I hadn't seen him since the accident. He told me they had retired Shawanni because she had become a bit of a handful. I told him, 'It was just one of those things.' He said he missed me riding at Ascot and that he was really sorry about what had happened. I told him, 'It's not your fault. Just one of the hazards of the job.' Luckily, one that doesn't happen very often. While it all might look glamorous, it can be a risky business riding such powerful horses.

Afterwards, I went back to the weighing room. I'd already said hello to everyone earlier on, and now I was really an outsider. I had to step back and ask myself, 'Is this really what I do every day?' It looked so crazy and disorganised, and I wondered whether it was just because it was Royal Ascot or was it like that every day? I realised that it was just the same as always: riding your last horse of the day, gathering up your stuff and sprinting for a car or a plane to get to the night meeting, keeping a ridiculously tight schedule.

Being with John that day also gave me a little insight into how things are for trainers and owners after a race, especially when a horse runs less well than expected. I could see from John's face that he was disappointed by Shantou. He hadn't got the best of runs and was in a poor position turning for home. Watching the race unfold, I felt helpless, not being able to do anything about it. He ran on at the finish for third. Normally, a jockey will come back, explain to the owner and trainer what happened, why it went wrong and then walk away to prepare for the next ride. The trainer has to start thinking out his reasons for the result not going his and the owner's way. For the first time, I saw the effect losing has on the owner and the trainer. Mick Kinane had left us and we were there going over everything in our minds. The jockey had done what he was paid for, the trainer is left with the post mortem, the new plan of how to get the best out of the horse on behalf of the owner.

I see the jockey's role, especially when he rides regularly for a stable, as something like that of a racing driver. When drivers compete in a Grand Prix or any race, they report back on all aspects of the car's performance so that the technical people can make adjustments to get a better result next time. I might say, 'Try a new distance – he wants further or shorter, try running him from the front.' Fine-tuning really.

Now we were back in our car, expecting a normal journey, but we had forgotten about the infamous M25 Friday car park. John had gone off with Sheikh Mohammed for a meeting, so I was with Rachel in the car. At the M3 junction with the M25, we looked right and the traffic going towards the Dartford tunnel was solid; we looked left to go north and it was solid. We went left and it took us three hours to go just over ninety miles. I called Catherine from the car and said I'd had a good day, but told her not to cook: 'Book a table at Number Nine,' which is a restaurant in Newmarket. She'd done enough all week nursing me.

I enjoyed the chat with Rachel going back to Newmarket. She's very smart and knowledgeable and interesting to speak to. I hope she wasn't bored listening to my life story. The next day I saw England play Spain on TV and when it came to the penalty shoot out I had tears in my eyes. I was scared for my friend David Platt when he had to take his penalty. I thought, 'You've got to be brave in front of 80,000 people and many millions more watching, like me, on TV.' As ever, David came up with the goods, and to see Stuart Pearce's face after his penalty had helped England win was one of the most emotional moments for me in sport. Afterwards, when I thought of it, the boys were not just taking their penalties, they were taking them for all of us who wanted them to win. What a responsibility. Imagine Gareth Southgate after the semi-final. If I get it wrong on the track, it's a loss to the people involved in the race and the betting public. A missed penalty affects almost everyone in the country. Even Henry Cecil watched the game. It was quite funny to think he'd never seen Gazza play before. Henry thought he played well and looked a good player. He knows more about roses – and horses, of course.

The following Sunday I suffered another blow. Colin telephoned to say he wanted to come round to see me. Colin and his girlfriend, Alex, had been with Catherine and me on holiday in Switzerland at the start of the year. At the time she'd seemed very happy and the four of us had had a great time. We were all looking forward to November when they planned to be married and I was going to be Colin's Best Man. But as soon as he arrived at my house I realised something was wrong: Alex had said she didn't want to get married. Colin was so sad, shattered really, and I could see the look of shock on his face. The day before he'd thought everything was going well for him and in the space of one minute his whole life was messed up. Now the tables were turned between us and this time it was me who had to be his big brother, unlike when I first came to Newmarket and Colin looked after me. He came and stayed with me for a while to get his head right. Gradually, he began to feel better. Life goes on, but it can be cruel all right.

9 Road to Recovery

The first two weeks of my own recovery seemed never-ending. The time went so slowly and the pain and discomfort were with me all the time. Then it was time to contact Mr Dodds, the consultant, to get a progress report on my elbow. He arranged to see me and I went to the hospital with Catherine and Andy. I wanted Catherine with me because ten years earlier, when the plaster had come off after I'd broken the other elbow, I'd taken one look at it and fainted. I wanted her there because I thought I might faint again, and was worried how it would look.

There were two or three people in the waiting room, all with plaster on various limbs. It was soon my moment of truth. A nurse very carefully removed the plaster and, to my relief and pride almost, I didn't faint. I was pretty pleased with myself. Like a proud little boy who doesn't cry after a bad fall. But I was surprised when I actually saw the arm. It looked awful. There was a woman there talking to her husband and she looked as though she would faint when she saw my arm. They were all trying not to look at me.

Then we went into Mr Dodds's office and he organised another X-ray. When eventually the pictures came back, he said, 'Everything's going to plan,' and told me that the bone should heal in another four weeks. It seems any bone takes six weeks to recover from a break: a broken leg requires twice as long. He said that the wounds seemed in good shape and that I could keep the plaster off. He told me to do everything very gently, never to force movement. So far, so good.

The next morning I made my first visit to one of my regular stopping-off points in Newmarket. Any jockey who needs to lose a couple of pounds has a number of alternatives. Some have saunas at home, others use the ones at racecourses, but I find it much better to use the facilities available at the Bedford Lodge hotel, which is just along from Stanley House stables, where John Gosden trains, on Bury Road in Newmarket. So I went to the swimming pool there and saw a few of the ladies who regularly use the Bedford Lodge sauna. They all wished me a 'speedy recovery'. It was obviously too soon to do anything there, but as I had been eating more than usual in those early days after the accident, I decided to walk the two miles from the town and across Newmarket heath to my house in The Drive. At that time of day, most of the horses have finished their exercise on the gallops and are already eating their late breakfast, but a few stragglers were still around, and it felt very strange to be on foot. I had become an outsider, but everyone who noticed me said 'hello', so that helped me believe I was indeed a jockey. Later that day I went to see John, and when he saw my arm he seemed very shocked. He told me to put some

Arnica on it to help reduce the bruising.

I thought that my recovery would be speeded up if I could get out into some sunshine, so I arranged to go on 25 June with Catherine to Gran Canaria, where my dad has an apartment. Before I went, the doctor said: 'The elbow is locked, so you have to unlock it. But don't try to unlock it with pressure. It's a very long, slow process.' At that stage, I could almost touch my nose with a finger, but I couldn't straighten my arm, which was locked in an L-shape. The only thing that concerned me was the scar from the operation, as I didn't want it to come open while I was away. But when he inspected it, Mr Dodds said that it seemed to have healed nicely and should be all right.

So we flew out to Gran Canaria and every day I spent the afternoons by the toddlers' pool. The first few days, I would go in and crouch under the water and do a 'pretend' breast-stroke, only gently at first, just to get the arm moving. By the third day, I had a little more confidence in my elbow and could use my strength to float on the surface. So much of it was to do with confidence. When you have an injury like that, you are always afraid that something will go wrong, and the injury will get worse. In my case, everything was going fine and by the fifth day there I was able to go into the proper adult pool and swim about forty lengths, each of which was probably twenty metres or so. The climate in Gran Canaria is always ideal, and whether it's June or December, the temperature seems to vary by only a couple of degrees, from between around twenty-six and twenty-eight degrees Celsius. So the sea is beautiful and by now every afternoon I was going to the sea with my dad and basically working. We'd swim a bit, and then float for a long while. To float in a wavy sea takes much more work than in a swimming pool, so you have to move your arms under the water to keep afloat. The elbow would therefore be kept moving, while the sea itself helps reduce the pressure on the arm. While we floated, for about thirty minutes each day, we would chat about life and racing, of course. After six or seven days, I was able to cope with swimming fifty lengths in the morning and another fifty in the afternoon and I could see that every day the arm was getting better. By now I could touch my shoulder and my arm was getting quite strong.

In the flat, my dad has a satellite TV and it has the BBC World Television channel, with Teletext. I used to punch up Teletext each night to see the racing results back in England, and I remember waiting anxiously on the Saturday of the Coral-Eclipse Stakes for the result. Eventually, the name Halling flashed up as the winner, with Bijou d'Inde second. I was angry and frustrated at missing a Group 1 win on a favourite horse of mine. I rushed out to the pool and did another twenty-five lengths to calm myself down. I was pleased he'd won, but at the same time I felt frustrated that I hadn't been involved in his big win.

By the tenth day it was obvious that there was great improvement in my arm. Now I was keen to start bringing the muscles in the arm back into shape. I wanted to get a spongeball to grip to work the muscles, but couldn't find one in Gran Canaria, so instead I got a sponge and began squeezing that the whole time. That helped, too, and I thought it was probably the right time to come home to see the doctor. It was still less than four weeks since my accident, so when I called him to say that I wanted him to see how much the injury had improved, he wasn't too keen. He said: 'You should come to see me after six weeks, as it takes that long for the bones to heal.' I still pressed him to let me come, saying, 'You want to look at this' and eventually he agreed. I was convinced the healing process was pretty advanced. He examined my arm, said that it looked great and then sent me for an X-ray. The X-ray proved a great disappointment to me, though. You could detect a line where the bones were put together – there were still signs of calcification. I was very disappointed. I had been taking calcium tablets while I was in Gran Canaria and eating lots of Parmesan (which also contains calcium), so I'd expected it all to have healed already.

My return to England was timed to coincide with a nice invitation I had received from the Ritz Club, who were going to present trophies to several sportsmen, each of whom were reckoned to be the sportsman of the various decades. I was the sportsman of the 90s, rather premature as we're only just over halfway there – and had someone kidnapped Eric Cantona? Gary Lineker was the man of the 80s; my great racing hero Lester Piggott was the man of the 70s; Henry Cooper, who had knocked Muhammad Ali down in a world title bout, was the man of the 60s; Sir Stanley Matthews, the great soccer star, represented the 50s; and Denis Compton was their sportsman of the 40s. I know nothing about cricket, except that England often lose Test matches, but I know Denis was a great player. What I didn't know, though, was that he played Test cricket for England before the war in the 1930s, yet was still good enough at football to play in a Cup Final for my team Arsenal in 1950 – twenty years before I was born. He must have been pretty special. To be considered to be in that sort of company was very flattering, and we had a wonderful evening.

We met up with Lester and had dinner. We met Gary Lineker and his wife and they seemed very nice. Jimmy Hill was doing the introductions and we were all asked a couple of questions. I was asked: 'What was your best day in racing?' and 'Who is your sporting hero outside your own sport?' I cheated really, saying, 'Because I'm very young, the only sport I know much about is racing. In racing, my hero is Lester Piggott.' Everyone cheered and Lester smiled. They went round to everyone and when it came to Lester's turn, nobody would have expected his answer. I'm sure I didn't. Lester is sixty years old now and you'd have thought that there were any number of people from when he was younger that he could have mentioned. But he said 'Damon Hill', a great compliment to Damon, and it also shows that Lester's a frustrated racing driver. Certainly, people who've been driven by him would think that! Anyway, it was a great night, and we ended up for the first time in my life at Annabel's night club. It looked a very nice place, but it was a Tuesday and we were the only people there. The next day I was back home in Newmarket to work with the Channel Four television people at the July meeting, one of the highlights of the year in English racing. The July course is very informal, the weather's always great and the racing is of a very high standard. The meeting is often chosen by the top stables to give their promising two-year-olds their first race – Alhaarth and Mark Of Esteem were first and second in a maiden there in the 1995 July meeting – and the Group 1 July Cup, on the Thursday, is one of the most important sprints of the entire season. One horse I would soon be riding which ran that week was David Loder's Bahamian Bounty. He, like Mark Of Esteem the year before, was not quite ready to win first time out, but within a few weeks I would be delighted to get the mount on him, with good reason.

By now I was having some regular physiotherapy, but, once the July meeting was finished, I didn't really want to stay around doing nothing, seeing horses I would have ridden win for others. So I saw John and said, 'I'm going to Sardinia. There's no point staying around and getting frustrated. I'll be able to do some more swimming in the sea and get some sun – it will be good for my arm.' Before we left I went to the local sports shop and bought a couple of light wrist-weights, just half a kilo each, and some springs to squeeze in my hand. We stayed at the family's house in Sardinia where I'd spent all those summers when I was a little boy. Dad was from there, and, apart from Milan, where he worked, it was my original home, so I felt very comfortable. Every day I would go into the sea. Where they live is on a bay and to swim across it's probably half a mile, and I would swim across. Then I'd relax in the afternoons in the sunshine. Catherine was great at that time. You need support when you are trying to overcome something like a major injury and she was always there. I wore the weights on my wrist and we would walk the beach. It was almost three miles there and back. While I walked, I'd move my arms up and down. I'd straighten my arm and then pull it up to the shoulder. I found that easy, but to put the hand behind my back and then attempt to lift the weights was much more painful. It really hurt the muscle at the back of the arm.

I would do that exercise at least one hundred times as I walked along the beach. It was painful, but I got to accept the pain as I realised that if I wanted to proceed I'd have to pay a price. If you do nothing, the muscle will not build up again. I wasn't going mad – there was only one pound on each wrist – but I could feel the benefit each day. By the end of the week I was doing the exercise two hundred times a day. By now my arm was around ninety per cent straight and I could touch my shoulder with no problems. I had planned to stay for ten days but because I was already feeling ready to start riding horses again, I cut the trip short by four days. I said to myself, 'You've done as much as you can with the weights and the swimming. Now it's time to get on the gee-gees.' We flew back that Thursday, and on Friday 25 July, I went to see John to show him my arm. He couldn't believe it.

I told him I'd like to give it a go the following Monday and ride out for the first time. That weekend, to prepare myself, I began a regular exercise programme in the gym at the Bedford Lodge. I started with forty lengths of the swimming pool, went on to pull a few weights (around five kilos), and then went on to the rowing machine. The hardest thing I tried at that stage was to push myself against the wall, when the arm felt quite sore.

The next Monday I went in early and John put me on a horse for the first time. As ever, he was considerate, and selected a great favourite in the yard, a horse nicknamed The Tortoise, which is a bit unkind, as he's won a couple of races, but he is pretty slow. It's probably best not to reveal his real name as his owner might not be too amused by the nickname. He's just the sort you'd expect him to be with that name, a lovely, quiet, easy ride, and for my first ride on Monday 29 July, I just went gently up the hill with him. On the Tuesday, I did a couple of canters, again with no ill effects and then the next day, the second day of the Goodwood summer meeting, I agreed with Julian Wilson to ride out at Lady Herries's stables, a few miles from the beautiful course up in the Sussex Downs. Julian was organising some filming which would be shown during the BBC coverage of the Goodwood meeting, another of the big highlights I would be missing. At least, by now, I could see some light at the end of my tunnel!

On the surface, my day at Angmering Park was fine, and

it all looked okay on the television screen. I rode Harbour Dues, who at the time was a short-priced ante-post favourite for the Tote-Ebor, the big handicap at the York August meeting. They told me Harbour Dues was a nice quiet ride, and he actually was, but for me the day was a disaster. After I got on the horse, my arm began to get really painful. After the first two days back on a horse, my hopes had been high, but all it took was one day with the pain again for me to lose confidence once more.

So, after Goodwood, I had to get back and increase the work in the gym. I was still riding out every morning for John and then I'd go down to the gym in the afternoons. Now it was a full hour and a half each day, starting with a forty-length swim, followed by the weights, a jog on the running machine for about one and a half miles, then a row on the rowing machine, and ending with fifty press-ups.

At this point, I was also having plenty of physiotherapy. Liz Minter, who was once married to Alan Minter, the former world professional boxing champion, now operates as a masseuse in Newmarket. I've known her for years, and she's great. She would work my arm so hard, it really helped me, and helped the arm relax. Liz is busy, so was not always available, but, by luck, I came across another physio, Mike Rogers, who'd been in charge of physiotherapy at Glasgow Rangers and some other big football clubs. He's nearly retired now, but he's still brilliant at the job. While he works, he's got a thousand stories about a lot of the footballers and what they used to get up to. Some of it made me blush! The hard work in the gym, Liz's and Mike's efforts and also a little extra assistance from an ultrasound machine, operated on me by Fiona and Rose, the girls at the Grosvenor House Clinic in Newmarket, meant that I soon felt ready. It was midweek in the first week of August and I felt really good. I said, 'I want to give it a go.' We agreed on a low-pressure evening meeting at Newmarket on the Friday night and a ride on a nice quiet two-year-old. I was back. Had I ever been away?

10 The Comeback

The horse I was to ride for my comeback was a backward youngster called Conon Falls, who would need an education and not too much hard riding from his unfit jockey in his first race. I'd had a sit on Conon Falls a few mornings before the race and he'd seemed a good, sensible horse to ride. On the morning of Friday 9 August 1996, looking forward to the comeback, I was very excited, and as I made the short drive to the track late that afternoon, I was very nervous, very excited. It was funny, but as I arrived in the weighing room I noticed everyone else's faces looking worn out. The other jockeys had been going through their summer agony, with their long days and evening meetings. As for me, while a little worried, I felt as fresh as a daisy, too fresh really, and I seemed to be jumping around everywhere. It must have irritated some of the jockeys, but they gave me a great welcome, and so did the crowd that night.

The race went fine for me, and though Conon Falls only

finished in the middle, we weren't expecting much more and the delicate first venture for both of us was safely achieved. Even an hour after the race I was still very excited and hyped up, as though I'd won a big race. I decided to take Catherine to the Hole in the Wall restaurant, just outside Newmarket. The food was excellent as usual, but all of a sudden I felt so tired. The adrenalin, which must have been pumping hard all day to keep me going, suddenly stopped. We went home and I was in bed by nine – exhausted. Luckily for me, the next afternoon's races were again at Newmarket. I had three rides, not expecting too much of any of them, and my expectations proved correct. Three unplaced horses.

At this time of year, top jockeys spend most Sundays travelling to race on the Continent, and that weekend, there was the choice of riding in Deauville or at Leopardstown in Ireland. David Loder had planned to run a nice two-year-old called Bahamian Bounty in the Heinz 57 Phoenix Stakes, a Group 1 race in Ireland, and the day before my comeback ride at Newmarket I had agreed to take the ride. Then David called the next day and told Matty that he would wait another week and run the horse in France. John had been happy for me to ride David's horse as he had Leap Of Joy in a Group 3 race the same day in Leopardstown, so once David's horse came out, I still flew across, but just for the one ride. Leap Of Joy didn't have much luck in running and finished third. So far, the comeback was not looking too good.

Next stop, on Monday, Windsor. During the summer, if it's Monday it has to be Windsor, and usually at night, but by the middle of August, as the days are getting ever shorter, we get a couple of afternoon meetings there. Windsor that day was the scene of another much-publicised comeback:

Walter Swinburn's return six months after his terrible fall in Hong Kong was even more momentous for him than my own comeback had been for me. Okay, I got hurt when Shawanni fell on me at Newbury, but when Walter crashed through the rails at Sha Tin back in February, for several days they thought he might die from his severe head injuries. His comeback to full health, starting in intensive care thousands of miles from home, was, literally, painfully slow and in the last few weeks, it was also frustrating as he had to accept a delayed return because of a technicality.

The race in which Walter was looking for a winning start on Talathath, a four-year-old horse trained at Newmarket by Chris Dwyer, was a handicap over one mile and I also had a ride, in my case on an old friend, the eleven-year-old Cape Pigeon. It was nice for Walter that an above-average crowd at Windsor gave him a great welcome, and there were plenty of TV cameras that day to see his comeback. We were all happy to see him back.

As I said, Cape Pigeon is a really nice horse and over the years I've ridden him quite a lot. He'd won a claiming race at Windsor very easily a little earlier in the season, and it's in that class that he is most likely to win. I usually end up riding him two or three times a year and I think I've won on him twice in selling or claiming races. He and another horse went off like scalded cats and I couldn't get him into the lead on his own for a couple of furlongs. I admit in hindsight I went too fast for the old boy and left nothing for the end of the race.

Meanwhile, Walter was coming to challenge and when I saw him I gave my horse a couple of back-handers. The poor old boy was knackered, and a furlong out Walter's horse went by and never looked in any danger. Because I burnt Cape Pigeon out in the early part of the race, he was very tired. So out of consideration for him – after all, he's an eleven-year-old – I just pushed him out to the line, before which Tony McGlone's horse caught and beat us by a short head for second. Perhaps in the eyes of some sections of the public, my riding at the end of the race did not look very good, but what they should have looked at to understand what I did was the entire race. If I did anything wrong – and underneath it there seemed to be the suggestion that I and maybe the other jockeys allowed Walter to win – it was merely that I went too fast at the beginning. When Cape Pigeon got tired, I thought it better not to hit him when he may then have weakened even more.

The stewards called me in to explain my riding. I did, and they accepted my explanation, which I think was the correct thing to do. They know I'm not a butcher and the poor old fellow, after all, is eleven years old and gives you everything on the bridle anyway. So, while Walter had his first win after his return at the first time of asking, I'd been riding four days without any luck. My next chance was to be at Salisbury on Wednesday, when John was running a nice filly called Altamura in a Listed race. It wasn't until after she had run a very good race to win the Upavon Stakes that day that I heard about a letter which Mr Eric Gadsden, who owns Cape Pigeon, had written to the newspapers. It said that I hadn't ridden to his orders, that the horse should have won, that it was disgusting that the stewards had done nothing about it, and that I was a disgrace, suggesting that we were all riding for Walter and not for our owners and trainers. He ended by saying that he would be selling all his horses – I think he owned one other apart from Cape Pigeon – and would not be buying any more – because of me.

Naturally I was very sad to hear about this and, like the

controversy after the 2,000 Guineas, in a way it spoiled my comeback winner. In the end, it took me almost a week to get over that particular upset, and it took a lot of the satisfaction from the fact that my first win had been in an important race for my boss. The next morning, as usual, the newspapers were all still talking about the Cape Pigeon incident – as far as I'm concerned there wasn't one anyway – and not my winner. It was a bit different for Walter. In his case they were all delighted for him and concentrated on his win. The thing that disappointed me most was the fact that here was an owner, still running an old horse and getting pleasure from him, but, reading his letter, it seemed to me he actually wanted his loyal old horse to be beaten up. I wrote him a couple of lines, saying I was sorry he thought that way. In my mind, I wanted that to finish the matter, but a week later Mr Gadsden was still making comments to the papers, and, astonishingly, those comments were still being printed.

The hardest part of anything is achieving the first milestone. It had taken almost a week to get my first winner, but within another ten days it all seemed like I'd never been away, and the winners kept clicking, as though I'd hardly missed anything. Before the flood of winners, though, there was a less than successful afternoon in Deauville, my first visit there of the year, when I would normally have made a number of day trips across for the top races at the picturesque track. The French really know how to relax in August and the jockeys also take their chance to mix business with plenty of pleasure. The life is comfortable, the races valuable, and the weather normally beautiful. We had two Godolphin horses entered on the Thursday, with Charnwood Forest our main runner in the Prix Jacques Le Marois, a Group 1 race over a mile, which is probably the highlight of the entire Deauville meeting in terms of quality. I had been very disappointed to miss the ride on Charnwood Forest when he'd won the Queen Anne Stakes, the opening race of Royal Ascot; he'd been the first horse to ram home to me what I was going to be denied in my enforced absence. He had been beaten since in the Sussex Stakes, by First Island, but I was going to have my chance of revenge for Godolphin against First Island in the Juddmonte International at York the following week. Now, though, this was my first really important ride. We'd also taken Wall Street, a decent three-year-old for a supporting race. Both horses finished fourth and by this time I was getting a bit grumpy because the winners weren't coming.

While I was flying home, Catherine got a call from John asking her to tell me, 'Just ride by instinct. You're thinking too much and trying too hard. Just go out and ride.' It was good advice, especially as, next day, Friday, would be my first visit back to Newbury where, just nine weeks before, the accident had occurred. As soon as I arrived there I had to admit it felt strange. Going into the paddock for the first race, it all came back again, and when I got on Catechism, the filly of John's I was riding in the two-year-old maiden race, I recalled the fall and decided to take my feet out of the irons, just in case. Perhaps you could accuse me of being over-cautious and by the end of the day I would have had to agree with you, as by then we were really rolling.

Catechism had raced twice already and finished second each time, but, with a few more fancied newcomers in a big field, I thought maybe a place would come our way. If your luck is out, you won't get a run, but this was going to be my day and, sure enough, the split came at exactly the right time. Catechism went through it and went on to win, when ninety-nine times out of 100 you wouldn't get the split from that position. My next ride was also for John, in a valuable three-year-old handicap over ten furlongs. I was on Greenstead, a horse who had won a maiden at Newmarket's big three-day July meeting. The bookies weren't too interested, and he started at 13–2, but won like an odds-on shot. Again we got the gap when we needed it and, by that time, confidence was really starting to go through my veins.

The big race of the day was the Hungerford Stakes, an important seven-furlong Group 3 race, and I was riding Bin Rosie, a bit of a character but a talented one, for David Loder's stable. David fancied his chances as Bin Rosie had been over to France and won a Listed race. He thought that the pace was sure to be fast with Green Perfume, a confirmed front-runner, in the field, and so it proved. For the third time, I got my gap when I wanted it, and again my horse ran all the way to the line. Three winners in a day on the track where I'd been hurt. John had said 'Ride by instinct' and it had worked. In one day my confidence was suddenly back. You can see how some jockeys, unlucky enough to have to live on three rides a day, find their confidence going when they get on a long losing run. When I'm busy, when the evening meetings come along, a run of thirty consecutive losers may mean as little as only three days without a winner. For me, though, having been off for eight weeks, it was especially important that the fears and worries that might have developed during my absence were quickly overcome. John was right, until Friday I was a little bit nervous, thinking too much and trying too hard.

I felt much more comfortable going to the track on the second day of the meeting. I rode Head Over Heels, a nice filly owned by John's wife Rachel. John was really keen for her to win and get the valuable black type a Listed win would entitle her to. For a filly, to get 'black type' is most important. When fillies and mares are sold, they are listed in catalogues printed by the respective bloodstock sales companies around the world. Keeneland in Kentucky, Tattersalls at Newmarket, Goff's at Kildare in Ireland and Deauville in France stage the major sales and that is where the 'black type' fillies are likely to appear, either to be sold, or in the pedigrees of other horses, most importantly, yearlings who are in their families. Black type means winning or being placed in either Group or Listed races, and when a filly achieves black type it is great news for her owner. As I said, John was keen for her to win, and actually gave me the riding instructions a week before the race. As instructed, I always had her close behind the leaders on the rails, again got a gap when I pulled her out to tackle Olympic Spirit, and got up on the line to win by a short head.

The day's main race was the Geoffrey Freer Stakes, over a mile and five furlongs, and my mount was the Queen's filly, Phantom Gold, who was making her last appearance as she is already in foal to the successful stallion Cadeaux Généreux. Like any expectant mother, an in-foal mare can feel very energetic for some time in the early part of her pregnancy. Many fillies do well when in foal, and Phantom Gold certainly showed her best form here. Lord Huntingdon, who trains her, had not been enjoying a great season, and neither had the Queen's horses been in brilliant form, but I was hopeful, as the only previous time I had ridden Phantom Gold had been in the 1995 Ribblesdale Stakes at Royal Ascot, which she'd won. This final race was meticulously and carefully planned by Lord Huntingdon and Lord Carnarvon, the Queen's racing manager, who is also Chairman of Newbury racecourse. They decided to run Whitechapel, a good stayer also owned by Her Majesty, to ensure the good pace needed for Phantom Gold to show her best form. The plan worked well, especially as Whitechapel found a friend, Reg Akehurst's Wayne County, to share the work.

Meanwhile, I sat at the back and took my time. The filly is a little tricky, as she needs to be settled, but when she comes through and gets in a challenging position she tends to be a little one-paced, and, when she hits the front, she tends to pull up. So, with her, timing is everything. You try to get her running, and get up there and then try not to allow her to stop when she does make her move. Crucially, it all worked out right because of Whitechapel, whose strong pace helped me time everything to perfection. It's always a thrill to ride for the Queen. I've been lucky riding her horses, and when I pulled up I remember thinking, 'I hope she was watching this on TV at Balmoral', where she has her summer holiday. I'm sure she was.

So we left Newbury on the Saturday night, with five wins to show for my first two days back at the track where I'd been badly hurt such a short time before. It was as if I'd never been away from riding, and with a Listed winner at Salisbury, a Group 3 at Newbury, and another Listed and a Group 2 on the second day at Newbury, I had to be delighted. Some jockeys would be delighted with that haul in a career. I'd been lucky enough to get it within three riding days in England.

I wasn't expecting too much as we set off for Deauville on the Sunday. The Prix Morny, over six furlongs, is the first leg of France's three top races for two-year-olds. All Group 1, they comprise of the Morny, over six, the Prix de la Salamandre at Longchamp, over seven, and the Grand Critérium, over a mile at the Prix de l'Arc de Triomphe meeting. Some top French-trained horses have won all three to become France's and Europe's unchallenged champion two-year-old, and as I set off with David Loder to ride Bahamian Bounty nobody gave us much chance of beating France's latest star Zamindar. David had switched his colt from his planned race in Ireland the previous weekend, and I wasn't unhappy with this, as the extra week had given me the chance to ride myself into form. But we knew Bahamian Bounty, who had made a promising start when second at Newmarket and then won well in modest class at Yarmouth, was trying to climb a mountain against the horse I called 'Baby Zafonic'. Zafonic was the horse which in 1992 dominated the two-year-olds in Europe, but instead of trying for the Grand Critérium, he came to England and easily won the Dewhurst Stakes. The next season, he won the 2,000 Guineas at Newmarket in brilliant style and while he then raced only once more (unsuccessfully) before retiring, he still has a great reputation. His first crop of yearlings were presented for sale in the autumn of 1996. Zamindar, like Zafonic, is owned and was bred by Prince Khalid Abdulla and trained by André Fabre, France's leading trainer.

The word from France was that 'Baby Zafonic' was 'as good as his brother', and 'a world beater' but David and Edward St George, who owns Bahamian Bounty, reckoned that if nothing took him on, no one would know how good he was. In the race, I tracked Thierry Jarnet, who was riding the favourite, a heavily-backed 5–1 on shot. Just before the furlong marker, I pounced and went by him, and although Zamindar kept after us, we won by a short neck. As I came back, I was dying to do my Angel Cordero leap again, even though I had resolved never to repeat it after all the hassle following the 2,000 Guineas. I reasoned that the French are not as fussy as can be the case in England, so I did the leap, and as usual the crowd seemed to enjoy it. Happily for me,

I didn't land on my elbow, like the last time I took an unorthodox exit from a horse!

When a champion is dethroned, the tendency, I'm afraid, especially from the pressmen who have been hyping him, is to look for something or someone to blame. It was like that in the 2,000 Guineas when they said the watering was uneven and Mark Of Esteem was a lucky winner because of it. There had to be a fall guy for Zamindar's defeat and this time it was the jockey. Mr Fabre and, I think, also Prince Khalid felt that Thierry Jarnet had been caught out by my manoeuvre. Certainly, once we went ahead there wasn't too much time for Thierry to get back, but I thought my horse idled when he hit the front and was probably value for a little more than a short neck. I saw the race myself from the perfect place, in the front seat, and I don't think Thierry did anything wrong. Maybe his horse will still become the star they thought. I know it hurt the Prince, because at York when I bumped into him after the Juddmonte International, which he so generously sponsors, he said, 'You didn't beat my horse, you beat my jockey.' I disagree, politely, I hope, with his opinion, but agree that what happens when horses meet on an individual day need not happen when they meet again. On that day, though, I believe most people did not give enough credit to my horse. It was nice to see David Loder coming back to form as his horses had been under a cloud for much of the summer. He was one of the guys who backed me when I most needed it, and I rate him very highly as a trainer. His misfortunes of the summer, when his horses were wrong, showed that, like everyone else, when things go wrong you just have to wait for them to come right again. If you have the talent, as David does, the success will come when the horses are back in good health. Getting back with a Group 1 winner so soon after Bin Rosie's good win at Newbury was, with some other important races coming up at York, the boost he needed.

11 The Race of the Year

Funnily enough, although I'd been in a good run, from the Saturday night before I left for France until Monday, when my horses did nothing, I was in a bad mood, as Catherine kept reminding me. I was tense, all right, and for a good reason: on Tuesday I would be back on one of my favourite horses and one of the biggest stars in European racing. I'd missed Halling's repeat win in the Coral-Eclipse Stakes at Sandown during my injury, but I'd won the Prix Ganay in France on him before my accident when he'd told me that he'd not been affected by those two defeats by Cigar on dirt. Now, though, was the real test. That Monday night, Catherine and I sat in the front room sulking to each other. Trying to put me in a better mood, she said, 'Don't worry, he's a certainty. He can't get beat.' I wasn't so sure, and in some cases I think it's good to take a negative view, believing a horse like Halling can get beat, so at least you pay more attention to all the possibilities. So I was looking at the field and thinking, 'If I make the running, would that help First Island (the horse that beat Charnwood Forest at Goodwood)? If the pace of the race is too slow, would that give the advantage to Bijou d'Inde, who has the turn of foot of a top miler?' I thought it all through, and was determined to get the tactics right, especially as this was one of the most important races I'd not won, and one that my dad had won on Wollow more than twenty years earlier.

When I ride for Godolphin, however important the race, I am given plenty of freedom on how to ride each horse. The Godolphin team sits down and debates and carefully plans the race. I decide I will try to do this and follow plan A. If that is not working in the early stages, then I'll go to plan B, C or D. I'm very lucky to have that freedom and that was reassuring for me when I went out for the ride on Halling. It was probably the race of the year, contested by five Group 1 winners. There was a lot of tension as we stood in the paddock beforehand, with Sheikh Mohammed and all the entourage, and there was a lot of discussion between them about how the race might go. They were all tense, and understandably, as no horse had ever achieved the feat of winning two Coral-Eclipse Stakes and two Juddmonte Internationals. I was tense, like them, but just to make myself feel a little more at ease, while I was standing there, Halling walked past, and I turned to Sheikh Mohammed, pointed to Halling and said: 'Is he any good?' He didn't answer, but I think it eased the pressure a little bit.

Halling cantered beautifully to the start, and felt great as usual. All the jockeys were concentrating hard on what they were doing, and, in a race like the Juddmonte International, each of the horses has a stalls handler allocated to him. There's an old guy in the north, called Sid, but whom we know as 'Vicious' because of the ill-fated member of the Sex Pistols group – they were before my time, of course. Vicious was looking after me, and as he came to greet me and check the horse's girth, I was thinking: 'I'm going out there and doing what I have to do.' I saw him coming over to me and said, 'Hi, Vicious, how are you?' He said, 'Guess what happened to me last week? My son, aged twenty-two, hanged himself.' I thought, 'Jesus Christ. Here I am worrying about a horse race and here's a man who's lost his son and still doing his job.' It helped put everything in perspective. Vicious was just going through the motions, really. I felt really sad, but, as you do, when we went into the stalls, I forgot all about it and waited for the gates to open.

As I waited, my one worry was that I was drawn near the rails. I wanted to make it, but if Halling was to miss the break and not get to the front I would have to switch to plan B. He didn't have to lead necessarily, just get a nice break. The stalls opened and Halling jumped off well and was quickly into his stride. The only thing going through my mind at that stage was that the pace needed to be even. That way there would be no advantage or disadvantage. That would suit me fine and I knew my horse was better than the others. 'They can't beat me,' I thought. You feel how comfortable he is and go at that speed. Not every horse is the same, and I quickened the pace entering the straight where I had a very nice rhythm.

He's an amazing horse. When John trained him to win the Cambridgeshire as a three-year-old, before he first went to Dubai and into the care of Godolphin at the end of 1994, he was very immature and had no gears. That's not quite right. He probably had them, but didn't know how to use them. As a five-year-old he is almost certainly an even better horse than he was at four.

When we came into the straight, I brought him to the middle of the track. He prefers to run right-handed and to have a rail to run down on his right-hand side. York, of course, is a left-handed track and by taking him out to the middle there would be less danger that he would hang right away from the rail on his left. If he were to do that when another horse came up alongside to challenge, the problem would be that he could interfere with them and lose the race in the stewards' room. I thought it was common sense, and the going in the middle of the track seemed just as fast. I'd given him a little breather before the straight, and now took a quick look under my legs at the other horses. I saw they were all in Indian file, and playing my game. It was time to stretch them as we got to the three-furlong pole.

Halling is a very intelligent horse and to make him go faster all I need to do is lean forward a little and he accelerates for me. You lean forward and he goes lower like a cheetah as it sprints. From going along evenly, he gets down. I asked for a gear but without asking for everything. After all, were was still two and a half furlongs to run. Then just before the furlong pole, I had a look, and then asked him again, and he found another gear and drew away to win by three and a half lengths. You have a good horse if he can quicken once. To do that is an achievement. To quicken twice, that's exceptional, and the mark of a true champion. Like Halling.

Coming back to the winner's enclosure I felt great. It was probably the performance of the year in one of the best races of the entire season. All the people had come to York to greet a great champion – Halling – and I was part of it. He'd more than fulfilled every expectation. I felt the crowd wanted me to do something. I punched the air a couple of times and got a great response from them. As we reached the winner's enclosure all the owners and their friends were there with big smiles on their faces and they were hugging each other in pure excitement at what they'd seen. I'd vowed never to do my Angel Cordero jump again in England, but the atmosphere overruled any such negative thought. I said to myself: 'What the heck?' There's a right time for everything in life. There's a right time to jump. I knew the horse would not worry about it, because he told me! It's a great feeling. I'll probably never get a welcome from a crowd at any time in my career like the one the enthusiastic Yorkshire people gave me that day. So I made the most of it. I was worried for a minute that Sheikh Mohammed and his elder brother Sheikh Maktoum would not like it, and I must confess that since the Guineas I had regretted my actions that day, having gone too far on that occasion, especially as I hadn't got back to the winner's circle. But their faces told me it was all right. I wasn't quite so sure about the stewards though. Funnily enough, as I jumped I just caught a glimpse of another Yorkshireman out of the corner of my eye. That was Mark Tompkins, ironically, going out with his saddle before running Even Top in the following race, the Great Voltigeur Stakes. I thought I saw his lips move, but it was too fleeting a glimpse. I suppose he was saying 'Silly booger' in his best Yorkshire accent. But then I reckon I might be forgiven by now for what he called being unprofessional, as I see he now has a horse running from his stable which he has called 'Frankie' and says he's named it after me. Of course, Mark has to have the last word and says the horse is not as silly as me!

After unsaddling and watching the presentation, I had a

lovely interview on Channel 4 TV with Brough Scott. They have an interview point at the entrance to the winner's circle and weighing room closest to the main stand where all the punters go, and there was a massive crowd on that side listening to us. I said that one of the most enjoyable things about racing at York was that the Yorkshire people all get so involved in the racing. They cheered me all the time, and every sentence seemed to bring another great cheer. As an Italian I now realise that Yorkshire people do not think that their country is part of England. They think that the rest of England is a small part of Yorkshire! The one disappointment, considering the race was so important, was that there was no memento for the jockey. You don't want anything valuable, but to have a little reminder for your old age that you won the Juddmonte International on the great Halling would be nice. Especially as my dad also won the race all those years ago.

The other main ride for me that day was Mons, who ran well in the Great Voltigeur, finishing second to Dushyantor. I'd tried to ride him like Halling, but that was unfair on him, and he did well as it turned out. Maybe I went a little too easily, as he was coming back again at the winner in the last half-furlong, but sometimes, when you ask a horse to go half a beat faster than is comfortable for him, he doesn't get home. That day he seemed a decent St Leger prospect to me.

The second day of the York Ebor meeting started with a double disappointment. The first setback was that Pricket, who would have been the assured favourite, had to miss the Yorkshire Oaks because of a minor problem. Luckily Godolphin had a decent deputy in Russian Snows, a filly which had been trained in Ireland by John Oxx as a three-year-old, but then went to Dubai for the winter. She'd run well in a race on the Nad Al Sheba track in February and although she hadn't run for six months, the team were hopeful of a good run and she started favourite. In the race, over a mile and a half, she was in a good position but when I tried to edge out to make her challenge at the two-furlong pole, I couldn't get out. Richard Quinn was on my outside and upsides and he had me boxed in. I couldn't do anything about it. Then Richard came off the bridle and started to lose ground on his filly, and gave me the sign to 'go on, take it'. I moved out a second too quickly and didn't allow him quite enough time to drop out. I brushed his filly and it didn't make any difference to Whitewater Affair, his mount, but it looked from the head-on camera that I'd barged my way out. That was the stewards' view and they banned me for four days for 'irresponsible riding'. I was upset by the decision, especially as it meant that because of my two earlier bans, in April and May, each of two days, I was getting close to the mandatory extra two weeks ban once a jockey gets twelve days in total under the same heading. I don't like the rule, which is a new one. I believe the jockeys have been doing their best to keep within the rules, but they are riding under a system which does not apply in any of the other countries. The thought of two extra weeks after all my missed racing during the year was a great worry coming to the other big races at York. The jockeys' representatives on the Jockeys' Association are keen to get a different system into operation. No one wants to see top jockeys banned for weeks at a time for marginal interference. The penalty, to my mind, is far out of proportion to the crime. It's a bit like having penalty points on a driving licence. The idea probably looked good in the first place, but in practice it's like having a gun to your head for a whole year.

I didn't have too long to dwell on this suspension, though, before I was back in action on another of David Loder's nice two-year-olds. I'd ridden Abou Zouz when he'd made a most impressive winning début at the Guineas meeting back in the spring. That day we'd thought he was pretty special, but then he'd run very disappointingly at Kempton and that was probably the start of David's bad time. He was ridden by John Reid that day and the horse was never happy, he was very sweaty and upset. He ran a terrible race for no reason at all it seemed and it puzzled all of us. Then, two weeks before York, Abou Zouz started to show his old sparkle again. For me and David it was third time lucky in the race. In David's first season, in 1993, Fast Eddy had finished a very good third behind First Island and Mister Baileys. The following year, I'd thought Fallow, owned by Sheikh Mohammed, had the race in his pocket when Chilli Billy came out of the clouds to win going away. This time, though, there was no mistake. I had Abou Zouz well there on the outside all the way. We hit the front with one hundred yards to go, and although he swerved a little to his left, he had a bit in hand. David, like me, was on fire, winning a Group 3, a Group 1 and then a Group 2 within five days. It showed how in racing just a week can change someone's life. In the previous three months, while his horses were wrong, he was starting to question whether he was still a good trainer. Just like for me, that was not the end of David's York story.

After the second day, Wednesday, at York, Catherine and I stayed up for the night, and it was a nice change to have an easy time. We had a very pleasant early dinner, but I was really tired and went to bed very early. I woke up and as the hotel was so close to the track – it is just at the end of the straight course – I decided to go to the weighing room to see how my weight was. So I left at nine thirty, and Catherine, who had been racing on the Wednesday, when she'd spent the day in the company of Johnny Murtagh's wife Orla, decided to have a day in town shopping and sight-seeing, as the Murtaghs had gone back to Ireland on Wednesday night. I was going to have to do 8st 6lb on one of John's horses, North Song, which is owned by Rachel, and because I wanted to do the best I could on him – he was running in a valuable handicap – did not want to put up any over-weight. So, after discovering I needed to lose just over a pound, I took a very steady run, really a light jog, around the track. I went from the weighing room down to the mile and a quarter start and then back around the course, about two miles in all, but very steady. Afterwards, I sat outside the weighing room in the sunshine, as I had been sweating and wanted to dry off while I read the papers. I weighed myself again and found I'd lost around one pound already, but so that I could be able to use a chamois on North Song – it's not something John's fussy about, but it's more comfortable for the horse to have a soaked chamois leather under the saddle when he runs – I needed to lose a bit more.

The chamois weighs about half a pound, so I decided on half an hour in the sauna. After the sauna, I was about 8st 3.5lb stripped, comfortably light enough to do the weight on North Song. I was doubly keen to take every advantage. As well as doing my best on John's horse, there was the matter of the London Clubs Charity Trophy, which goes to the jockey who rides the most winners at the big meetings. I knew that Pat Eddery was going to be a threat as we were on the same number of wins going into the final day, and in the event of equal winners the biggest number of seconds decides it. It was still early, so I took the chance to grab a short sleep in the ambulance room and then began to prepare for my full book of rides.

Looking at my rides, I reckoned I had a great chance, especially as the day was beginning for me with another of David's good two-year-olds. I had ridden Indiscreet in a gallop the previous week and on what we'd seen that day we all thought a lot of him. The one thing we weren't sure of was whether when he was asked to lengthen he would be able to do so. The race was the Convivial Maiden, always one of the hottest two-year-old maiden races of the year, and the race in which such great racehorses as Danehill, In The Groove and Owington had got their winning ways going. I doubt if any of them was more impressive than Indiscreet, a colt from the first crop of St Jovite (one of the best mile and a half horses of the past decade, when you consider he won the Irish Derby by twelve lengths and the King George by six).

All the papers were saying Indiscreet would need more than six furlongs and his breeding certainly said the same thing. No one told Indiscreet though and we were always going really sweetly on the outside. There were three or four others, all from stables with good lines to two-year-old form, who were reportedly well fancied, but Indiscreet simply blew them out of the water. I did my lean forward when Willie Carson started to work on the favourite and we went clear in a few strides. Imagine my shock then that he broke the two-year-old track record, first time out, without me ever having to get after him. He shocked everyone, including me. I knew he was nice and I love the way he tries to give everything to you. That made it three for the meeting and another winner on the way to the Trophy.

If we weren't sure how good the track record was that Indiscreet had set, we didn't have long to wait to find out. David ran Bianca Nera, a filly that had won her only race just a week before at Beverley, a track where we've had a lot of success together. He didn't decide to run at York before I'd already accepted the ride on a filly of Michael Stoute's and for most of the week David was pestering me to see if I would become available. I rode Moonshine Girl for Michael and she's a nice filly, keen to please. In the race she was a bit buzzy, which can often happen with a filly there because the York track is so open. She pulled a bit and didn't feel right and later we found she'd been struck into. I was disappointed, and especially as I could have ridden the winner. Bianca Nera won in really determined style. The Lowther is a Group 2 race and is always hard to win and I was pleased in one way for David, but disappointed for myself. Bianca Nera saw off several challenges in the last furlong and had a much harder race than Indiscreet, so the fact that she took a second longer to run the same distance put the colt's great first run into perspective.

I was back with David on his sprinter Struggler for the third race, the Nunthorpe Stakes, one of the biggest sprint races of the entire year, and the most important five-furlong race in England. This was the race that gave Sir Mark Prescott his first ever win in a Group 1 race after many years' trying. Pivotal was the horse who came late and fast to win from Eveningperformance.

Before the race, it was beginning to get hot and I started sweating freely. I'd not taken any drinks because I was doing light later on, just a sip of Coca Cola. Struggler was fine going to the start. David told me he had been missing the break lately – he was left in the stalls at Royal Ascot – and told me to watch for that. Unfortunately, he jumped too good, pulled for three furlongs when I was hoping to be covered up behind the leaders. Struggler is usually strong in five-furlong races, but this time after taking me along for three and a half furlongs, he died on the bridle and finished unplaced.

At York, when you finish in the first four you unsaddle right in front of the weighing room. When you are unplaced it's quite a walk back from the paddock, and I was trudging back when I bumped into John. 'Hurry up,' he said, 'I've got two to saddle.' That meant he wanted me to go straight into the jockeys' room, change into his horse's silks, change the weights in the saddle cloth and be ready to give the saddle back to him as soon as possible. I kinda snapped at him a little bit. Obviously, the heat and the thought of not being able to have a drink or any food all day was getting to me and I was a bit tetchy. I went straight into the room, got my light saddle out, changed and weighed out. I was 8st 6lb with a chamois. No bother! I gave the saddle to John and I could hardly believe it when he said: 'Come straight out, he's going down early.' So, instead of having a few minutes' rest, I had to go and put my hat on and then was out in a minute.

It was getting hotter all the time. There were plenty of runners in the race, so we went down really early and North Song was great, no trouble at all going to the start. Unfortunately, when I got there we had at least ten minutes to wait, so I got off and then had to keep leading him round so he wouldn't stiffen up. So there I was out in the sun for what seemed an unnecessary length of time. He's not the easiest of horses at the walk and, as we were walking, he was dragging me around, all the time sapping a little more of my strength. Eventually, the others came down and, when they started, North Song jumped off well. I decided to let him make the running and he was in a nice easy lead. When we turned for home, I came out to the middle of the track where I thought the ground was a little faster. A couple went by me a furlong or so out, but I saved a bit and they must have gone a bit early because North Song got back to beat them. Unfortunately, another horse came from way off the pace and came down the wide outside and we were second.

North Song had been fine in the race, but that wasn't the end of that particular story. The fun had not really started. When I went to pull him up, North Song bolted towards the stables. It was my fourth ride of the afternoon. I'd been leading him round for ten minutes under the hot sun and then pushing him all the way to the straight. Anyway, he wouldn't stop. Whatever I tried to do to stop him, he simply went faster and faster. By now his mouth was dead. I had no control, and we continued to head straight for the stables. We were still flat out and at the same time the starter was coming back in his car towards the finishing line and for a minute I thought my horse was going straight for the car and we were in for a spectacular collision. I wondered what I could do and thought: 'My God, my big accident!' I imagined the horse running into the car and maybe breaking his legs and whatever might happen to me. It had been just ten weeks since my major operation and it was at that point that my arm started to give – I didn't have any strength any more. Luckily, just when it seemed a crash was inevitable, he stopped all by himself. I took a deep breath, took him round and galloped him back. I was in a state. I was exhausted, my arms were aching, my hands burning having been rubbing on the reins in the heat, and I was sweating ever more. I was knackered. More importantly, I was also back late and, still grumpy, told John he'd given me a bad ride. It was not his fault, but obviously I was a little upset. I went into the jockeys' room. Again I was looking for a little recovery time before riding Daunt, another horse of John's, when John popped his head round the door and said, 'He's early too!' I tried to make it, but I was still late getting out and missed going down early. So John said, 'Ask to go down last, then.' Daunt is the biggest horse in John's stable, stands a full eighteen hands (six feet) high and is simply huge. Before going to the start, the horses trot down to the winning post from the paddock exit before cantering back. The York lead-up got to Daunt, however, and he was really buzzing. I tried to trot him across to the start, but couldn't hold him so I decided to get off halfway and walk the rest of the way to the start. Eventually, we were there, and once loaded, he jumped out and immediately started taking me on so much. When we came to the straight I started pushing, and did so all the way from the four-furlong pole to the winning post. We finished fifth. I went to stop him, and, like North Song, he didn't want to stop, but luckily this time I ran into the back of Jimmy Quinn, who'd finished just ahead of me in third. Jimmy was very nice to me and kinda towed me back. Lord Hartingdon, the owner, who was the first Chairman of the British Horse-Racing Board and is a very nice man, came to see his horse and on the spur of the moment I threw my saddle on the floor and said: 'You can't do this to me, John. Everything I ride today pulls.' Daunt had 9st 12lb and to carry the saddle back would have meant my carrying almost a couple of stones' dead weight. I was in no condition really to carry myself, let alone a heavy saddle the long way back to the weighing room. I told John: 'I'm knackered. I'm exhausted!' John kindly took pity on me and carried the saddle back for me.

I wanted to stop there and then and probably should have

done, but there was still the matter of the London Clubs Trophy. I should have won the Royal Ascot one this year, so I was anxious not to let this one slip away. North Song's second place added to my three winners meant that Pat couldn't beat me, but if Kevin Darley rode the last two winners, he'd sneak up on the rails. I was completely wiped out, but I felt that Annaba, one of the favourites for the Galtres Stakes, could help me clinch it. So I had a little excitement to help keep me going. I checked the weight, had a couple of minutes' rest and a glass of Coca-Cola before going out to the paddock once more. In the canter to the post, Annaba took me on. I couldn't believe it. Another horse pulling me all the way down to the start. In retrospect, I must have got to the stage where I could do nothing about it. Even a Jack Russell would have run away with me.

By now, I couldn't help making the running. I stayed out in front until three horses went by and I could do nothing about it. I was fighting to keep fourth for the whole of the last furlong and missed that, too. I'd pushed myself too far. When I pulled the filly up I couldn't get my breath back. I felt exhausted, gave the horse to her lad and simply sat down where I was. I took off the colours where I sat and was pouring with sweat. I told John I would have to give up my last ride, Forest Cat, a filly I'd done well on before, in the last race, and asked John to apologise to Julie Cecil, her trainer, and owner George Ward. I was taken to the ambulance room where they gave me Coca-Cola with sugar in an attempt to pump some energy into me. Then I had five cups of tea with lots of sugar, and rested there for forty-five minutes. While in there I saw Forest Cat finish third in the last race. Luckily, Kevin didn't win either race and thanks to North Song, who gave me one second place more than Pat,

I'd won the Trophy. I wasn't in the mood to collect it after the race so I flew straight back to Newmarket with John. On the way, I apologised to him for the day.

Re-thinking, I realised there is a difference between being fit and being fit to ride under duress. The time I'd had off meant that I needed a longer recovery time. After being unfit for more than two months, to go through such a severe schedule at the start of my come-back, culminating in three really busy days in York, drained my energies. I still thought my recovery rate was just as quick as before the accident, but I would have cause to reconsider that opinion very soon. On getting home, I thought, 'There's one remedy. Pasta and plenty of carbohydrate.' I ate a big plateful and went to bed. I had a good night's sleep and in the morning still felt a little under the weather, but I decided to go ahead and ride that day at Newmarket. I thought, 'Well, I've only got six easy rides at Newmarket.' It wasn't the case. After the third one, I felt like something had sucked all the strength out of me. The previous day's exertions had taken a lot more out of me than I'd thought. I took all the rides and kept going because I knew that I'd look a fool if I stopped halfway through the day. They would all have said, 'He had a bad day yesterday, he should have taken today off', and they would have been right. Luckily, all my rides were dream rides. Mick Channon, the former England footballer who is doing so well as a trainer, gave me two fantastic rides which took me through the race by themselves. After racing, I saw the doctor, who advised me to 'get some food into you'. I didn't want to miss the next day, when I would be renewing my association with another old friend – Mark Of Esteem, in the Tripleprint Mile at Goodwood.

12 Super Saturday

By the Friday night of my busy week at York I was beginning to worry. For the second day I'd felt very weak and
when I saw the racecourse doctor at the end of the
Newmarket meeting he asked whether I had been getting a
good night's sleep. I told him I'd been a little edgy and he
said it would be all right to take a sleeping tablet to help me
relax. When I got back I called John and asked if I could
take Saturday morning off. He was fine as usual and after
having a nice salad I went to bed very early and took a sleeping pill. It must have worked because I slept through until
nine the next morning and when I got up I felt much better
than the previous day, properly rested and ready for another
big day.

Today was going to be important for me and all the
Godolphin people because, at Goodwood, Mark Of Esteem
was having his first race since failing at Royal Ascot, and I
was going to have my first ride on him since the 2,000

Guineas, which he'd won, but which had become a very controversial race for everything that had happened afterwards. He was one of a few nice rides I had scheduled that day at Goodwood and then later in the season's last evening meeting at Windsor. Peter Burrell, my business manager, had some time earlier arranged a day-long session with a video cameraman, who would come with us in Neil Foreman's plane, taking shots for a film which would be shown on airline magazine programmes and things like *Transworld Sport*, I think. It would be a 'day in the life' and the cameraman, a very nice man called Matt, could not have picked a better day to show me looking good!

As I looked through the papers before flying down to Goodwood from the July course at Newmarket, I thought, while I drank my coffee, that I had some good rides. Although Mark Of Esteem was the one to look forward to, and the most important as he was running in a Group 2 race, the Tripleprint Celebration Mile, I reckoned Sharaf Kabeer was my best chance of a winner. I'd ridden him at Kempton the day before the accident at Newbury and he'd won by miles. He was well beaten, when I was out of action, in the Irish Derby, but as I made a close study of his opponents in the Sport on Five race, which is a trial for the St Leger and run over a mile and three-quarters, I didn't think the opposition was very strong for a race of that type. I knew, judging on his win at Kempton, that the distance would be no problem and I fully expected him to win.

We got to the course at twelve-noon, having landed at Goodwood on the strip in the middle of the old car-racing track, which used to have Grand Prix races in the old days. Because I was so hopeful about Sharaf Kabeer, I told Matt that this should be the race to concentrate on with the filming, and as it was a little relaxed at the start of the day I sneaked him into the jockeys' room (not allowed, strictly speaking) for him to film me getting changed. I said, 'Build everything around that race.' I'm not sure whether Matt was a betting man, I reckon he might be, but after Sharaf Kabeer came home an easy three and a half length winner at the good price of 11–4, Matt had a stunned look on his face, which never really left it all day. This meant Godolphin would have another shot at the St Leger which we'd won the year before with Classic Cliché. Sharaf Kabeer was much less mature than Classic Cliché had been at this stage of his career, but he's a nice stayer with a good future, I'm certain of that.

Now we were ready for the big race. Mark Of Esteem had given us the biggest thrill of the year so far in the Guineas but he hadn't run well at Royal Ascot. At the back of my mind, there was a worry about him because of that, but I remembered that two weeks before Ascot he'd been meant to run in the Derby but had been ruled out because of a temperature. I think that was probably the main reason for his disappointing run, which clearly wasn't his form – much more logical than not liking the firm ground. He was beaten too far for it to be that. A week before Goodwood, Mark Of Esteem had a nice workout with me on the Limekilns gallop at Newmarket. One of my favourite phrases in racing, always used by over-excited stable lads when their horses work well, is that the horse is 'catching pigeons'. That day, Mark Of Esteem worked so brilliantly that after three furlongs he caught the pigeon, after five he cooked it, and, at the end of the seven-furlong gallop, he had indigestion!

On the work, then, he had to run well at Goodwood, but the Ascot defeat still played on my mind a bit, and I wondered whether he would be as good as on Guineas day. As with Halling in the Juddmonte International four days earlier, there was some tension in the paddock beforehand, and one worry for me was that I was drawn on the inside of the seven runners, right on the rail. I explained to Sheikh Mohammed that from that draw, the one thing I had to try to ensure was getting a run. Some tracks are difficult in that respect and Goodwood is one of the most difficult. If you are trapped, there's sometimes no way out and jockeys can be made to look foolish through no fault of their own. Mark Of Esteem is exactly the type of horse who could get into trouble. He comes from behind with a great burst of finishing speed. The only problem is getting him in a position to use it.

In the race, from that draw, all I could really do was track the leaders, and it was my old rival Alhaarth, with Willie Carson, and Gothenberg, ridden by Jason Weaver, who shared the lead. Alhaarth was one of the horses who, on 2,000 Guineas day, was said to have been at a disadvantage by racing away from the rails. Many people had complained about the 'uneven watering' as they'd called it, and said that Nick Lees, the clerk of the course, had produced 'unfair ground' for those drawn in the middle. At the time I'd thought it was nonsense, as Alhaarth had been only a couple of horse widths wide of me, and nearly level, as we'd all made our efforts that day. After the Tripleprint race at Goodwood, all those arguments would be dead and buried.

As we came to the crucial stage of the race, I knew I had the first two covered, as I still had plenty of horse and Willie and Jason were already working. But on my outside, Walter Swinburn seemed to be going pretty well on Bishop of Cashel and it soon became obvious that he would not be doing me any favours and letting me out. As I said to the press afterwards, 'Walter had me in prison and I didn't have the key to get out.' Luckily, though, at the furlong and a half point, Gothenberg was starting to weaken and left me a little gap on the inside of Willie and Alhaarth. Remembering what had happened at York just two days before on Russian Snows, I didn't want a repetition, as the consequences could be very difficult. At Goodwood, because of the nature of the track, which is very undulating, horses suddenly left in front on their own, as Alhaarth was about to be, tend to roll on to the far rail. Because I was worried Alhaarth would do that, I had to make my move about twenty yards earlier than I would ideally have done. Jason kind of had to check for a stride, but once Mark Of Esteem went through the gap, he quickened even better than he had in the 2,000 Guineas.

The horse won easily, but as we were pulling up, I saw Jason, who said, 'I had to check when you went for the gap.' I asked him, 'Did I touch you?' and when he replied, 'No, you didn't', that was good enough for me. I thought, 'I'll get away with it.' Obviously, at the back of my mind, there was a little worried voice, because the stewards are getting a bit strict nowadays, and the result wasn't yet official. In fact, it took them fifteen minutes after Jason and I went in to see them. Jason was great, like a good old friend, saying there was no blame on me whatsoever. Then, after the delay, the announcement, 'The placings remain unaltered.' You can imagine how delighted we all were. First Halling and now Mark Of Esteem, two champions showing how good they were in the same week.

Meanwhile, Matt, still looking stunned, and still filming away, and Peter were beginning to look edgy. Because of the inquiry we were between fifteen and twenty minutes late setting off in the taxi for the air strip. Neil was waiting for the short flight to Windsor, and the weather up there was terrible, with heavy rain falling.

I had three rides that night, starting with one for Ian Balding at my minimum 8st 6lb. Because I had been pretty weak the day before and with big rides like Mark Of Esteem and Sharaf Kabeer at Goodwood, I hadn't wanted to weaken myself with a sweat in the morning, but had planned half an hour in the sauna at Windsor. Getting there late meant I had just ten minutes, but I was in there on my own, and got a real good steam going, pouring plenty of water on the fire until it was very hot in there. I gave it a really good bashing, but ran out of time. My natural weight, as I've said before, is at least a stone heavier than the weight at which I manage to ride, and to keep near my riding weight I have to be careful. At the same time, there is nothing I hate more than doing overweight. Over a season of around 1,000 rides, I'm annoyed if I'm ever overweight, and usually three or four times a season, I might be slightly over. I think it's unprofessional, but here I was just a quarter-pound over the limit when I sat on the scales and the form books will record the dreaded words: one pound overweight; 8st 7lb. Ian was very understanding and when the filly I was riding in a handicap race finished well down the field, nobody worried too much that the overweight had made any difference.

When I'd set off in the morning from Newmarket, I'd said to Matt and Peter, looking at my rides, that this was the day of the old-timers. Maybe I should have said 'a reunion of old friends'. Mark Of Esteem, Sharaf Kabeer and Shantou, my ride in a nice conditions race which was coming up next at Windsor, had all done me proud the last time I'd ridden them before my accident. Shantou of course was the horse on which I'd had such a great ride, finishing third in the Derby, but like Mark Of Esteem and also Annus Mirabilis, my final ride of the day half an hour later, he is a bit of a character. I quite enjoy trying to find the key to this type of horse, I find them more interesting. Mark Of Esteem needs to come very late; Shantou is a nice horse, but you have to leave him alone and then ask him for his one run at the two-furlong pole. He was also very disappointing when we thought he would win the King Edward VII Stakes at Royal Ascot and even worse in a less important race at Haydock. I followed my own blueprint for riding him, in what was a pretty good race for a conditions event, and he quickened really well at the two pole and drew clear to win by three and a half lengths from Double Leaf, showing that he liked the easy ground. It was really good to see him back in the winner's circle.

And now to the biggest character of them all and my most difficult ride of the day, the Winter Hill Stakes, a Group 3 race and the most valuable race of the year at Windsor. In fact, Annus Mirabilis, that Saturday night, was probably the most difficult and testing ride for me of the year. He has never run a bad race in his life, but all his tough races against very good opponents may have made him a difficult horse to win with. In the race, I sat behind the leaders and was going well enough to hit the front two furlongs from home. A furlong later, first Storm Trooper and then Salmon Ladder went by me, and nobody could have expected what was going to happen. I still didn't really ask for a final effort until 100 yards from home, and Annus Mirabilis just gradually edged back and got up in the last twenty-five yards, and I don't think I hit him once in that final effort. As far as I was concerned, apart from Mark Of Esteem at Newmarket, when we were in a Classic race and success was so important, this was the best ride of the year. I really kidded him home. It's funny – the day before I'd felt lousy and the thought of having a cameraman follow me around hadn't interested me at all. Matt couldn't have chosen a better day. As we left Windsor, Matt still looked stunned. I'd won a Listed race, a Group 2, a Group 3 and a good conditions race. Overall, in one week, the horses I'd ridden had won more than £400,000 in prize money. My seven per cent of that was not looking too bad. That's what's called timing your comeback, but it's not always like that.

That night, after we flew back to Newmarket, I decided to take Peter and his wife Lucinda out to dinner at the Number Nine restaurant. I didn't watch too closely what Peter ate, but I had Caesar salad and some grilled salmon. As ever, the quality was great. I was really on a high after a great week, and began to look forward to another good Sunday back in Deauville.

The last Sunday of the month-long meeting always features the Grand Prix de Deauville. I was riding for André Fabre, but we finished only fifth behind Paul Cole's good horse Strategic Choice, who was given a lovely ride by Richard Quinn. Then I had another try on Leap For Joy, my ride at Leopardstown soon after the start of my comeback. In the two seasons I've ridden her, Leap For Joy has hardly ever been lucky with getting a run during a race just as she hadn't in Ireland. So I was determined that she would get every chance this time and got her plenty of room to challenge at the two-furlong pole. This time I went too early and she was well beaten by the finish. Already the day wasn't going particularly well and when I rode Chantilly Fashion in the Tiercé race – the horse finished fifth, as usual – it didn't get any better. Chantilly Fashion runs for one of the smaller French stables and they always book me to ride in races like this. If it's Sunday, it's France, and if it's France, it seems, I ride Chantilly Fashion. Tiercé races are always contested by big fields. The French betting public focuses on the Tiercé, where the punter has to get the first three in the correct order. In recent years, the Quarté, first four, and Quinté, first five, have given France's small punters the chance of a big win for small stakes. Racing in England is worried about the effect on betting turnover of competition from the National Lottery. If racing could organise its own regular bet like the Tiercé, Quarté or Quinté, all as in France, all three on the same race, the small punters might come back. At least they can see how their money is going through a race, unlike the lottery, which is just a bag of balls!

The funniest part of my day in Deauville was left for last. The two Bints (Arabic for daughter or girl), Bint Shadayid, ridden by me, and Bint Salsabil, ridden by Willie Carson, formed a strong British challenge for the Prix de la Nonette, a valuable race for fillies run over ten furlongs. Both carry the colours of Sheikh Hamdan, who had the good fortune to own their respective mothers Shadayid, a very good horse, and Salsabil, a great one. They were coupled under the French betting rules, which at present – they are about to change it to the same system as in Britain where all the horses run as individuals – means that a punter backing one coupled horse, wins the bet if the other part of the couple wins the race. So if someone wanted to back Bint Salsabil, and I won instead on Bint Shadayid, the punter would still collect. Two for the price of one! We, jointly, were second favourite behind Luna Wells, a good filly trained by André Fabre and ridden by Thierry Jarnet.

We were both prominent from the start, and as we came to the straight, Willie was lying second and I was third. There had been racing all month at the track, which was beginning to show signs of wear and tear, and by now everyone was beginning to search for better ground away from the inside rail. My rides earlier on convinced me it would be a good idea to get towards the stands side, and, as we turned in, I angled my run towards the stands while Willie stayed up the middle. We had less than two furlongs to go and there were at least four horse widths between us. Then, suddenly, my filly started to see the crowd and began to hang towards Willie. As I was anxious to correct that, I pulled my stick through to my right hand to tell her to go straight. As I did, my whip hit the face of Luna Wells, on whom Thierry Jarnet was trying to come between us. She jerked her head and stopped for a moment. By now the gap is already down to just two horses wide, and then Willie's filly starts to go left looking for company herself. Thierry still persisted going for the gap, but Willie and Bint Salsabil kept hanging towards me so Thierry had no option but to switch round us. At the line, which came up almost immediately, Willie won by a neck, with Luna Wells a length back in third.

As we came back to unsaddle I felt very disappointed to be beaten in a close finish, but the worst was yet to come. Thierry objected to both of us, so we all went into the stewards' room. They showed us the video, and it looked bad. In fact, on the screen, it looked so bad that if you had wanted to do a 'team job' to stop the favourite you couldn't have done it better. Out there, though, it's every man for himself. I was trying to win, Willie Carson was trying to win, and we were out to beat the favourite. We were already out again for the next race when we heard the results of the long stewards' inquiry. We were both demoted – to second and third – and, more painfully, when I came back after the race, I discovered we were banned for four days each. I must say, I can't remember ever being involved before in a race where the first two were disqualified, especially the first two for the same owner in a Group race. I cannot believe that my actions deserved a four-day ban. All I tried to do was correct my filly and unfortunately my whip accidentally caught Luna Wells. Once again, racing, the great equaliser, had thrown a dampener on a great winning spell.

The one saving grace was that the French ban did not get included in my by now worrying 'totting-up' score of eight points. If it had, I would already have been on my way to Portman Square and at least fourteen days' extra holiday. Because of the four days and York, and the French, which fortunately overlapped by one day, I had a total of seven days out of action. I was free to ride, though, in the middle of that on my old friend Germany, back in the same Baden-Baden race he'd won the year before.

I'd already asked John to let me have a couple of days off, so when I returned the following Tuesday to Deauville for the final day of the August meeting I arranged to stay there with Catherine for the rest of the week. I'd gone from doing virtually nothing to going flat-out straight away. The break was a great help before building up to Kempton and the September Stakes with Classic Cliché, then the St Leger meeting and all the important races of the autumn in Europe and around the world.

13 The St Leger

Back in June, when I first had time to think about the implications of my fall, the furthest thing from my mind was being able to ride in the summer at all. In fact, I thought the St Leger meeting was an impossibility, so there would be no chance to wear the famous St Leger hat again.

Of course, my recovery had been so rapid that I had already won plenty of nice races before the 1996 St Leger meeting, and the whole week at Doncaster went very well. I won on a nice two-year-old of John's called Benny The Dip on the Wednesday; won the Doncaster Cup on Thursday on that great stayer Double Trigger because Jason Weaver was suspended; and completed a first and last race double on the Friday.

I did have a little regret on the Friday, though, as I did mess up one race, on Daunt. Immediately after the race I felt it had been a good ride and we'd been beaten fair and square, but, on reflection, if I had allowed him to go on when he was travelling so well at the two-furlong pole, I'm sure we'd have won. Instead, I waited half a furlong – he did have 9st 12lb to carry, after all – and the response when I asked him was a little disappointing.

When I got home that night I had a quick glance at the draw for the following day's Pertemps St Leger. I noticed that I'd drawn stall ten, near the outside, on Shantou, while Dushyantor, the horse I thought our biggest danger, was immediately to my left, in nine, with Gordi and Heron Island, the only two outside us, at eleven and twelve respectively.

Inside myself I was in terrible form. Perhaps I was feeling the race the next day, because at the back of my mind I knew I had a good chance. There was a lot of talk about Shantou being ungenuine. Timeform even gave him a squiggle after his rating, which denotes an ungenuine horse, but to my mind he's just a little bit of a character.

I was very untalkative (you might say unusually so!) that night and went to bed at nine o'clock after Catherine and I had had a light dinner. I had a lot think about. I needed to go through the race in my mind and how best to win it. It was a Classic race after all.

Just as well I had a good night's sleep, because I needed to be up very early the next day. In fact we finished the first lot gallops at John's by six thirty and I came home to study the paper for the day's races. I still wasn't absolutely clear how to approach this race, though, so I decided to go back to John's for breakfast. I had a few questions to put to him and wanted to see if he had the answers. I wanted to race on Dushyantor. He was, after all, the horse to beat, and I reckoned my best chance was to follow him. But John wasn't quite so sure as Shantou is a horse who, if you ask him to do something he doesn't want to do, you would ruin his chance. John said, 'Follow Dushyantor if you can, but take the race as it comes.'

During Doncaster week, I had been booked to do a couple of talks to some guests. On St Leger day, although I didn't have a ride in either of the first two races, I was due to make an appearance for some racegoers, so I left home earlier than I would normally need to do. Lucky I did. The journey took three and a quarter hours, an hour more than usual, and I only just made it in time for the first race. The traffic got even worse later on, and Oscar Urbina, the young Spanish jockey who is doing so well now with my old boss Luca Cumani, arrived only just in time for his first ride in the St Leger, on Mons. When you are preparing yourself for a big race, having to rush and be anxious about whether you are going to be on time is the worst possible thing to happen.

I did have one ride before the big race, in the two-year-old sprint on Head Over Heels. This filly is owned by John's wife Rachel and loves fast ground. The day before, John was hoping the ground would be a little easier for the St Leger than on the other three days, when a couple of track records were set, one by the great Double Trigger. He told the press: 'I hope they leave the taps on all night!' and the reports from the jockeys who rode in the first two races were encouraging for Shantou if not for harmony in the Gosden household. All the family, including John's mother, were there for a family outing, but Head Over Heels was as much in their minds as Shantou.

Head Over Heels finished fourth, as the ground was indeed a little softer than she likes, so now it was all up to Shantou. I came back and reported to John that the ground was very good. Shantou was fine in the build-up and very good at the start. He jumped so well from the stalls that I was actually about a length in front of Dushyantor. I waited four or five strides for Dushyantor to get into a prominent position inside me but he didn't. Shantou was already travelling really well and I managed to get into a prominent position. I noticed Mons and Sharaf Kabeer were in front of me; on my inside was the outsider Samraan – who I thought had no chance – and Gordi was to my right.

Once the race took its rhythm I accepted my position, so even though I had wanted to track Dushyantor, I tried to keep Shantou happy. There wasn't much change until we came to the straight. Obviously, from the position in which I was racing, I was completely boxed in and I was already looking for several horses, especially Dushyantor, to come round and pass me on the outside. Just after the four-furlong pole, so still with a long way to go, I could see Pat and Dushyantor making very good headway and pulling double. I thought: 'We're a long way from home – don't panic!' My main concern at this time was to make sure we got a clear run. Meanwhile, when Pat got to the leaders, he sat on Dushyantor for a bit.

At that stage we were approaching the two-furlong mark and I was hoping to find a way out. Luckily, I found a split and immediately started to feel Shantou move – he came alive. As we made ground towards Pat at the furlong pole, I could see Dushyantor was still going well. Once we passed the furlong, the race was really on. Both horses were going for gold. When we reached half a furlong out, we were going stride for stride, until which time neither Pat nor I had gone for 100 per cent. Till then, we'd asked our horses for ninety-five per cent. Now we both asked for everything, me with my stick in my left hand, Pat with his in his right hand. In the last fifty yards, Dushyantor could not manage to give him any more, but Shantou galloped all the way to the line.

I was lucky to have ridden Mons against Dushyantor in the Great Voltigeur at York a few weeks before. That day

Dushyantor had found extra because he'd been spurred on by the sight of Mons close to him. I was aware of that, so wanted to challenge three or four horses wide of Dushyantor, and keeping the whip in my left hand – the arm I'd broken not so long before – meant Shantou would edge away from Dushyantor towards the stands. It was still only in the last ten yards that we were definitely ahead, and we crossed the line a neck in front. So, once more, the thing I'd been working for, for all those years, came to fruition. I've always thought, 'It can't get better than this', but it always does. As we crossed the line, I screamed and waved at the stands, but really to John. The feeling was pure ecstasy. It was an amazing sensation.

As we came back to the winner's enclosure, I was accompanied by the same two policemen and their police horses who had escorted me on my walk back after Classic Cliché the year before. Bob Herrick, the lad who has done so much to settle Shantou and who rides him out on his own every day, came to collect me. I had worn two pairs of goggles in the race, and gave one to Bob and threw the other into the crowd, which, as at York, gave me the full Yorkshire welcome. While we were still walking in, I couldn't see John as I scanned the crowd. I'd already decided to mark another great occasion with a great jump, and, judging by the picture in the following Monday's *Daily Telegraph*, it was one Angel Cordero would have been proud of!

I landed, gave Sheikh Mohammed, who owns Shantou, a hug and took the saddle off. Then John came in and was grinning from ear to ear. If he didn't have ears, his mouth would have gone all the way round. Then, afterwards, when I'd been in the weighing room for a few seconds, I came out to collect my own trophy, the much-treasured St Leger hat, something every jockey would like to get once. I had two in two years. I was interviewed before the presentation by Brough Scott on Channel 4. I told him what a special moment it was – as good as winning the Derby – for the staff and something I'd wanted so much for John, after all that undeserved criticism.

Then came the presentation. I received the hat. I'll never forget the feeling of standing there on the podium. Then I looked to the left and John was standing off the podium. It was hard to describe the look on his face. A mixture of shock and emotion. It was surprising to see such emotion on the face of such a big, powerful man. I had to walk off the podium and back into the weighing room. If I had stayed, the lump in my throat would have turned to tears. It was all too much for me.

I bought a dozen bottles of champagne for the boys in the weighing room, and at once they all started to come out of the woodwork. There were some big fields for the handicaps that day, and it was soon obvious that the twelve bottles were not going to be enough. I bought another six, and, what with the jockeys, the valets, and a couple of the stall handlers, these soon went too.

Throughout 1996, the good times and the bad times have gone hand-in-hand. I was still on a high and rode two more winners in the last two races for a treble with combined odds of more than 600–1. A few punters struck it rich that day, but, as ever, I was soon coming down to earth. Pat and I both had to see the stewards because, in their opinion, our riding had breached the controversial rule H9 on use of the whip.

I'd been down that path already when I'd won my first Classic of the year, the 2,000 Guineas, when Philip Robinson and Jason Weaver had also paid the penalty for a thrilling finish to a Classic race. Now Pat and I were again in the dock. We watched the video, and I gave Shantou thirteen strokes with the whip, but I explained to the stewards that they were only back-handers and flicks with the whip and not at all severe. The rule, which none of the jockeys thinks is reasonable, meant I could expect a two-day ban for unreasonable frequency – that's what Pat got. But even after I'd explained about the back-handers, they gave me an extra two days for force. I was perplexed by this, because it meant they believed I'd hit the horse harder than anyone else – I had not and seldom do. As Pat said later, unless the stewards of the Jockey Club sort it out, the top jockeys will get banned after every important race.

So once again I paid the price and took it on the chin. Sheikh Mohammed was happy, John was happy, the staff were happy and I'm sure the racing public thought we had put on a great show. It's so ironic.

We drove home and met John later for a quiet drink. I was proud of him, and was so pleased that we had achieved such a great triumph together. He had got his first, much-deserved English Classic winner. I hope to ride for him for many years and, as I told him that night, 'The first one is always the hardest, there's plenty more Classics to come.'

For me this has been an extraordinary year in so many ways. The ups have been great, but there've been far too many downs. Injury, bans and disappointment mixed with some amazing spells of great success. My resolution for 1997 is to have a much more consistent year, free of injury, and, if you're reading this Pat and the rest of you, I'm going all out to get back the title. It was only lent.

A Selected List of Non-Fiction Titles Available from Mandarin

☐ 7493 0692 0	**A History of God**	Karen Armstrong	£8.99
☐ 7493 2098 2	**Running with the Moon**	Jonny Bealby	£6.99
☐ 7493 1744 2	**The Orion Mystery**	Robert Bauval / Adrian Gilbert	£6.99
☐ 7493 1328 5	**Among the Thugs**	Bill Buford	£6.99
☐ 7493 1028 6	**In the Psychiatrist's Chair**	Anthony Clare	£6.99
☐ 7493 1691 8	**Mind Over Matter**	Ranulph Fiennes	£5.99
☐ 7493 1899 6	**The World Economy Since the Wars**	J. K. Galbraith	£7.99
☐ 7493 1454 0	**Fingerprints of the Gods**	Graham Hancock	£6.99
☐ 7493 0186 4	**The Sign and the Seal**	Graham Hancock	£8.99
☐ 7493 1491 5	**The Erotic Silence of the Married Woman**	Dalma Heyn	£4.99
☐ 7493 2019 2	**On Being Jewish**	Julia Neuberger	£6.99
☐ 7493 2347 7	**The Troubles**	Ulick O'Connor	£7.99
☐ 7493 1954 2	**To War With Whitaker**	The Countess of Ranfurly	£5.99
☐ 7493 1902 X	**Modern Philosophy**	Roger Scruton	£8.99
☐ 7493 2015 X	**Tomorrow is Another Country**	Allister Sparks	£6.99
☐ 7493 1625 X	**London at War**	Philip Ziegler	£6.99